The Demand
for Durable Goods

This volume is a publication of the
Research Group in Public Finance

✱

STUDIES IN ECONOMICS

of the

ECONOMICS RESEARCH CENTER

of the

UNIVERSITY OF CHICAGO

The Demand
for Durable Goods

Edited by

ARNOLD C. HARBERGER

With Essays by

ARNOLD C. HARBERGER

RICHARD F. MUTH

MEYER L. BURSTEIN

GREGORY C. CHOW

ZVI GRILICHES

YEHUDA GRUNFELD

THE UNIVERSITY OF CHICAGO PRESS

Library of Congress Catalog Number: 60-7236

THE UNIVERSITY OF CHICAGO PRESS, CHICAGO 37
Cambridge University Press, London, N.W. 1, England
The University of Toronto Press, Toronto 5, Canada

Preface

This volume presents a series of studies of durable goods demand done under the auspices of the Research Group in Public Finance at the University of Chicago. This group was formed in 1954 with the purpose of undertaking econometric research which would shed light on some of the principal problems and issues of tax and expenditure policy in the United States. The work of the group has ranged over a wide variety of topics, some of them connected only tenuously with the field of public finance. The five studies in this volume were designed in part to provide insights into the cyclical process in the United States; the wide fluctuations in durable goods demand make the durables sector a danger spot in which cyclical fluctuations may be initiated, and it is also likely that the responses of durables demand to income changes initiated elsewhere significantly amplify the extent of our cyclical swings. Furthermore, an understanding of the mechanisms determining changes in demand for durable goods is important for estimating the probable effects of proposed stabilization schemes. Two of the studies here presented also fall into another category of the group's research: the estimation of demand functions for commodities subject to excise taxation. Here, in addition to Chow's chapter on automobiles and Burstein's work on refrigerators, the group has produced two studies by William Niskanen, one on the demand for cigarettes and the other on the demand for alcoholic beverages.

Of other broad areas, the group has worked most intensively on the corporation income tax and the capital market. Under this general rubric, Lawrence Fisher has completed a study of the determinants of risk premiums on corporate bonds, Haskel Benishay one on risk premiums on corporate equities, and Marshall Kolin one on the market valuation of dividends and retained earnings. I have contributed a study of the effects of the percentage depletion provisions of the corporation income-tax law and one on the over-all effects of the corporation income tax.

In a further effort to improve our understanding of cyclical movements, John W. L. Winder has contributed a study of inventory fluctuations in copper, and Walter Y. Oi a study of cyclical responses in the labor market. To obtain some insights into the effects of our agricultural price-support program and of possible changes in it, Marc Nerlove has made estimates of the long-run elasticity of supply of particular agricultural products, and Lester Telser has completed a study of hedging, storage, and the futures markets for cotton and wheat. In a study aimed at providing a point of departure for an analysis of the role of the federal government in the market for forest products, Richard Crowther has estimated demand functions for these products. Martin Bailey has contributed two significant theoretical studies, one on the response of saving to changes in the rate of interest and the other on the welfare cost of inflationary finance.

While the studies undertaken in the Research Group in Public Finance are in every respect the products of their individual authors, there exists nevertheless a general indebtedness of each of the members to the group as a whole. A typical study will have been in process for eighteen months or more, during which period its author will have reported his progress and problems and consulted with the group in at least ten two-hour formal sessions and informally on many more occasions.

The formally constituted faculty of the group has consisted of Professors Martin Bailey (since 1955) and Yehuda Grunfeld (1957–58), in addition to myself. However, the group has had the benefit, during most of its history, of the contributions of several other faculty members, whose participation was in every respect as intensive as that of the formally constituted members. These include Professors Carl Christ (since 1955), Zvi Griliches (since 1956), John Muth (1956–57), and Jerome Rothenberg (since 1957); their participation is partly the result of the close collaboration which has existed between our group and the Econometrics Workshop, directed by Professor Christ.

Three of the studies in this volume were presented as doctoral dissertations, and their authors owe particular debts to faculty members not associated with the group. The volume as a whole has benefited from a careful review by the Publications Committee of the Department of Economics, consisting of H. Gregg Lewis, Earl J. Hamilton, and Margaret Reid.

Arnold C. Harberger

Table of Contents

I

Introduction

ARNOLD C. HARBERGER

Introduction

I

In THE growing mass of empirical demand studies durable goods are poorly represented. Minor food items have been studied far more intensively than major durable items. The share of durable goods demand studies in the total of all demand studies is only a picayune fraction of the share of durable goods purchases in the gross national product or the share of durable goods "consumption" in the national income. Yet a case could be made that the durables are actually deserving of a more than proportionate emphasis in our professional research effort. Durable goods, even in the United States, but more especially abroad, seem to have attracted excise taxation, tariff duties, quantitative trade controls, license fees, and other policy measures far out of proportion to their weight in the national output or expenditure. Housing is almost everywhere subject to a property tax, and the return on business capital to a corporation income tax as well. Durables demand, moreover, fluctuates so violently, in comparison with the demand for other sectors' products, that most modern theories give it a key role in causing and/or exacerbating business fluctuations.

There can be little doubt that the paucity of durable goods demand studies is to be explained by the difficulty of making them rather than by any lack of interest in the quantitative relationships they seek to explore. The difficulties are, indeed, both substantial and numerous. In the first place, the data are far from ideal. Comparatively negligible errors are made in measuring wheat in bushels or salt or haddock or beef in pounds. It is quite another thing to measure housing by the number of dwelling units, refrigerators by the number of machines, or cars by the number of vehicles. At any point in time great differences in quality exist among the major durables, and, furthermore, there are much greater changes in quality over time in the durables sector than in, say, the basic foods. Price data, too, tend to be shaky in the durables field. On the one hand, this is merely the counterpart of the quality problem on the quantity side: the market prices of dwelling units at any one time cover an enormous range, while the market prices of different bushels of wheat cluster narrowly about their mean. On the other hand, the price data suffer from a different problem in that for such items as automobiles and refrigerators the published prices tend to be manufacturers' suggested

3

list prices, actual transactions prices being clouded from our view by such devices as trade-in allowances, cash discounts, and what-not.

Second, durable goods studies face a set of problems peculiar to themselves, arising from the Hydra-headed nature of durables demand. At any point in time there is the demand for the ownership of houses, and also there is the demand for newly constructed dwellings. These two demands are obviously interrelated. The stock of houses on hand cannot be increased without new construction, and, indeed, new construction is necessary to maintain a given stock in the face of normal depreciation and natural disasters. But the precise nature of the interrelation is not clear. A desire on the part of the public to increase the stock of housing by 10 per cent can be accommodated by constructing all the added houses in a single year or by adding 1 per cent to the stock of housing each year for a ten-year period. And there are good reasons to doubt the obvious offhand reaction that the adjustment will be immediate. Not only does construction take time but a major decision like the purchase of a new house is likely to be weighed carefully, and the alternatives well explored, before the move is finally made. Thus different patterns of change in the demand for new construction are consistent with given patterns of change in the demand for houseownership, depending on the speed of adjustment to changes in ownership demand. If adjustment is slow, of course, the possibility emerges of differences between the actual stock of housing and the "desired" stock, adding a further complication to the problem of estimating demand.

The problems associated with estimating "stock demand" (comparable to the demand for houseownership) as well as "flow demand" (comparable to the demand for newly constructed housing) are present throughout the durables area. Many of these problems arise from the inadequacies or unavailability of stock data. Only in the case of automobiles do we have really good information as to the size and composition of the available stock, year by year. For housing, our data on the number of dwelling units are fairly reliable, but we have only sketchy and sporadic information about the age and quality composition of the stock. For refrigerators we do not even have information as to the number in use, year by year, let alone their distribution by age and quality. In such cases it is necessary to build up a set of stock data by applying an assumed pattern of depreciation to the purchases of past years. Errors and inaccuracies are obviously introduced by this procedure, the more so in a case like refrigerators, where the market provides very little information on the pattern of depreciation.

We cannot get away from the problems of measuring the existing stock by focusing on "flow" demand, because of the crucial influence which the existing stock has on the rate of new purchases. For any given level of demand for the services provided by a durable, new purchases in a given period will be lower the higher is the level of services obtainable from the existing stock carried into the period. Moreover, it is not clear that the service yield obtainable from the existing stock can be measured easily. If cars of all ages really have the same service yield, the aggregate service yield of the existing stock of cars would be measured by their number; if, on the other hand, the service yield of individual cars is proportional to their value, the service yield of the stock would be measured by its aggregate value. We can get an indication of which of these two possible measures is more correct by looking at the pattern of depreciation. If cars tended to depreciate by a constant dollar amount per year, this would indicate that the service yield tended to be about the same for cars of different ages, and the "numbers" measure would be preferable. If, as appears to be in fact the case for cars, they tended to depreciate by a constant percentage of their value each year, the "aggregate value" would be the preferable measure of service yield. But either of these measures is at best only a rough approximation, not only because the depreciation pattern in any practical case will fit into neither mold precisely, but also because interest charges (actual or imputed), maintenance costs, and taxes are also components of what people pay for the use of a car for a period. Furthermore, maintenance costs can "substitute" for new purchases by raising the capacity of the existing stock: we cannot know precisely in advance how much service the stock carried into a year will yield in that year. Thus, even when the data on the depreciation pattern are good, as in the case of automobiles, we can in practice get only a measure of the stock which approximately captures what we seek. The situation is far worse in a case like refrigerators, where we must almost arbitrarily assume a depreciation pattern before we can generate any measure of stock at all.

Finally, there are the problems associated with the comparatively great volatility of durable goods demand. Not only is it true that relatively small random shifts in stock demand lead, at least for a time, to much larger percentage shifts in flow demand but also, even when stock demand changes for some "systematic" reason, such as an income change, the pace at which this will be reflected in flow demand through altered purchases will vary from situation to situation. We can at best hope to capture the average effect of, say, a 5 per cent rise in income upon flow demand; the fact that the actual effect is sometimes greater and sometimes less than average operates to introduce an added "error component" into the relationship we estimate. The volatility of durables demand also raises questions as to the "identifiability" of the relationships we try to measure. May not the relationship we measure between income and construction catch, in part, a causal connection which goes from swings in construction activity to resulting income movements, thus obscuring or at least blurring the "demand" relationship we seek, which runs from changes in income to resulting movements in construction? And may not shifts in durables demand *cause* price movements in the same direction, similarly blurring or obscuring the demand relationship by which price changes lead to quantity movements in the opposite direction?

All in all, the difficulties facing those who estimate durables demand are numerous and severe enough easily to explain why so few finished studies have emerged. They also, however, serve to warn both those who undertake and those who read studies in this field of the pitfalls along the way.

II

The studies which follow were undertaken in full awareness of these pitfalls. They do not attempt to achieve precise and unequivocal estimates; rather they seek to sift through the available evidence, using a number of alternative approaches, in an effort to answer certain rather broad questions. Is the demand for automobiles comparatively insensitive to changes in price (elasticity in the neighborhood of zero), moderately sensitive (elasticity in the neighborhood of unity), or very sensitive (elasticity of, say, 2.0 or more)? Is the income elasticity of housing demand near 0, near 1.0, or near 2.0? Can changes in the farm demand for tractors be plausibly explained as responses to changes in the prices of farm inputs and outputs and in the interest rate? Is the widely observed correlation between industrial profits and industrial investment due to a close causal connection between these two variables, or do other variables appear to be the dominant causes of changes in investment? Do holdings of durable goods adjust rapidly to changes in the determinants of demand, or are there significant lags in adjustment? The above questions illustrate, though they do not exhaust, those examined in this volume.

Although each of the studies was independently conceived and executed, and although no two would fit into precisely the same mold, the studies do have a certain flavor in common. All are based on an explicit recognition that the fundamental demand for durables is the demand for the services provided by the "stock"; the demand for purchases of new durables is derivative from the fundamental stock demand, purchases serving the dual role of replacing the stock as it deteriorates and of adjusting its size to accommodate changes in the demand for services. All, at one stage or another, explore the possibility that the adjustment process may be slow rather than instantaneous. All exhibit a skeptical attitude toward the basic data, exploring the consequences of using alternative available series, examining the nature and effects of possible biases, and, at times, laboriously constructing new series of their own.

In the course of their experimentation with various series, all three studies of consumer durables test the effect of substituting Milton Friedman's "expected-income" variable for the more conventional disposable-income series. The expected-income series is intended to be an empirical approximation to the subjective concept of "normal" or "permanent" income. It is in fact a weighted moving average of disposable income, in which current income gets one-third of the total weight and past incomes get weights which decline progressively and roughly exponentially, income of nine years ago and earlier receiving zero weight. This variable was found to explain a larger percentage of the variation in total consumption than did disposable income or any of a large number of differently weighted moving averages which were tested by Friedman. The theoretical support for a variable of this type comes from the conjectures that consumption will conform to what the consumer considers his "normal" income to be rather than to the quite possibly transitory movements of his current income and that the consumer's view of his normal income position will be conditioned largely by his past experience and revised only gradually when current disposable income differs from its expected norm.

Durable goods play a special role in Friedman's system. He treats the consumption of their services as the "durables component" of aggregate consumption and their acquisition as assets as a form of saving. He anticipates durables purchases to be highly sensitive to transitory variations in disposable income and the consumption of the services of durables to be mainly (though, because of the savings effect just mentioned, not exclusively) dependent on expected income. The three consumer durables studies in this volume provide some evidence on the validity of this conjecture, in addition to showing to what extent estimates of elasticities and adjustment coefficients are sensitive to changes in the income concept.

All the studies rely exclusively, though not naïvely, on the least-squares method of estimation. Least-squares bias can result either from errors of measurement in the variables treated as independent in the estimated regressions or from shifts in the functions being estimated. As long as the measurement errors in the different independent variables are reasonably random—that is, as long as they are not too highly correlated with the true values of the independent variables or with each other—they tend to introduce a downward bias into the absolute magnitudes of the estimated regression coefficients. Price elasticities and income elasticities obtained using quantity as the dependent variable will accordingly tend to be underestimated. On the other hand, a price elasticity obtained using price as the dependent variable will tend to be overestimated, as will an income elasticity obtained treating income as dependent, for in these cases the estimated elasticity is based on the reciprocal of the regression coefficient.

Shifts in demand functions tend to have a direct effect on both price and quantity, so long as the elasticity of supply of the commodity in question is less than infinite and greater than zero. This effect also operates to introduce a downward bias into price-elasticity estimates obtained using quantity as dependent and an upward bias into those obtained using price as dependent. Thus, both from the standpoint of errors of measurement and from the standpoint of shifts in the functions, the quantity-dependent estimates can in a sense be regarded as "lower limits" and the price-dependent estimates as "upper limits" to the true parameter sought. Muth, Burstein, and Chow all present estimates based on both regressions, thus bracketing the range in which the true elasticities probably lie.

While shifts in demand functions presumably have no effect on real income in full-employment situations and may have no effect in situations of less than full employment (in cases in which demand for one commodity is increased at the expense of demand for other commodities), there exists a presumption that at least some of the shifts in demand in situations of unemployment will be at the expense of savings. Such shifts will tend to have an effect on income in the same direction and naturally will also tend to be positively correlated with the quantity of the commodity in question. The bias produced in this case is positive, tending toward an overestimation of the income elasticity regardless of whether quantity or income is taken as dependent. The three studies of consumer durables accordingly did not rely on time-series estimates of income elasticities using income as the dependent variable (in which case both the bias due to errors of measurement and that due to shifts in the functions are in the same direction) but used instead income-elasticity estimates obtained using either price or quantity as the dependent variable. Here the bias resulting from shifts in the function is positive, while that stemming from errors of measurement is in the opposite direction.

In cross-section analyses (e.g., among states at a given time), the possibility of shifts in the demand function for a given commodity having significantly affected the pattern of income differences among states is negligible. Hence the principal problem of bias is that of errors of measurement in the variables. In Burstein's cross-section studies of refrigerator demand, regressions using income as dependent accordingly were computed, along with those using quantity as dependent, the two yielding "upper" and "lower" limits after the fashion indicated above. Beyond the sources of bias discussed here, there is also the problem of errors of specification: of omitting variables which have significant independent effects on the demand for the commodity in question. The danger of such errors always exists and can be coped with only by sensible experimentation with reasonable alternative formulations. They are not specifically associated with the least-squares method and accordingly will not be discussed further here.

All the studies place major reliance on time-series analysis. Where, as in Muth's study of housing and Burstein's study of refrigerator demand, cross-sections are used, they play a distinctly supplementary role. The comparative neglect of cross-section methods stems mainly from the nature of the problems which the authors set themselves and should not in any way be taken to reflect on the usefulness of such methods in general. Such variables as prices and interest rates tend to exhibit little variation cross-sectionally at a given point in time, and hence cross-section analysis is not often useful in measuring the response to changes in them. In the investment field there are substantial variations in some important variables (e.g., profit rates) among firms at a given point in time, but there is little reason to expect that the reactions of firms to given changes in these variables will be the same as we move from industry to industry. Here Grunfeld's approach, of following individual firms through a period of years, avoids the possible dangers both of lumping heterogeneous data on many firms together before embarking on a time-series study and of trying to draw inferences from cross-section comparisons of what may be substantially unlike observations.

One relatively new and promising approach, based on sample surveys of consumer and investor intentions, was neglected entirely. This approach has special merit for short-term forecasting. It can be used to warn in advance of impending declines in the principal spending categories and, as evidence accumulates on the factors which lead people to behave differently from their stated intentions, can lead to quite subtle insights into the cyclical responses of our economy. At least at the present stage, however, intention survey data give little help in the estimation of the fundamental stock-demand relationships for particular durables. Focusing on purchases rather than holdings, and more often than not on gross rather than net purchases, these data do not easily lend themselves to studies of stock demand or of net changes in the stocks of different durables. This explains in part their neglect in the present studies, though it does not in any way deny their importance in the area of cyclical movements, on which the present studies also bear.

III

The principal findings of Muth's study of housing are that the price and income elasticities of stock demand are probably in the neighborhood of unity (perhaps even greater), that the interest elasticity is substantial, and that the adjustment of the stock of housing to a change in the determinants of demand takes significantly more than a year. When it is assumed that the adjustment process is completed within a year, the price- and income-elasticity estimates are only in the neighborhood of 0.5. A substantially better explanation of variations in the stock of housing is obtained when the adjustment coefficient is estimated from the data. Muth's first regression of this type, equation (10), yields price and income elasticities of stock demand of around 0.9 and an adjustment coefficient of around .33 (indicating that a third of the full adjustment to a given change typically occurs within a year). A trend term, introduced in part to check on the possibility that trendwise biases in the data distorted the estimates, turns out (in eq. [11]) to have little effect on the coefficients of price and income and to be insignificant statistically. When disposable income is substituted for expected income (eq. [12]), the estimated price and income elasticities remain about the same, but the adjustment coefficient is cut to about 15 per cent, and the explanatory power of the equation is reduced. Muth concludes from a series of experiments that Friedman's expected-income concept is superior to disposable income in explaining variations in new construction activity.

Muth then turns to an examination of the ratio of a rent index to the price of housing as a determinant of the rate of construction. Given the interest rate, construction varies directly with the ratio of rent to price, these two variables explaining some 70 per cent of the variation in the ratio of construction to the stock of housing (eq. [18]). When, instead of the current ratio of rent to price, an "expected" ratio is used (based on a weighted moving average of current and past ratios), 85–95 per cent of the variance in construction relative to the existing stock of housing is explained (eqs. [23] and [24]). In Muth's next formulation rent is viewed as the price which rations the existing stock of housing in the market, and the regression is taken of rent against the stock of housing and expected income. Here the price elasticity of demand for housing services is estimated to be about 1.5, and the income elasticity near 1.0 (eq. [26]). Next, the average quality of new housing is studied; over 70 per cent of its variation through time is explained in Muth's equation (27), which yields a price elasticity of about 1.25 and an income elasticity of near 2.0. Finally, in equations (28) and (29), the average quality of dwelling units is compared as among cities. Here 80 per cent of the variation is explained, and price and income elasticities are estimated to be over 1.5.

The elasticity of demand for the stock of housing with respect to the interest rate is estimated at -0.13 in equations (9) and (10) and at -0.18 in equation (11). This suggests that a change in the interest rate from, say, 6 per cent to 4 per cent would ultimate lead to an increment of some 5 per cent in the nation's stock of housing. The initial response of construction would be more pronounced; the flow-demand elasticities of -0.80 and -0.95 obtained in equations (10) and (11) imply that, in the initial year following the change in the interest rate, construction would be between a fourth and a third greater than it otherwise would have been. The regressions using the rent-price ratio and the interest rate as explanatory variables yield estimates of the elasticity of construction with respect to the interest rate which are not grossly different from the above—around -0.40 in equation (18), -0.74 in equation (23), and -1.22 in equation (24). In equation (27), the elasticity of the average quality of housing with respect to the interest rate is measured at -0.45. Only in equations (12) and (16), where disposable income replaces (12) and supplements (16) the expected-income variable, does the coefficient of the interest rate fail to exceed its standard error, and even in these cases its sign is negative.

The key problems which determine the structure of Burstein's study of refrigerator demand are the related ones of price and quality. Quality has had a pronounced upward trend, making the problem of expressing "refrigeration" in equivalent units a serious one. Apart from the fact that we must solve the quality problem before we are able to obtain a time series of the price of equivalent units, price presents an additional difficulty in that most available data refer to "suggested list prices" rather than the average prices at which actual transactions took place. Burstein attacks these problems simultaneously by constructing a price index from Sears, Roebuck mail-order catalogue data. Sears's prices are actual transactions prices, uncolored by discounts or trade-ins, and external evidence suggests that they are reliable indicators of transactions prices for refrigerators in general. Burstein's index compares, in chain-link fashion, the prices of models with similar specifications in adjacent years. In each adjacent-year comparison quality is thus held constant; the quantity of "refrigeration" purchased by consumers, year by year, is then obtained by deflating the dollar volume of annual sales by the price index. Burstein next generates stock series, under several alternative assumptions as to the rate and pattern of depreciation, from the series on quantities purchased.

Regressions of stock (=consumption of services) on relative price and real income are taken under a wide variety of assumptions as to the depreciation pattern, with two alternative price indexes and two alternative income variables. Each of these regressions (IV–XVI) succeeds in explaining at least 97 per cent of the variance in the stock; the price-elasticity estimates range from −1.07 to −2.06, and the income-elasticity estimates from 0.82 to 2.54. If the war years (data for which are more dubious) are excluded, the range of price-elasticity estimates is from −1.58 to −2.06 and that for income-elasticity estimates is from 1.23 to 1.64.

Though all the coefficients emerging from the above regressions are highly significant statistically, the possibility exists that the price and income variables, both of which have strong trends, are in these regressions "explaining" a trendwise change in tastes. When trend is introduced (Regressions I–III) as a separate variable, in addition to price and income, the price-elasticity estimate falls to around unity but remains highly significant. The income elasticity falls to 0.83 under the disposable-income variant and remains highly significant, but under the expected-income varient the income-elasticity estimate falls below 0.5 and becomes statistically insignificant. (This is partly explained by the fact that the averaging procedure used to generate the expected-income variable smoothes out extreme fluctuations and makes the movements of expected income more trendlike than those of disposable income.)

When the regressions are taken in first-difference form (Regressions XVII–XXI), the multicollinearity problem is largely avoided. Both price and income elasticities remain highly significant regardless of whether a trend is introduced or not, the range of income elasticities here being 0.70 (disposable income, with trend) to 1.60 (expected income, without trend). The upper and lower limits of the price-elasticity estimates in all cases span the range obtained in the earlier regressions.

Burstein also estimated regressions in which a trend in tastes was imposed. When a "high" trend (implying an increase in per capita demand of over 300 per cent in twenty-four years) was imposed, estimated income elasticities ranged from 0.72 to 1.1, and estimated price elasticities from −1.19 to −1.58. With a "medium" trend (implying a 180 per cent increase over twenty-four years), income elasticities ranged from 0.97 to 1.57, and price elasticities from −1.32 to −1.87. When slow adjustment of actual to desired stock was allowed for, price elasticity was estimated at −1.4, income elasticity at 1.9, and the adjustment coefficient at .46. When both slow adjustment and trend are allowed for, the price-elasticity estimate becomes −0.7; the income elasticity, 1.5; and the adjustment coefficient, .73. When disposable income is used in the slow-adjustment variant, the price-elasticity estimate becomes statistically insignificant (−0.37), the income-elasticity estimate very large (3.0), and the adjustment coefficient is estimated at .36.

The final section of Burstein's study uses cross-section data in an effort to gain further evidence on the income elasticity of demand for refrigeration. A forty-eight-state cross-section study yields estimates of 0.4 using stock in 1954 as the dependent variable and 2.5 using income as dependent. This range is narrowed by taking weighted Regressions XXX*a* and XXX*b*, which yield elasticity estimates of 0.96 and 0.73. When the percentage changes in stock by state between 1940 and 1950 are related to the percentage changes in state incomes, a high estimate of income elasticity (over 2.0) emerges. When family budgets are used as the basis for estimating income elasticity, an estimate of around 0.7 results. This excludes freezers, which appear to have a higher income elasticity than refrigerators. Burstein's modest conclusions are that "the price elasticity is between −1.0 and −2.0 and, somewhat less conclusively, that the income elasticity is between 1.0 and 2.0."

Chow's paper is an extension and further test of the model presented in his earlier study of automobile demand. Here the stock of automobiles is expressed in new-car equivalent units on the basis of the relative market prices of cars of different ages. On the assumption of instantaneous adjustment of actual to desired stock Chow estimates the price elasticity to be between −0.6 and −1.1 and the income elasticity at from 1.5 to 1.7 under the disposable-income variant and at from 1.8 to 2.0 under the expected-income variant. The expected-income variant succeeds in explaining 90–95 per cent of the variance of the stock of cars, while the disposable-income variant explains 85–90 per cent.

When the possibility of slow adjustment of stock is allowed for, the estimated price elasticity of stock demand ranges around −0.7; the income elasticity, around 1.8. In this case purchases are the dependent variable in regression, and the disposable-income variant explains a substantially larger fraction of their variance than the expected-income variant (86 versus 63 per cent). According to the disposable-income variant, the adjustment coefficient is .48; according to the expected-income variant, it is .55.

The above estimates were derived from data on the years 1921–53. The 1921–53 relations are then extrapolated to the 1954–57 period and appear to hold as well in this "forecast period" as they did in the observation period. A further extrapolation into the recession year 1958 turns out to be substantially above the actual figure, indicating the possibility that automobile demand shifted downward "autonomously" in that year.

Chow also constructs a projection of automobile demand for the year 1968: according to his estimates, the normal annual demand for new cars in the United States will at that time be between 8.9 and 9.7 million units, if the relative price of cars remains unchanged.

In Griliches' study the focus is shifted from consumer durables to a durable productive input. The demand for farm tractors is taken to depend on tractor prices relative to agricultural product prices, on the interest rate, and (in some variants) on other factor prices, on the stock of horses and mules on farms, on farmer's equity, and on a time trend. When instantaneous adjustment of actual to desired stock is assumed, the price elasticity of stock demand is estimated at −0.5, and the interest-rate elasticity at −4.9. When slow adjustment is allowed for, the estimates of price elasticity of stock demand come to exceed unity in absolute value, averaging around −1.5, and the estimates of interest elasticity come to exceed −5.0 in absolute value, averaging around −6.5. The adjustment coefficient is estimated to be about .17. The main variables affecting tractor demand appear to be the price of tractors relative to agricultural product prices and the interest rate. When the other variables listed above were tried, they turned out to be statistically insignificant. Relative price and the interest rate alone explain about 80 per cent of the variance in tractor stock; together with lagged tractor stock (in the slow-adjustment models), they explain about 99 per cent of this variance. When tractor purchases rather than tractor stock are taken as the variable to be explained, relative price, interest rate, and lagged tractor stock explain over 90 per cent of the variation (in purchases).

Griliches, like Burstein, was faced with rather unsatifactory data on the pattern of depreciation. The official series on the stock of tractors used a depreciation rate which declined gradually from 40 per cent in 1910 to 18.5 per cent in the 1950's. Yet market data on used tractors appear to indicate a depreciation rate of around 11 or 12 per cent. Fortunately, the estimated-price and interest-rate coefficients are rather insensitive to changes in the assumed rate and pattern of depreciation. However, the estimated adjustment coefficient is somewhat sensitive to alternative assumptions, ranging from .10 to .26 in Griliches' different formulations.

One puzzle that emerges from Griliches' study is the high value of estimated interest elasticity of stock demand as compared to the price elasticity. Interest being only a fraction of the total imputed cost of using a tractor, we would expect the interest elasticity of stock demand to be smaller than the price elasticity. Yet Griliches estimates the interest elasticity to be much larger than the price elasticity. Part of the explanation lies in the fact that the interest-rate series used (that on farm-mortgage rates) is probably more sluggish in its movements than an ideal measure would be; if the measure used understates the extent of the true percentage movements in the relevant rate, it thereby introduces an upward bias into the elasticity estimate. A second possibility is that the lag in achieving a full response to interest-rate changes is shorter than the lag associated with, say, changes in the prices of agricultural products. In this case, the procedure of assuming the lag to be the same regardless of which variable caused desired stock to deviate from actual stock would tend to yield a too-low estimate of the price elasticity and a too-high estimate of the interest-rate elasticity.

Grunfeld's study takes as its point of departure the high correlation observed by many investigators between profits (either lagged or current) and investment. Working with time-series data for each of eight large manufacturing corporations, he finds also that investment tends to move with profits. However, he is led quickly to suspect the validity of this relationship. Recognizing that the stock of capital equipment should exert via replacement an independent influence on gross investment, he introduces a measure of this stock side by side with profits in an equation explaining investment. The partial correlations of investment with profits turn out to be negligible. This suggests that, in the observed correlations between profits and investment, profits may have to some extent acted as a surrogate for "stock of capital equipment" or "size."

Grunfeld then examines the possibility that profits may have acted as a surrogate for other variables as well. First, he tests "liquidity" hypotheses by introducing the stock of liquid assets and other possible liquidity variables into the equations explaining investment. Liquidity variables appear in this investigation to have no significant effect on investment. Second, he turns to a variable aimed at measuring profit expectations. This variable, the "value of the firm," is the sum of outstanding debt plus equity as valued in the market. It gives the market's assessment of the value of the firm, while Grunfeld's measure of the "stock of capital equipment" attempts to approximate the value of the assets of the firm at replacement cost. Expectations are favorable when the market places a high value on the firm relative to the replacement cost of its assets and vice versa. Thus, for a given cost of assets, the market value of the firm measures the state of the market's expectations. Grunfeld finds the value of the firm to be superior to either current or lagged profits as an explanatory variable for investment.

There follows an investigation of the role of the rate of interest in determining investment. Grunfeld notes that the market value of the firm, being the discounted value of expected earnings, actually contains an interest-rate effect. He attempts to separate out this effect by using two distinct variables in place of the market value of the firm: first, the expected flow of earnings, measured by the market value of the firm times the rate of interest and, second, the rate of interest itself. In this variant the rate of interest appears to have significant effects on investment for most of Grunfeld's companies. The elasticity of investment with respect to the long-term rate of interest on bonds is estimated as being between -0.5 and -2.1 for seven of the eight corporations.

Grunfeld tests in several ways the model in which "stock of capital equipment" and "market value of the firm" are used to explain variations in investment. For all but one of the eight corporations Grunfeld's model gives predictions superior to the "naïve" prediction of "no change from last year to this year." The model correctly predicted the direction of change of investment in 64 of 73 turning points; in fact, in a considerable fraction of the cases, it overpredicted investment the year after a trough and underpredicted it the year after a peak. After extrapolating the equations to two years (1955 and 1956) not used in estimating, Grunfeld concluded that the new observations were consistent with all but one of the relationships estimated previously. For these years, comparison with "naïve" predictions did not fare so well, the model doing better in only four of the eight cases. On the other hand, a test of the model on three additional corporations not included in the original sample confirmed strikingly the main hypothesis that, once the value of the firm and the stock of capital equipment are introduced, profits variables do not add significantly to the explanation of movements in investment.

IV

Viewed as a group, the studies leave some fairly clear impressions. First, the price and income elasticities of demand for consumer durables appear to be rather substantial—in the neighborhood of unity at least and in some cases perhaps quite a bit greater. Second, the interest rate appears to be an important variable in determining the demand for housing, for tractors, and for business plant and equipment. Third, in the places where Friedman's expected-income variable was "tested" against disposable income as a determinant of demand for holdings of consumer durables, it came off the winner (except possibly in the case of refrigerators). Disposable income provided a better explanation of variations in purchases than expected income for automobiles and refrigerators but not for housing. These results are not inconsistent with the expected-income hypothesis, which anticipates that durable goods *purchases* will be sensitive to transitory variations in income.

Finally, the studies provide a substantial body of evidence in favor of viewing durable goods purchases in any given year as providing for the replacement of the stock plus *some fraction* of the difference between actual stock at the beginning of the year and its equilibrium level. This fraction appears to be 0.50 or less for most durables: Muth estimated it at 0.32 for housing using the expected-income variable and at 0.15 using disposable income; Chow estimated it at 0.55 for automobiles using expected income and at 0.46 using disposable income; Burstein estimated it at 0.46 for refrigerators using expected income and at 0.36 using disposable income; Griliches estimated it to be in the range between 0.10 and 0.25 for tractors. This relatively slow-adjustment process helps to dampen somewhat the cyclical responsiveness of durable purchases.

V

In this section, I attempt to trace briefly the role which these studies suggest is played by durable goods in cyclical fluctuations in the United States. The three consumer durables studies provide direct evidence on the way in which the desired stocks of durables seem to react to changes in disposable income and on the manner in which purchases of new durables operate to bring actual stocks into line with desired stocks. Table 1 presents the reactions implied by these three studies for a "typical" postwar recession.

The entries in the table refer to percentages below normal; I assume the normal situation to be one in which gross national product (GNP) and disposable income grow at 3 per cent per year, or $\frac{3}{4}$ per cent per quarter. In the model recession of Table 1, GNP is assumed to fall below its normal growth path by 1 per cent in the first quarter, 3 per cent in the second, 5 per cent in the third, and 7 per cent in the fourth quarter and then to rise back to normal by similar quarterly steps. Because of built-in stabilizers such as corporate saving, the corporation income tax, the personal income tax, and unemployment compensation, personal disposable income does not fall below its norm by an equal amount, or even by an equal percentage, as GNP. In the table the effect of these stabilizers is taken roughly into account by the assumption that the percentage gap between disposable income in any quarter and its full-employment norm is six-tenths of the corresponding percentage gap between GNP and its norm.

The normal rate of growth of the stock of a durable good is assumed to be $3e$ per cent per year, where e is its income elasticity of demand. Normal purchases are the fraction $(d + 0.03e)$ of normal stock, where d is the percentage annual rate of depreciation (replacement); because normal purchases are a constant fraction of normal stock, they also grow at $3e$ per cent per year, or $\frac{3}{4}e$ per cent per quarter. Table 1 shows the percentages by which purchases of each durable fall below their normal growth path in successive quarters of the model recession. The first three coefficients given for each durable at the bottom of the table are derived from the studies in this volume, taking in each case that equation which allowed for slow adjustment, while using disposable income as the income

TABLE 1

IMPLIED BEHAVIOR OF DURABLES DEMAND IN A "TYPICAL" RECESSION
(Based on Estimates Using Disposable Income)

Time (in Quarters)	GNP (Per Cent below Normal)	Disposable Income (Per Cent below Normal)	Residential Construction (Per Cent below Normal)	Refrigerator Purchases (Per Cent below Normal)	Automobile Purchases (Per Cent below Normal)
0..........	0	0	0	0	0
1..........	1.0	0.6	1.5	3.2	2.1
2..........	3.0	1.8	4.5	9.4	6.0
3..........	5.0	3.0	7.3	14.8	9.5
4	7.0	4.2	10.1	19.8	12.8
5..........	5.0	3.0	6.8	12.2	7.6
6..........	3.0	1.8	3.5	5.2	3.0
7..........	1.0	0.6	0.4	− 1.0	− 1.1
8..........	0	0	− 1.1	− 3.7	− 2.7
9..........	0	0	− 1.0	− 3.2	− 2.3
10..........	0	0	− 0.9	− 2.9	− 1.9

COEFFICIENTS USED

Income elasticity of stock demand (e).........	.9	2.9	1.7
Quarterly adjustment coefficient (k)..........	.04	.1	.15
Quarterly replacement coefficient (r).........	.0075	.03	.06
Initial ratio of normal purchases to GNP (f)...	.0384	.0036	.0390

variable. The annual replacement coefficients assumed are 3 per cent for houses, 12 per cent for refrigerators, and 24 per cent for automobiles; the quarterly replacement coefficients are simply one-fourth of the annual ones. The quarterly adjustment coefficients are derived from the annual ones estimated in the studies. If 4 per cent of the gap between actual and desired stock is filled each quarter, some 15 per cent (the figure Muth estimated in eq. [12]) will be filled in a year; if 10 per cent is filled each quarter, some 35 per cent (Burstein's figure was 36 per cent) will be filled in a year; if 15 per cent is filled each quarter, some 48 per cent (Chow's figure was 0.46) will be filled in a year.

The method by which the last three columns of Table 1 are derived from the three key coefficients for each durable is illustrated in Table 2 for the case of automobiles. Table 2 divides the response of purchases into three effects: the desired stock effect, the actual stock effect, and the replacement effect. The net change of stock in any quarter, it will be recalled, is the quarterly adjustment coefficient, k, times the excess of desired over actual stock. The desired stock effect on purchases is simply k times the difference between desired stock and its normal level, while the actual stock effect is $-k$ times the difference between actual stock and its normal level. (Differences between recession value and normal value

TABLE 2

INDUCED RESPONSES OF AUTOMOBILE DEMAND IN A "TYPICAL" RECESSION

(Amounts below Normal in Billions of 1957 Dollars at Annual
Rates; Norms for Quarter 1 Are 1957 Values)

Time (in Quarters)	GNP	Purchases, Desired Stock Effect $(0.082 \times [1]_{-1})$	Purchases, Actual Stock Effect $(-0.15 \times [4]_{-1})$	Actual Stock $([2]+[3]+ +[4]_{-1})$	Purchases, Replacement Effect $(0.06 \times [4]_{-1})$	Total Purchases $([2]+[3] +[5])$
	(1)	(2)	(3)	(4)	(5)	(6)
1....	4.403	0	0	0	0	0
2....	13.308	0.361	0	0.361	0	0.361
3....	22.345	1.091	−0.054	1.398	0.022	1.059
4....	31.521	1.832	− .210	3.020	.084	1.706
5....	22.685	2.585	− .453	5.152	.181	2.313
6....	13.683	1.860	− .773	6.239	.309	1.396
7....	4.575	1.122	− .936	6.425	.374	0.560
8....	0	0.375	− .964	5.836	.385	−0.204
9....	0	0	− .875	4.961	.350	−0.525
10....	0	0	− .744	4.217	.298	−0.446
11....	0	0	−0.633	3.584	0.253	−0.380

will hereafter be referred to as "shortfalls.") The percentage shortfall of desired stock is simply the income elasticity of demand, e, times the percentage shortfall in disposable income, or $.6e$ times the percentage shortfall in GNP, g. To express the shortfall of desired stock as a percentage of normal purchases, we simply divide $0.6eg$ by $(r + 0.0075e)$, the normal ratio of quarterly purchases to normal stock. Here r is the quarterly replacement coefficient, and the factor $0.0075e$ makes allowance for the normal growth component of purchases. The shortfall of desired stock as a percentage of normal purchases is thus $0.6eg/(r + 0.0075e)$. To express the shortfall of desired stock in dollars, we multiply the above expression by normal purchases, obtaining the expression $0.6efG/(r + 0.0075e)$, where f is the normal ratio of purchases to GNP, and G is the absolute shortfall of GNP. The desired stock effect on purchases being k times the absolute shortfall of desired stock, we obtain column (2) by multiplying the short-fall of GNP of the previous quarter by the factor $m = 0.6efk/(r + 0.0075e)$. This factor, equal to 0.082 in the case of automobiles, can be regarded as a sort of cyclical marginal propensity to invest in the durable good in question.

The shortfall of actual stock (col. [4]) at the end of period 2 is simply the shortfall of purchases in period 2. The influence of actual stock on purchases in period 3 is accordingly $-k$ times this figure. Net purchases being the sum of the entries in columns (2) and (3) for any period, the shortfall of actual stock at the end of period 3 is obtained by adding this sum to the shortfall of actual stock at the end of period 2. Columns (3) and (4) are thus generated on the basis of column (2). It is in column (3) that the accelerator effect is revealed, the shortfall in actual stock operating first to limit and ultimately to reverse the tendency for purchases to fall below normal. Column (5) reflects the fact that it takes less replacement to maintain a subnormal stock than to maintain a normal one; it is simply the quarterly replacement coefficient times the previous quarter's shortfall of actual stock. (This assumes that service yield declines in proportion to the market value of a durable good as it ages; as indicated earlier, the pattern of depreciation for automobiles suggests that this is true, but in any event the figures involved are so small that altering the assumption would not have a significant effect.)

The total effect on purchases in any quarter is the sum of the desired stock, actual stock, and replacement effects, that is, the sum of the entries in columns (2), (3), and (5). This is presented in column (6) of Table 2. To obtain the percentage figures given in Table 1, the figures in column (6) of Table 2 are expressed as percentages of normal purchases. Normal purchases for period 1 are assumed to be at the 1957 annual rate; they are assumed to grow at the rate of $0.75e$ per cent per quarter.

The results of Table 1 indicate substantial responsiveness of durable goods purchases to cyclical movements. Where the trough of GNP is 7 per cent below normal and the trough of disposable income is 4.2 per cent below normal, the trough is 10.1 per cent below normal for residential construction, 12.8 per cent below normal for automobiles, and 19.8 per cent below normal for refrigerators. By the end of the recession at the beginning of quarter 8, it has entailed a loss of total product equal to 6.25 per cent of a year's GNP, and consumers have suffered a loss equal to 3.75 per cent of a year's disposable income. Meanwhile the "loss" of automobile production has been 10 per cent of a year's normal output, that of residential construction has been 8.5 per cent, and that of refrigerator production has been 15.9 per cent. (These figures are obtained by adding the quarterly shortfalls of production for the first eight quarters and by dividing by four to express the cumulated loss as a percentage of normal annual rather than normal quarterly production.)

The percentage loss in automobiles, in the example of Table 1, was some 1.6 times the percentage loss in GNP. The corresponding multiple for residential construction is 1.36; for refrigerators, 2.54. These multiples depend to some extent on the pattern through time of the changes in GNP. It is thus worthwhile to know that, given the replacement coefficients, income elasticities, and adjustment coefficients used in Table 1, the percentage loss in automobiles could never exceed 2.1 times the percentage loss in GNP, while the corresponding multiples could never exceed 1.52 for residential construction or 3.36 for refrigerators, whatever may be the pattern or size of the percentage shortfalls of GNP and whatever may be the length of the period for which the losses are accumulated, starting with the beginning of the recession. These multiples, equal to $0.6ek/(0.0075e + r)$, express the desired stock effect on purchases as a percentage of normal purchases; so long as k exceeds r, the sum of the actual stock and replacement effects must be negative or zero throughout a recession in which actual stocks were initially at normal levels.[1]

Some observations and qualifications are in order before we draw inferences or conclusions from Tables 1 and 2. First, these tables apply in a recession situation demand functions for durables which are based on time series covering prosperity and depression periods as well as mild recessions. There exists the possibility that the relationships applicable in recessions differ systematically from those applying in other periods. For example, if a recessionary fall in income is regarded as temporary, desired stocks of durables may not fall as much as our income-elasticity estimates imply.[2] On the other hand, the postponement of durable goods

---

[1] The pattern of changes in GNP which elicits the maximal response is a drop below normal lasting for just one period, plus an infinitesimal shortfall in the subsequent period. Then the full desired stock effect of the initial shortfall takes place while the recession is still under way, while the rise of durables demand above normal, resulting from the operation of the actual stock effect, takes place after the recession is over and does not contribute to the numerator of the ratio.

[2] If the results obtained by Muth, Burstein, and Chow in their expected-income rather than their disposable-income variants are used to generate a table similar to Table 1, the pattern of response changes quite drastically. The troughs of purchases are less than 7 per cent below normal levels for all three durables, but the recession pattern is flatter and more prolonged, purchases being still below normal for all three durables in the twelfth quarter rather than rising above normal in the seventh or eighth quarter, as in Table 1. In automobiles and refrigerators the aggregate shortfall of demand, during the whole period before demand rises above normal, is only a little more than half as large in the expected-income model than in the disposable-income model. But for residential construction, the only case in which the expected-income variant provided a better explanation of purchases than the disposable-income variant, the aggregate short-

purchases in a recession may reflect a higher adjustment coefficient than that governing movements between full-employment periods. We have, however, not had sufficient recession experience to warrant the separate estimation of durable goods demand functions for just such periods. Second, the model underlying the tables takes account only of income-induced changes in durables demand during a recession. In any real recession these will be compounded with the autonomous fluctuations to which durables are particularly subject and with movements induced by changes in relative prices and interest rates which may well be the products of the recession itself. To the extent that the underlying relationships do hold in recession periods, however, they give us some insights into an important part of the mechanism by which our cyclical movements are propagated and may enable us at least roughly to divide the observed changes in durables demand in a recession into the categories "autonomous" and "income-induced." Third, a caveat is in order with respect to the income-elasticity estimate used in the case of refrigerators. The great bulk of Burstein's evidence pointed to an income elasticity of stock demand somewhere between 1.0 and 2.0, yet his income-elasticity estimate, obtained using the disposable-income, slow-adjustment formulation, was 2.9. I am quite confident that this is an overestimate and suspect strongly that the true cyclical volatility of refrigerator demand is less than that revealed in Table 1. I made no adjustment to Burstein's results, however, because of the possibility that the high-income elasticity estimate is solely the result of a downward bias in the estimate of the adjustment coefficient.[3] If this were the case, the simultaneous correction of both the

---

fall of demand is slightly greater when expected income is used than it is when disposable income is used. Thus, had expected income been used for construction in Table 1, while disposable income was used for the other durables, the main results would not be greatly altered.

[3] Griliches ("Distributed Lags, Disaggregation, and Regional Demand Functions for Fertilizer," *Journal of Farm Economics*, XLI [February, 1959], 95–99) has demonstrated that there exists a presumption of downward bias in estimates of adjustment coefficients obtained in the manner of those presented in this volume. This bias would result in an overestimation of income elasticities of stock demand, which are obtained by dividing the regression coefficient of purchases on income by the estimated adjustment coefficient. It would not of itself affect the cyclical volatility revealed in Table 1, for this depends essentially on the product of the income elasticity and the adjustment coefficient (i.e., on the regression coefficient of purchases on income directly). It is hard to establish a strong presumption of bias in this latter coefficient, an argument along Griliches' lines and an argument proceeding from the effects of shifts in demand on income both suggesting an upward bias, while errors of measurement in the income variable conduce to a downward bias. In the net, there is probably a weak presumption that the estimates of cyclical volatility are slightly excessive.

income elasticity and the adjustment coefficient estimates would lead to no significant reduction in cyclical volatility.

One striking result of Table 1 is the relatively low cyclical volatility of residential construction. In simple expositions of the acceleration principle, cyclical volatility is usually asserted to vary inversely with the rate of replacement; we would accordingly anticipate housing to show the most extreme movements. Our example differs from the simple textbook models in two respects: first, in taking account of the component of normal purchases which provides for the secular growth of stock; second, in allowing for the gradual rather than instantaneous approach of actual to desired stock. It is this latter factor which explains the "anomalous" behavior of residential construction. The adjustment coefficient in the case of residential construction is sufficiently low, together with the income elasticity, to outweigh the tendency for high volatility stemming from construction's low replacement coefficient.

The table also reveals a notable tendency for the percentage shortfalls of purchases to bear a reasonably constant relationship to the percentage shortfalls of GNP, particularly in the downswing. In construction the shortfall is around one and a half times, in refrigerators around three times, and in automobiles around twice the percentage shortfall in GNP. Only when the recession has been under way for a considerable time— indeed, in this example, only when it is nearly over—does the self-reversing tendency implicit in the accelerator mechanism assert itself seriously.

VI

In the preceding section the reactions of particular durables to an assumed set of changes in GNP were explored. In this section, I attempt to broaden the horizon to include the whole durable goods sector and to get an idea of the role of this sector in the multiplier-accelerator process. Again a "typical" recession is assumed, but in this case only the course of autonomous movements in demand is known in advance; the paths of GNP and of demand for durables and non-durables are generated by the model. Autonomous changes are assumed, which, by themselves, would carry GNP down to 4 per cent below normal within four quarters and then back to normal within four additional quarters. Disposable income is again assumed to fall below normal by six-tenths of the percentage shortfall of GNP. The normal ratio of disposable income to GNP is assumed to be three-fourths, and the marginal propensity to consume non-durables to be 0.4; thus the induced shortfall of non-durables demand in period t is taken to be 0.18 ($=0.6 \times 0.4 \times 0.75$) of the absolute shortfall of GNP in period $t - 1$.

For the durables a process like that outlined in Table 2 is assumed, desired stocks falling below normal by some fraction of the lagged shortfall of GNP, net purchases falling below normal by the adjustment coefficient times the difference between the shortfalls of desired and actual stocks, and replacement demand falling below normal by the replacement coefficient times the lagged shortfall of actual stocks. Two alternative sets of coefficients were used, one leading to high and the other to low volatility. For residential construction the coefficients were taken to be the same as in Table 1 under both alternatives. For automobiles the same values as in Table 1 were assumed for the high-volatility case, but the income elasticity was reduced from 1.7 to 1.0 for the low-volatility case. For "other consumer durables" reference was made to Burstein's study of refrigerators, and an income elasticity of 1.5 was assumed together with an adjustment coefficient of .1 in the high-volatility case, while in the low-volatility alternative the income elasticity was reduced to 1.0 and the adjustment coefficient to .08. In both alternatives a replacement coefficient of .03 was assumed. For non-residential construction the alternative income elasticities were 1.0 and 0.8, while for producer durable equipment they were 1.2 and 0.8. These assumptions are partly based on the observed secular tendency of capital stock to maintain a reasonably constant ratio to GNP. Both Grunfeld's and Griliches' results suggest that the adjustment coefficients are quite low for investment in plant and equipment. I have assumed alternative coefficients of .05 and .04 for "other construction," and of .10 and .08 for producer durable equipment. For both of these categories desired stock was taken to depend on GNP directly rather than on disposable income; that is, the percentage shortfall of desired stock was taken as eg rather than the $0.6eg$ figure used for the consumer-demand categories. The value for m, the "cyclical marginal propensity to invest," is for these durables $efk/(0.0075e + r)$, rather than 0.6 times this expression as in the consumer categories.

In spite of the rather substantial differences between the high- and low-volatility assumptions used, some generalizations appear warranted regardless of which set is employed. On the high-volatility assumptions, the aggregate loss of product by the time the recession is over at the close of the ninth quarter is 2.64 times the sum of the autonomous disturbances appearing in column (1) of Table 3; on the low-volatility assumptions the loss of GNP is 1.94 times this sum. Durables do indeed amplify our recessions (if there were no induced response of durables, the loss of GNP would be only 1.22 times the sum of autonomous disturbances) and extend them somewhat (were it not for the durables response, the recession of Table 3 would be over after eight rather than nine quarters). But they do not, under "reasonable" assumptions about autonomous disturbances, respond in capricious ways. Even when an autonomous disturbance is assumed which lasts but one quarter and then disappears, the resulting loss of GNP is not a very different multiple of the autonomous loss from that emerging from Table 3. Though this "recession" lasts six quarters under the high-volatility assumptions and five under the low-volatility assumptions, compared with two in the case where there is no durables response, the GNP loss is but 2.75 and 1.96

TABLE 3

THE MULTIPLIER-ACCELERATOR PROCESS IN A "TYPICAL" RECESSION

(Amounts below Normal in Billions of 1957 Dollars at Annual Rates; Norms for Quarter 1 Are 1957 Values)

TIME (IN QUARTERS)	AUTONO- MOUS DE- MAND	HIGH-VOLATILITY ALTERNATIVE			LOW-VOLATILITY ALTERNATIVE		
		GNP	Non- durables	Durables	GNP	Non- durables	Durables
1.......	4.4	4.4	0	0	4.4	0	0
2.......	8.9	12.1	0.8	2.4	11.3	0.8	1.6
3.......	13.4	22.1	2.2	6.5	19.4	2.0	4.0
4.......	18.0	33.7	4.0	11.7	28.3	3.5	6.8
5.......	13.6	37.0	6.1	17.3	28.4	5.1	9.7
6.......	9.1	33.9	6.7	18.1	23.5	5.1	9.3
7.......	4.6	26.0	6.1	15.3	15.9	4.2	7.1
8.......	0	14.8	4.7	10.1	6.9	2.9	4.0
9.......	0	6.0	2.7	3.3	1.8	1.2	0.6
10.......	0	−0.5	1.1	−1.6	−0.9	0.3	−1.2
Σ....	72.0	189.5	34.2	83.3	139.0	25.2	41.8

TABLE OF ASSUMED COEFFICIENTS

	HIGH-VOLATILITY ALTERNATIVE					LOW-VOLATILITY ALTERNATIVE				
	e	k	r	f	m	e	k	r	f	m
Residential construction	0.9	.04	.0075	.0384	.0582	0.9	.04	.0075	.0384	.0582
Other construction...	1.0	.05	.01	.0372	.1064	0.8	.04	.01	.0372	.0744
Producer durable equipment......	1.2	.10	.03	.0630	.1940	0.8	.08	.03	.0630	.1120
Automobiles .	1.7	.15	.06	.0390	.0819	1.0	.15	.06	.0390	.0529
Other consumer durables	1.5	.10	.03	.0515	.1123	1.0	.08	.03	.0515	.0659

times the autonomous loss in the two cases, respectively, as compared with 2.64 and 1.94 obtained from Table 3.[4]

The picture thus emerges of a normal recession pattern in which the aggregate loss of product probably lies between 2 and 2.5 times the aggregate autonomous reduction in demand. The induced shortfall or non-durables demand probably lies between one-third and one-half of the aggregate autonomous reduction, while the induced loss of durables demand probably amounts to between two-thirds and five-fourths of the autonomous reduction. In this picture the effects of the built-in stabilizers are already taken into account. In the autonomous category are inventory investment, exports, and government purchases of goods and services plus changes in demand for durables and non-durables stemming from other causes than the recession's income movement. Naturally, many obvious qualifications must be attached to so simple a picture. But I believe that these qualifications are not of the kind which would seriously shake the rough conclusions stated above. The studies in this volume suggest strongly that the mechanism of adjustment in the durables field is of the general type employed in this and the preceding section; they also give ample evidence of the orders of magnitude of income elasticities and adjustment coefficients for particular durables, which in turn suggest ranges of plausible values for broad categories of the type treated in this section. It seems to me that, insofar as the picture presented above errs, it probably exaggerates the actual response of durables demand in a recession, the actual response being influenced additionally by the favorable movements in purchase and credit terms which normally take place in recession periods.

[4] The computations underlying the above statement and those for Table 3 were carried out using an exceedingly convenient method which approximates very closely the results which would emerge by pursuing the calculations for each durables category separately. The desired stock effect is estimated exactly by multiplying the lagged shortfall of GNP by the sum of the marginal propensities to invest in the particular durables. The actual stock effect on purchases and the replacement effect are approximated by applying average coefficients of adjustment and replacement to the preceding quarter's shortfall in the aggregate stock of durables. The appropriate averages are $\bar{k} = \Sigma m_i k_i / \Sigma m_i$ and $\bar{r} = \Sigma m_i r_i / \Sigma m_i$; these weight k_i and r_i by roughly the ith durable's contribution to the shortfall of aggregate stock.

II

The Demand for Non-Farm Housing

RICHARD F. MUTH

The Demand for Non-Farm Housing

I. Introduction

IN THIS study an attempt is made to estimate the responsiveness of housing demand to changes in income and in the price of housing. Probably because of the intractability of the data in this field, little work on these questions has been done in the past.

Opinions about the price and income elasticities of demand for housing vary widely. On the one hand, there is the view that housing is a "necessity," in some sense, and that the quantity of housing demanded changes less than proportionally in response to changes in price or income. On the subject of income elasticity, Morton asserts that, "because of the absolute necessity of shelter, housing stands with food very high in the order of urgency. . . . Housing expenditures, accordingly, do not bear a constant but a decreasing ratio to income."[1] This is in direct contradiction to Marshall's classic comments that "house room satisfies the imperative need for shelter from the weather; but that need plays very little part in the effective demand for house room" and that "where the condition of society is healthy . . . there seems always to be an elastic demand for house room, on account of the real conveniences and the social distinction which it affords."[2]

Morton's assertions and similar opinions expressed by Winnick,[3] among others, are based mainly on evidence of the type presented in Table 1, column (2). This column shows the percentage of current income spent for housing as computed from data from the 1935–36 consumer budget study. This percentage declines steadily as current income increases, as does the percentage of current income spent for all items shown in column (1), suggesting that the income elasticity of demand for housing as well as for all current consumption is less than unity. However, recent research on the consumption function suggests that the relation of consumption to

[1] Walter A. Morton, *Housing Taxation* (Madison: University of Wisconsin Press, 1955), pp. 42–43. Sherman J. Maisel in *Housebuilding in Transition* (Berkeley: University of California Press, 1953), p. 274, offers a similar statement to justify his belief that housing demand is highly inelastic with respect to price.

[2] Alfred Marshall, *Principles of Economics* (8th ed.; New York: Macmillan Co., 1950), pp. 88 and 107.

[3] Louis Winnick, "Housing: Has There Been a Downward Shift in Consumer Preferences?" *Quarterly Journal of Economics*, LXIX (February, 1955), 87–88. Both Morton and Winnick suggest a value of about +0.5 for income elasticity.

current income as between income classes at a given point in time yields misleading results when attention is focused upon the income elasticity of demand as between different years. This is because the income a consumer receives in a given year may differ from his expectations about his normal income level, and it is the latter which is the more important determinant of consumption.[4] Friedman, in particular, has suggested the hypothesis

TABLE 1*

TOTAL CONSUMPTION EXPENDITURE AND EXPENDITURE ON
HOUSING IN RELATION TO INCOME, 1935–36

INCOME LEVEL	PERCENTAGE OF INCOME SPENT ON		RATIO OF EXPENDITURE (COL. [2] ÷ COL. [1])
	All Items (1)	Housing (2)	(3)
Under $500.............	149.3	28.9	0.194
$500–$750.............	112.7	19.9	.177
$750–$1,000...........	104.6	18.5	.177
$1,000–$1,250.........	100.6	18.1	.180
$1,250–$1,500.........	96.5	16.9	.175
$1,500–$1,750.........	93.8	16.6	.177
$1,750–$2,000.........	92.1	16.5	.179
$2,000–$2,500.........	88.6	15.7	.177
$2,500–$3,000.........	84.8	14.9	.176
$3,000–$4,000.........	80.4	14.3	.178
$4,000–$5,000.........	74.6	13.0	.174
$5,000–$10,000........	64.8	11.4	.176
$10,000–$15,000.......	53.7	10.6	.197
$15,000–$20,000.......	52.7	8.6	.163
$20,000 and over.......	35.4	6.5	0.184
Average, all levels........	85.6	15.3	0.179

* Source: National Resources Committee, Industrial Committee, *Consumer Expenditures in the United States: Estimates for 1935–36* (Washington, D.C.: Government Printing Office, 1939), Table 6A, p. 78.

that consumption is proportional to normal or "permanent" income.[5] If this is correct, the comparison of expenditures for housing with all consumption expenditures would give an estimate of income elasticity more useful for comparisons between different years—the elasticity with respect

[4] While the literature bearing on this topic is too extensive to cite here, the reader is referred to Milton Friedman, *A Theory of the Consumption Function* (Princeton, N.J.: Princeton University Press, 1957), and Franco Modigliani and Richard Brumberg, "Utility Analysis and the Consumption Function: An Interpretation of Cross-Section Data," in *Post-Keynesian Economics*, ed. Kenneth K. Kurihara (London: George Allen & Unwin, 1955), pp. 388–436.

[5] *Op. cit.*

to permanent income. Column (3) of Table 1 shows that, for these same data, the ratio of expenditure on housing to all current consumption is nearly constant and does not vary systematically with the level of income. This observation suggests an elasticity of about unity with respect to permanent income.[6]

The only published estimate of the price elasticity of housing demand is that of Duesenberry and Kistin.[7] They estimated price elasticity for housing as well as for food and clothing by comparing changes in expenditure in the same city between successive budget studies with changes in the appropriate Bureau of Labor Statistics city price indexes, holding real income constant. They found significant correlations between expenditures and price for food and clothing; but for housing the correlation coefficient was −.06 and the estimated price elasticity −0.08, neither of which was statistically significant.

This study focuses on housing services as the fundamental object of the "demand for housing." Since these services are provided by the stock of houses in existence at any point in time, we attempt to explain the variations in the stock of housing over time and to estimate how much this stock would ultimately change in response to changes in the price of housing or in income. We view new construction as the means by which the stock of housing is adjusted to changing conditions and attempt to estimate simultaneously from changes in the rate of new construction both the pace at which adjustments take place in the housing market and the responsiveness of stock demand to changes in price and income. Our emphasis on stock demand, as derived from the demand for services, distinguishes this effort from a number of studies of new construction which have appeared in recent decades. These studies have been motivated by the interest in short-run fluctuations in aggregate economic activity and have largely neglected the relation of the demand for new construction to

---

[6] This comparison is meant only to illustrate the point that previous comparisons of housing expenditure with current income by income class at a given time may give a misleading impression as to the elasticity of housing demand with respect to permanent income. If consumption expenditures depend upon the transitory income component, the difference between current and permanent income, as well as upon the permanent income component, and if all current consumption is more sensitive to variations in the transitory component than expenditures for housing, then the comparison made here would result in an underestimate of the permanent income elasticity of demand for housing. And, of course, in this comparison no account has been taken of price or other variables that might affect housing demand.

[7] James S. Duesenberry and Helen Kistin, "The Role of Demand in the Economic Structure," in *Studies in the Structure of the American Economy*, ed. Wassily Leontieff (New York: Oxford University Press, 1953), pp. 451–82.

stock demand. The emphasis adopted in this study will, I believe, lead to a better understanding of fluctuations in the rate of new construction and their place in the structure of over-all economic change.

II. A Model of Housing Demand

This section sets out the model which serves as the framework for the empirical investigation into the demand for non-farm housing discussed in later sections.

UNITS OF MEASUREMENT

Before formulating the model of housing demand itself, it is necessary to define precisely certain magnitudes. This is particularly important for the unit of measure of housing stock, since in the real world there is virtually infinite variation among residential structures as to size, type of construction, floor space, and other characteristics to which consumers attach value. Much of the discussion in the literature on housing and several empirical studies have used the dwelling unit as the unit of stock. But these are patently non-homogeneous; a one-room slum apartment and a suburban mansion certainly contain different quantities of "housing" in any reasonable sense, yet both count as one dwelling unit. Because of the infinite variation in dwelling units, it is difficult to find any classification in terms of technological or legal characteristics which results in homogeneous units. One way out of this difficulty is to accept the judgment of the market: to treat as identical those units of "housing" which command identical prices. Thus, to measure the total stock of housing, the market price of each structure might first be observed. (Throughout this study only structures are considered, and land is excluded, unless otherwise noted.) A particular structure would then be selected as standard, that is, as containing one unit of housing, and its price divided into the price of each other structure. The resulting ratios would give for each structure the number of units of housing in standard house equivalents. The total stock of housing would then be the sum of the number of standard house equivalents. But this total is simply the constant dollar value of the stock of housing—the current dollar value deflated by the price of the standard house.[8] Similarly, the price of a unit of housing is defined as the price of the standard house.

In what follows, a unit of quantity of housing service is needed as well. One unit of housing service is defined as that quantity of service yielded by one unit of housing stock per unit of time. The price per unit of housing

---

[8] This solution to the problem of measurement of stock suffers from the defect common to all index-number solutions. It yields no unique measure if the relative prices of the different units being aggregated change over time.

service, or rent, is the price paid by consumers for the flow of services from one standard house per unit of time. In addition to the net return received by the owner of the structure, this rent includes an allowance for depreciation, maintenance and repair, and taxes.

DEMAND FOR SERVICES AND STOCK DEMAND

The fundamental demand for housing relates the quantity of housing services, h, to rent, R, income, y, and other relevant variables.[9] This function is shown diagrammatically (for given levels of explanatory variables other than rent) in Figure 1. Now at any instant of time the quantity of housing stock is fixed; thus, by assumption, the quantity of housing services is also fixed. This quantity, say, h_1, together with the position of the demand schedule, determines the level of rent, R_1.

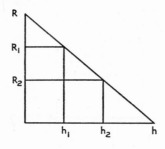

FIG. 1

To derive stock demand from the demand for services, we must explore the relation between rent and price per unit of stock. To do so, it is convenient to consider first only positions of long-run equilibrium in the market for stocks. By long-run equilibrium I mean a set of conditions—stock, price, income, and other factors—under which there would be no tendency for the quantity of stock (per capita) to change over time. In such a position, newly constructed housing would only be sufficient to offset depreciation and to provide for additions to population. The stock associated with such a set of conditions is described as the long-run equilibrium, or, for a more convenient term, the *desired* stock of housing, h_d. Now, since the demand for stocks is derived from the demand for services, the desired stock demand will depend upon the long-run equilibrium rent and income. But, if there is to be no net addition to the stock of housing over time, the long-run equilibrium rent, net of depreciation, maintenance and repair

[9] Throughout this study I use lower-case letters to refer to per capita magnitudes of stock and income; capital letters, to refer to the corresponding total or per household magnitudes. Income, rent, and price are all defined in real terms.

expenditures, and taxes per unit of stock must be just sufficient to induce owners of housing to hold this stock. That is, in long-run equilibrium, rent divided by price per unit of stock, p, must be equal to the sum of (1) the rate of depreciation, maintenance, and repair expenditures; (2) the tax rate; and (3) the long-run equilibrium net rate of return on housing. The last of these depends upon the mortgage rate of interest. The ratio of long-run equilibrium rent to price is described as the long-run equilibrium gross rate of return on housing.

Given the gross rate of return on housing, it is easy to derive the desired stock-demand schedule from the demand for services. Take any point on the latter, say, h_1, R_1, and find that price p_1 such that the ratio R_1/p_1 just equals the long-run equilibrium gross rate of return on housing. This price,

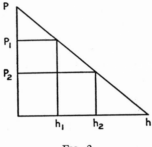

FIG. 2

along with h_1, gives one point on the desired stock-demand schedule, viewed as the relation between price and quantity of stock, given the depreciation rate, the tax rate, the rate of interest, and the variables determining the position of the demand-for-services schedule. The desired stock-demand schedule is illustrated in Figure 2. It is the same curve as the demand-for-services curve in Figure 1, except that the units on the vertical axis are different. That is, if the long-run equilibrium gross rate of return is, say, 10 per cent per year, the point on the vertical axis of Figure 2 which would be labeled "Ten dollars" corresponds to the point on the vertical axis of Figure 1 which would be labeled "One dollar per year."

Because the units of quantity of service and stock are numerically equal, the partial elasticities of the demand for services and desired stock-demand function are equal. An x per cent change in the consumption of housing services as a result of a 1 per cent change in income can come about only through an x per cent change in the stock of housing. Likewise, if in equilibrium rent bears a constant ratio to price, a 1 per cent rise in price must carry with it a 1 per cent rise in the equilibrium rent. Service demand will in response be reduced by y per cent, and the equilibrium stock of housing by the same percentage.[10]

So far only positions of long-run equilibrium, as defined above, have been considered. But at any instant of time the actual stock of housing, h, may not be equal to the desired stock, h_d. Suppose that the price per unit of additional stock is fixed by conditions of supply of newly constructed housing at p_2 and that actual stock is h_1, both in Figure 2. The level of rent as determined by the schedule of demand for services in Figure 1 is R_1 if the actual stock of housing (which is numerically equal to the flow of housing services per unit time) is h_1. The long-run equilibrium rent, that amount just necessary to induce owners of structures to maintain the stock of housing corresponding to the price p_2, is R_2. Hence, if the desired stock of housing exceeds the actual stock, the current level of rent exceeds the long-run equilibrium rent. Thus there is an incentive to add to the stock of housing. As actual stock increases over time, the current rent falls. When actual stock has reached h_2, rent will equal the long-run equilibrium rent, R_2 in Figure 1, and the ratio of rent to price will equal the long-run equilibrium rate of return. There will no longer be any incentive to add to the stock of housing, and the market for stocks will be in long-run equilibrium.

Thus any excess of desired over actual stock means an excess of current over equilibrium rent and therefore an incentive to add to the stock of housing. An excess of desired over actual stock can come about through a fall in price, a rise in income, or a fall in the rate of interest or in taxes.

THE DEMAND FOR NEW CONSTRUCTION

In dealing with the pace of adjustment of actual housing stocks to the desired or equilibrium level, we assume that a certain fraction, d, of the gap between actual and desired holdings will be filled in a year. If adjustment is rapid, d will be close to 1.0; if it is sluggish, d will be close to 0.

The reasons for slow rather than instantaneous adjustment can relate to either the demand side or the supply side of the market for new housing. On the demand side an increase in income may give, say, 10 per cent

---

[10] The elasticity of desired stock demand with respect to the rate of interest is but a fraction of the elasticity with respect to price. To see this, suppose that the rate of interest is 5 per cent per year and the depreciation and tax rates 3 and 2 per cent per year, respectively. In these circumstances the gross rate of return on housing in equilibrium is 10 per cent per year. A 1 per cent fall in the rate of interest will lead to a 1 per cent fall in that fraction, here one-half, of rent required to cover interest charges, or to a fall in rent of one-half of 1 per cent. Thus a fall in the rate of interest of z per cent will lead to only one-half the increase in service demand and desired stock that would result from a z per cent fall in price.

of households an incentive to buy new homes or to seek to rent new quarters. But this does not mean that all 10 per cent will try to move to new dwellings in the first year after the income change. It is in the nature of housing decisions that they should be considered carefully, and often moving into new quarters must be meshed with other events—children starting or finishing school, marriage, birth or death of family members, etc. On the supply side it is clear that changes in the scale of the home-building industry may entail changes in price.[11] Likewise, as the demand for mortgage funds to finance new housing increases, the mortgage market may become "tighter." Mortgage rates may rise, or, what seems equally likely under today's institutional arrangements, other conditions of mortgage loans may become more stringent.

We may legitimately ask at this point whether these "supply-side" causes of slow adjustment really fit here in our framework. Have we not already taken account of the effect of price through its effect on desired stock demand? The answer to this question is twofold. First, as a theoretical matter, the changes in demand which follow upon such price changes are governed by a mechanism quite distinct from the long-run price elasticity of demand for housing which we attempt to measure. It is my contention that desired stock demand is determined by the "long-run normal" price of housing, while short-run deviations of price from the long-run normal price govern in part the *rate* at which this desired stock is approached. Short-run price fluctuations about their long-run normal level are by their nature temporary. Houses may be "artificially" dear for a time after demand has risen, but, when sufficient additions have been made to stock, the normal price will be restored.

Second, as a practical matter, the changes in price which come about from even a sharp rise or fall in demand for new housing are likely to be too small to be captured and isolated by available price indexes. Suppose, for example, that a housing shortage caused by a sudden increase in desired stock demand leads to an increase in rent of 10 per cent and gives an incentive to expansion of home-building. Suppose, further, that conditions of mobility into the home-building industry are such that it can achieve any given output at the normal price within two years[12] but that expansions of output in periods of less than two years entail some price rise in order to hasten the movement of resources into the industry. How far can

---

[11] It is also possible that they might entail some deterioration in the quality of newly constructed dwelling units. In our framework, this is reflected in a rise in price of units of given quality.

[12] There is impressive evidence that resources are indeed quite mobile. This evidence is discussed in a later section.

price rise under these circumstances? The 10 per cent premium in rents cannot last more than two years under our assumptions, so the premium people would be willing to pay for new housing would certainly be no more than 20 per cent of the annual rent. But, since houses usually sell for about ten times the annual rent, the premium for new houses could be no more than 2 per cent.

The argument of the above paragraphs may be illustrated graphically, as in Figure 3, which shows the (total) net demand for new housing, H', as a function of the excess of current over the long-run equilibrium price, p^*, with the mortgage rate of interest held constant at its long-run equilibrium level. The position of the demand curve depends upon the excess of desired over actual stock, E, since E determines the excess of current

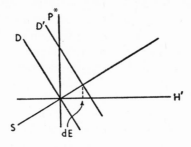

Fɪɢ. 3

over long-run equilibrium rent. With an increase in, say, income and hence desired stock, the demand curve shifts from D to D' by an amount measured along the horizontal axis which is generally some fraction of E. In long-run equilibrium D, of course, passes through the origin, since, in such a position, there is no incentive to add to stock. With the shift in demand for net additions to stock, the price of new housing tends to be bid up, as indicated by the supply schedule S. Because of the rise in price some consumers who desire new quarters tend to put off acquiring new housing in anticipation of a future fall in price. In fact, for short-run equilibrium to be attained, the increase in price would have to be such that individuals would be indifferent as between acquiring new housing now or in the future. The rise in price in the short run rations additions to the housing stock, so that new construction is less than that quantity indicated by the intersection of D' with the horizontal axis, which is itself but a fraction of the initial excess of desired over actual stock. Thus new construction during the first year after the initial rise in desired stock is dE, where the value of d depends partly on the slopes of the demand-and-supply schedules in Figure 3. Now in the following year the demand curve for new construction shifts downward from D'. This is because the net increase in stock during the first year leads to a decline in the gap between actual and desired stock and, hence, to a fall in current rent.[13]

In an empirical analysis of the housing market, such as is undertaken in later sections of this study, it would be desirable to estimate the short-run supply schedules for new housing and for mortgage funds and the demand function for additions to the stock of housing. There are two reasons, however, why this is not done. First, it is quite unlikely that the measures of price and the interest rate used in this study would reflect changes in these variables accompanying the rate of new construction in the short run. At best, they might be interpreted as measures of the long-run equilibrium values of these variables. And, second, as was indicated above, such short-run changes are likely to be so small as to be difficult to measure at all. However, Figure 3 suggests that to a linear approximation the net increase in stock per unit time will be proportional to the excess of desired over actual stock, either in total or in per capita terms. Stated in symbols, where h' is the per capita net rate of increase in stock per unit time and d is the constant of proportionality,

$$h' = d\,(h_d - h)\,. \tag{1}$$

Here, of course, the numerical value of d depends upon the length of the time period for which net additions to stock are measured. Also it is assumed that replacement demand—depreciation, maintenance, and repair expenditures—is proportional to actual stock. Thus the per capita gross rate of construction of housing per unit of time, h'_g, is given by

$$h'_g = d\,(h_d - h) + kh = dh_d - (d - k)\,h\,, \tag{2}$$

where k is the rate of replacement demand. Equation (2) is referred to here as the flow-demand equation; actually, of course, it is a "reduced form" of the demand function for new housing and the supply functions for new housing and for mortgage funds.

---

[13] We shall not go into the effects of a short-run rise in the rate of interest in detail. It is sufficient to point out that, if the supply of mortgage funds is not infinitely elastic in the short run with respect to the rate of interest, the latter will rise with any increase in the demand for funds accompanying the increase in the rate of new construction. Also, to the extent that the increase in the rate at which new housing is acquired is accompanied by an increase in borrowing relative to net worth, the risk premium on mortgage loans might rise even if the mortgage rate net of this risk premium remained unchanged. A rise in the interest rate, like a short-run rise in price, will serve to ration additions to the housing stock. In fact, if in Figure 3 and the text above the rate of interest is substituted for price and the schedule S is interpreted as the supply of funds, the argument remains essentially unchanged.

While equation (2) specifies the rate at which the stock of housing increases over time, it is of no use for empirical analysis because it contains the desired stock variable, and the latter is not observable. Desired stock per capita can, however, be expressed as a function of its determinants: long-run equilibrium price, p, per capita income, y, and the long-run equilibrium interest rate on mortgages, r.[14] To a linear approximation this function may be expressed by

$$h_d = b_0 + b_1 p + b_2 y + b_3 r \ . \tag{3}$$

Substituting (3) into (2) to eliminate the non-observable h_d, we have

$$h_o' = d b_0 + d b_1 p + d b_2 y + d b_3 r - (d - k) h \ . \tag{4}$$

Equation (4) is referred to as the "excess form" of the flow-demand equation; it relates the per capita gross rate of new construction per unit of time to the determinants of per capita desired stock and to actual stock per capita. If desired stock increases as income increases, *ceteris paribus*, gross new construction increases as well, since the coefficient of income in (4) is equal to the coefficient of income in (3) multiplied by the adjustment coefficient, d.[15]

However, in interpreting the elasticities of (4), it is important to realize that they depend both upon the point in time of the process of adjustment of actual to desired stock and upon the length of the time period for which additions to stock are measured. To illustrate, consider an initial position of long-run equilibrium and let income increase by 10 per cent. If the income elasticity of stock demand is equal to 1.5, desired stock would increase by 15 per cent. Suppose that in a year's time one-third of the difference between desired and actual stock is added to stock and that the rate of replacement demand is $3\frac{1}{2}$ per cent per year. During the first year after the initial increase in income the net increase in stock would be 5 per cent of the initial stock, while in the second year the net increase in stock would be $3\frac{1}{3}$ per cent of the initial stock. Construction would rise sharply in the year of the change in income, but it would fall from this peak in the

[14] Of course, desired stock also depends upon the property-tax rate, but I omit explicit consideration of this variable here because I have been unable to find satisfactory data to measure it. Also, I assume that the rate of depreciation, k, is constant.

[15] We might just as well relate the end-of-year actual stock, h_f, to beginning-of-year stock, h, and the net increase in the year. Thus

$$h_f = h + h' = d h_d + (1 - d) h \ .$$

We could then substitute (3) and obtain an equation analogous to (4). I prefer to place primary emphasis on (4) because I feel that the data on new construction are of much better quality than the stock data.

second and subsequent years, approaching a new equilibrium level 15 per cent higher than in the initial equilibrium, and in which construction served only to provide replacement for the now higher equilibrium stock. Thus, in response to a given percentage change in income, we would observe a variety of relative changes in construction, depending on the stage of the adjustment process we looked at. In this study, when estimates are presented of the elasticity of house construction with respect to a given variable, they will refer to the responsiveness of demand during the first year. Hence estimates of, say, the income elasticity of equation (4) refer to what the relative increase in construction would be in the same year as the change in income if prior to the income change the housing market were in full equilibrium.

Another point relating to equation (4) should be noted here. In examining this equation, we note that the coefficients of the desired stock-demand function, the b's in (3), and the adjustment coefficient, d, are not identifiable. That is, to estimate, say, b_2, the coefficient of income in (3), we need an estimate of d. The latter can be obtained from an estimate of the coefficient of h in (4) only if the value of k is known. However, to estimate the *elasticity* of h_d with respect to per capita income, no independent information about the value of k is needed. This elasticity is equal to b_2y/h_d, which, of course, is equal to $(db_2y)/(dh_d)$. But, comparing (3) and (4), it is easy to see that dh_d is given by (4) with the last term omitted. Hence its value and the income elasticity of desired stock demand can be obtained directly from estimates of (4) without any prior knowledge about k.

In the paragraphs immediately above it is seen that the gross rate of new construction can be expressed as a function of the determinants of desired stock and the actual stock of housing. This formulation is especially useful, since it permits estimation of the desired stock-demand elasticities. But for studying the rate of new construction another formulation of the flow-demand equation—the "ratio form"—is useful. Dividing each member of equation (2) by h, we have

$$(h_g'/h) = -(d-k) + d(h_d/h) . \qquad (2')$$

Now the analysis of the preceding section of this chapter suggests that the ratio of desired to actual stock may be approximated by the ratio of current rent to long-run equilibrium price, given the long-run equilibrium mortgage rate

$$(h_d/h) = c_0 + c_1(R/p) + c_2r . \qquad (5)$$

Substituting (5) into (2'), we obtain

$$(h_g'/h) = [(c_0-1)d + k] + dc_1(R/p) + dc_2r . \qquad (6)$$

According to (6), the ratio of gross construction to actual stock varies directly with the ratio of current rent to long-run equilibrium price and inversely with the rate of interest.[16] Estimation of (6) will provide another test of the analysis of this section.

The principal purpose of this study is to estimate stock-demand elasticities for housing from time-series data. At this point the implications of the analysis of this chapter for so estimating housing demand will be noted. The other comparisons to be made will be discussed when the empirical results are presented.

If, in the real world, individuals tried to add to the stock of housing at such a rate as to make actual stock at the end of any given calendar year equal to desired stock, estimation of desired stock-demand elasticities from time-series data would be similar to estimating the demand function for the services of any commodity. We would, simply, compare the end-of-year actual stock with price, income, and the interest rate. The set of observations of these variables for any year would give one point on the desired stock-demand function, apart from a random residual. This special set of circumstances will be referred to in this study as the "case of complete adjustment." If it were true that the economy actually operated in this way, new construction could be explained wholly by changes in the determinants of desired stock.

However, we advanced several reasons at the beginning of the last subsection why actual stock might not adjust completely within a year's time to changes in, say, price or income. If the lag in adjustment of actual to desired stock is long enough relative to a year, none of the observed combinations of end-of-year stock, price, income, and the interest-rate needs coincide with a point of the desired stock-demand function. Rather they would lie on a path of dynamic adjustment to the long-run equilibrium stock level. It is precisely for this reason that we considered the dynamics of adjustment at such length in the last subsection. The analysis there indicated that the rate of new construction in any year depends upon two considerations: desired stock expressed as a function of price, income, and the interest rate and the rate at which the actual housing stock moves toward it. Our equation (4) shows how these variables are interrelated. And, as we have shown, from estimates of it we can estimate the partial elasticities of the desired stock-demand function, even though that de-

[16] The formulation in equation (6) is similar to that of Charles F. Roos, "Factors Influencing Residential Building," *Dynamic Economics* (Bloomington, Ind.: Principia Press, 1934), chap. vi.

sired stock corresponding to any particular set of conditions might never be observed. From knowledge about the rate of depreciation parameter, *k*, the coefficients of the desired stock-demand function, as well as its partial elasticities, can be estimated, as can the rate of adjustment parameter, *d*. If *d* were really less than 1.0, and it will be seen that it seems to be substantially less, then new construction can be explained not only by changes in the determinants of desired stock but also by the dynamic lag of adjustment of actual to desired stock. The case where *d* is less than 1.0 will be called the "case of incomplete adjustment."

III. The Supply of New Housing

While important in its own right, an understanding of the conditions of supply of home-building is essential for interpreting the response of new construction to changes in the demand for housing. In the last section we saw that reactions on the supply side of the market for new homes provide one reason why the stock of housing might not react immediately to changes in desired stock demand. Likewise, desired stock may itself depend upon conditions of supply, since even in the long run supply might not be perfectly elastic; if it were not, the long-run normal price of housing would increase with an increase in desired stock demand. The evidence presented in this section, however, strongly suggests not only that the supply of new housing is highly elastic in the long run but also that even over short periods of time there is a high degree of mobility of resources into the home-building industry.

In examining the supply of new construction, several factors have to be considered. First, the price of new housing might rise with an increase in the demand for new construction if the prices of materials and labor were to rise along with the rate of new house-building. Even in the absence of this, variations in the price of housing might result from barriers to entry into or exit from the industry or because firms in the industry have differential advantages in producing new housing. Either of these factors would lead to changes in the profits of construction firms, so their importance might be judged by examining profit data. Direct evidence on the behavior of factor prices and rate of entry of firms into the industry is available.

The best time period for examining the relation of factor prices to variations in the level of new construction is that from 1922 through 1929. During this period there was comparative stability in the general level of prices and substantially full employment, as well as large changes in the rate of home-building. Likewise, while residential construction turned down following the middle of the decade, non-residential construction tended to rise well into the latter half. In other periods fluctuations in residential construction were closely related to fluctuations in the general price level and in the gross national product (GNP) as well as to non-residential construction, so that a comparison of annual changes in factor prices and output is less meaningful.

Data on new residential construction and building-material prices are shown in the first two columns of Table 2.[17] Examination of these data

TABLE 2

RELATION OF NEW CONSTRUCTION TO RELATIVE
FACTOR PRICES, 1922–29*

| YEAR | NEW CONSTRUC-TION (MILLIONS OF 1935–39 DOLLARS) | INDEX OF BUILDING-MATERIAL PRICES (1935–39 = 100) | WAGE RATES | |
			Unskilled Labor (1935–39 Dollars per Hour)	Ratio: Skilled/Unskilled
1922	4,239	90.7	0.369	2.26
1923	4,799	99.6	.425	2.12
1924	5,544	93.4	.454	2.14
1925	6,088	90.5	.429	2.27
1926	6,198	88.3	.434	2.32
1927	5,926	85.4	.447	2.38
1928	5,609	85.6	.454	2.43
1929	4,443	86.9	0.446	2.49

* All current dollar factor prices were deflated by the Consumer Price Index, 1935–39 = 100.

shows little or no relationship between new construction and building-material prices. In only three of seven cases did the two series change in the same direction from year to year; in fact, material prices reached a peak in 1923 and declined almost to the end of the decade, while construction continued to rise until 1926. Likewise, the data on the real hourly earnings of unskilled construction workers shown in the third col-

[17] Building-material prices are measured here by the Bureau of Labor Statistics index of wholesale prices of building materials, 1935–39 = 100. New construction is measured by the Department of Commerce data, and it includes new dwelling units, additions and alterations, and maintenance and repair expenditures. These are from U.S. Department of Commerce, Business and Defense Services Administration, *Construction and Building Materials, Statistical Supplement, May, 1954* (Washington, D.C.: Government Printing Office, 1954). To convert these value data to quantity terms, they were deflated by the Boeckh index of residential construction costs (brick), which is published in the same source.

umn indicate very little relation to new construction.[18] Except for the years 1925 and 1929, the earnings of unskilled construction workers increased steadily throughout the twenties, despite the fluctuations in residential construction. Sobotka, in examining the influence of unions on the wages of construction workers, has shown that the ratio of average hourly earnings of unskilled construction workers to those of all manufacturing workers remained virtually constant from 1919 to 1950[19] This finding indicates a high mobility of labor from construction to other employments and suggests that, for unskilled labor at least, wages are fixed to the home-building industry. While Sobotka's study concluded that unions have influenced the wages of skilled construction workers, the data in the last column of Table 2 suggest that union influence on their wages did not vary with the level of new construction. The ratio of the average hourly earnings of skilled to unskilled workers rose steadily from 1923 to 1929, despite the downturn of home-building following 1926. Here, too, we must conclude that factor prices do not vary systematically with the output of the home-building industry.

Granted that materials and labor are highly mobile into the industry, what about entrepreneurs themselves? There is little evidence to indicate that barriers to entry or exit of firms are a significant source of variation in the price of new housing. Data given by Colean and Newcomb indicate that both the entry and the exit of firms were far more rapid in the construction industry than in any other industrial group during the period 1945–50.[20] According to a recent Bureau of Labor Statistics study, 27 per cent of the dwelling units started in 1949 were built by owner-builders and 20 per cent by commercial builders who derived income from some source other than construction.[21] Of the operative commercial builders, who started between 45 and 50 per cent of new residential units built that year, 40 per cent had entered the industry in 1949 and 22 per cent had entered

[18] Both the wages of unskilled and the wages of skilled workers in Table 2 are measured by the *Engineering News-Record* series on average hourly earnings, which are published in the *Survey of Current Business*. It is claimed in the source that these measure wages actually paid rather than union scales.

[19] See Stephen P. Sobotka, "Union Influence on Wages: The Construction Industry," *Journal of Political Economy*, LXI (April, 1953), 127–43.

[20] Miles L. Colean and Robinson Newcomb, *Stabilizing Construction* (New York: McGraw-Hill Book Co., 1952), Appendix T, pp. 274–75. These data refer both to residential and to non-residential construction.

[21] U.S. Department of Labor, Bureau of Labor Statistics, *Structure of the Residential Building Industry in 1949* (BLS Bull. 1170 [Washington, D.C.: Government Printing Office, 1954]), Table 1, p. 21, and Table 10, p. 26.

in the years 1946–48.[22] It is not surprising that there is such apparent easy entry into the industry. Legal barriers are few, and little specialized knowledge is required, as evidenced by the large numbers of amateurs who built their own homes in the immediate postwar period. Likewise, capital requirements are very low; data gathered by Colean indicate that equipment per employee averaged only $68 for operative-builders (mostly residential) in 1929.[23] All this suggests that firms, as well as other factors of production, are highly mobile into and out of the home-building industry.

If there were barriers to entry and exit of residential construction firms or if firms enjoyed differential productive advantages, one would expect to find cyclical fluctuations in the profits of construction firms accompanying fluctuations in new construction. This would mean that the price of new housing would fluctuate more over the construction cycle than an index of construction costs. Some evidence on this point is provided by comparing the Department of Commerce GNP deflator for residential construction with the Boeckh index of residential construction costs. The Boeckh index is a fixed-weight index of material and labor costs (it will be discussed further in following sections and in Appendix B). The GNP deflator is, essentially, the Boeckh index adjusted for changes in profits and certain other costs of construction firms.[24] The comparison of the two indexes made in Appendix B reveals only a slight tendency for the ratio of the adjusted to the unadjusted Boeckh index to vary directly with the level of new home-building in the thirties and with no such tendency in the post–World War II period. Since material and labor costs account for about 90 per cent of the total cost of new housing, it is not surprising that fluctuations in price resulting from changes in profits appear to be minor.

Further evidence on conditions of supply can be obtained by a regression analysis which compares the variables in the supply function for new housing: total new construction in constant dollars, H_g'; the relative price of housing, p'; an index of relative building-material prices, m; the relative wage of unskilled construction workers, u; and the ratio of wages of skilled to unskilled workers, s. All these, except price, are measured by the same

[22] *Ibid.*, Table 7, p. 25. Operative commercial builders are those who build to their own specifications for future sale, as compared with general contractors, who build to the specifications of a specific buyer.

[23] Miles L. Colean, *American Housing* (New York: Twentieth Century Fund, 1949), Table 20, p. 385. Even for excavating subcontractors, for whom equipment per employee was greatest in the residential construction sector, this figure was only $1,491—very small indeed when compared with capital per worker in manufacturing.

[24] See U.S. Department of Commerce, Office of Business Economics, *National Income, 1954 Edition* (Washington, D.C.: Government Printing Office, 1954), p. 156. The details of this adjustment are described in Appendix B.

data as are presented in Table 2. Price is measured by Blank's index of house prices.[25] Since Blank's index is available only for the period ending in 1934, the regression comparison is limited to the period 1915–34, with war years omitted. Taking H'_g and p' in turn as dependent, the least-squares regression estimates are

$$H'_g = -111p' - 50.1m + 1{,}920u + 4{,}800s, \quad R^2 = 0.100 , \qquad (7)$$
$$\quad\;\; (138) \quad (62.0) \quad\; (3{,}710) \; (10{,}400)$$

$$p' = -0.000425H'_g - 0.0336m + 21.6u + 54.9s,$$
$$\quad (0.000530) \quad\;\; (0.124) \quad\;\; (4.26) \; (13.7) \qquad\qquad (8)$$

$$R^2 = 0.804 .$$

The first of these shows no relation between the quantity of new construction and the other variables in the supply function, and the regression equation explains only 10 per cent of the variation in new construction. The second indicates that about 80 per cent of the variation in price can be explained by the other variables in the supply function for new housing, but the quantity of new construction contributes nothing to this explanation.[26] Taken together, these results reinforce the conclusions of the earlier parts of this section, namely, that the supply of new housing is highly elastic. While the profit data considered above indicate that, in the short run, prices may show minor fluctuations with changes in the rate of new construction, the evidence is impressive indeed that, in the long run, the price of housing is substantially independent of the scale of the home-building industry.

IV. The Demand for Housing: Complete Adjustment

We turn now to estimating the stock demand for housing. If the housing stock were to adjust so rapidly to changing prices and incomes that at the end of any given calendar year actual stock would equal the level desired under currently prevailing conditions, estimating stock demand would be no different from estimating the demand for the services of any commodity. Each observed combination of end-of-year stock, price, in-

[25] David M. Blank, "Relationship between an Index of House Prices and Building Costs," *Journal of the American Statistical Association*, XLIX (March, 1954), 67–88. This is an index of the market prices of new and existing houses rather than a construction-cost index. Blank's index was not used in the demand analysis presented later because it is not available for years after 1934.

[26] That the coefficient of building-material prices in (8) is not significant is not surprising, since there was very little variation in the index of material prices in the period to which the regression refers.

come, and the interest rate would, apart from sampling fluctuations, give us one point on the desired stock-demand curve. Estimates of stock demand assuming these conditions are considered in this section.

In making these estimates, we used the following data:

h_f = end-of-year per capita non-farm housing stock—Grebler, Blank, and Winnick estimates of the non-farm housing stock deflated by the non-farm population of the continental United States[27]

p = Boeckh index of residential construction costs (brick)

y_p = Friedman's per capita expected-income series

r = Durand's basic yield of ten-year corporate bonds[28]

Throughout this study all monetary magnitudes are adjusted for changes in the general level of prices, the base period being 1935–39. Where deflation was necessary, the BLS index of consumer prices was used.

Although a more detailed evaluation of these data will be made in the following section and in Appendix B, their essential features should be noted. First, with respect to the stock series, comparisons which Grebler, Blank, and Winnick make with bench-mark-type data for a few selected years suggest that, although their estimates are reasonably close to others for the period prior to World War II and any discrepancies tend not to be cumulative over time, they seriously underestimate the housing stock in the postwar period.[29] For this reason, the time-series analysis of this study is restricted to the period 1915–41 (with war years omitted).

Second, the measures of price and the rate of interest used here are interpreted as measuring the long-run normal values of these variables. Since the analysis of the last section suggests that any short-run fluctuations in price are likely to result from changes in the profits of construction firms, such price changes would not be reflected in an index of material and labor prices. While it might seem surprising that a bond-yield series is used to measure the cost of mortgage funds, there is good reason for this. A measure of mortgage rates would be highly unsatisfactory, since other conditions of mortgage contracts—length of the loan and required down

[27] Leo Grebler, David M. Blank, and Louis Winnick, *Capital Formation in Residential Real Estate: Trends and Prospects* (Princeton, N.J.: Princeton University Press, 1956), Table D-1, pp. 360–61.

[28] David Durand, *Basic Yield of Corporate Bonds, 1900–1942* (New York: National Bureau of Economic Research, 1942).

[29] *Op. cit.*, Appendix D, pp. 365–76, and especially Table D-3, p. 370. Except for 1950, their estimates diverge from bench-mark estimates by no more than about 10 per cent. For 1950 their estimate is about 22 per cent less than an estimate derived from 1950 housing census data.

payments—have a significant influence on the cost of mortgage funds.[30] For this reason the bond-yield series, which is a measure of opportunity costs to mortgage lenders, was used.

Finally, with respect to the income variable, it is a matter of common knowledge that people's housing does not change with every short-range change in their income. At the same time it is generally true that individuals' housing is in tune with their normal level of income. This suggests that we need an income variable that is insulated from short-range fluctuations in money receipts and aims at approximating what people appear to believe is their normal income level. Such a variable is provided by Milton Friedman's series of expected or permanent income.[31]

Turning now to stock-demand estimates assuming complete adjustment, the least-squares regression with h_f as the dependent variables yields

$$h_f = -4.66p + 0.820y_p - 24.7r, \quad R^2 = 0.448, \quad \delta = 0.592,$$
$$\quad (1.45) \quad (0.219) \quad (11.4) \tag{9}$$
$$E(h_f) \quad -0.570 + 0.553 \quad -0.131,$$

where δ stands for the Durbin-Watson statistic (see below) and $E(h_f)$ for the partial elasticity of h_f with respect to the several determining variables, as estimated from the slope parameters of (9) and the mean values of the variables for the sample period. Equation (9) indicates that end-of-year stock varied directly with income and inversely with price and the rate of interest, as would be expected a priori. All the coefficients of (9) are numerically greater than twice their standard errors, and the regression equation explains almost half the variance of end-of-year stock. The estimated stock-demand elasticities for income and price are numerically about equal to 0.5. We shall see that these probably seriously underestimate the true elasticities, but even this estimate suggests that housing demand is much more responsive to price changes than the Duesenberry-Kistin estimate, -0.08, would suggest.

In evaluating these results, we note the high positive serial correlation in the residuals, as seen from the Durbin-Watson statistic.[32] An examina-

---

[30] Data presented by R. J. Saulnier, *Urban Mortgage Lending by Life Insurance Companies* (New York: National Bureau of Economic Research, 1950), Table B5, pp. 132–34, suggest that these other conditions changed drastically over the period we are considering. Apart from degrees-of-freedom considerations, measures of mortgage rates, length of contract, and required down payments are highly intercorrelated during this period so that it would be quite difficult statistically to measure the influence of each.

[31] *Op. cit.*, chap. v, esp. pp. 142–52.

[32] For twenty-five observations and three independent variables, the bounds on the 5 per cent point for this statistic are 1.12 and 1.66. Hence we would in this instance reject the hypothesis that the true residuals are serially uncorrelated (see J. Durbin and G. S. Watson, "Testing for Serial Correlation in Least Squares Regression. II," *Biometrika*, XXXVIII [June, 1951], 173, Table 4).

tion of the residuals computed from (9) indicates that they are negative—that is, computed stock exceeds the observed stock—in 1926 and earlier years and positive for the period 1927 through 1935. Now the period 1922 through 1926 was one of greater-than-average home-building, while for most of the period 1927 through 1935 the rate of home-building was below average. This means that, when new construction was proceeding rapidly, the actual housing stock was relatively small for given values of price, income, and the rate of interest and conversely. But this result is just what would be expected if the housing stock did not adjust completely to changed conditions of demand within a year's time. If the housing stock does not respond completely within a year's time to changes in, say, income, then the coefficients of (9) and the elasticities based upon them might seriously underestimate the ultimate response of the housing stock.

V. The Demand for Housing: Incomplete Adjustment

The results of the preceding section strongly suggest that, if housing demand is to be correctly understood, account must be taken of the dynamics of the adjustment of the housing stock to changing conditions. Our earlier analysis suggests that both the ultimate response of the housing stock to changed demand conditions and the pace of adjustment in the housing market can be determined by comparing new construction, h_g', with the determinants of desired stock and the stock actually in existence, h.[33] When we do so, we see that housing demand appears to be much more responsive than the preceding section suggests and that a period much longer than one year is needed for complete adjustment.

THE BASIC ESTIMATES OF STOCK DEMAND

Taking the least-squares regression with h_g' as dependent yields

$$h_g' = -2.49p + 0.438y_p - 8.34r - 0.282h,$$
$$(0.589)\ (0.0919)\ (4.47)\ (0.0695)$$

$$R^2 = 0.621,\ \delta = 1.01\ ,\quad (10)$$

$E(h_g') -5.54 +5.38 \quad -0.805 -5.13$

$E(h_d) -0.904 +0.879 \quad -0.131 \quad \ldots .$

---

[33] Here, the per capita gross rate of non-farm residential construction, h_g', is based upon estimates of the current dollar value of new dwelling units, additions and alterations to existing dwellings, and maintenance and repair expenditures, as published in U.S. Department of Commerce, Business and Defense Services Administration, *op. cit.* To convert to quantity per capita, these estimates were deflated by the Boeckh index and the non-farm population of the continental United States. The variable h is simply the beginning-of-year per capita housing stock and, as such, is h_f lagged one year.

New construction varied directly with income and inversely with price, the interest rate, and stock. The coefficients of price, income, and stock in equation (10) are all at least four times as great numerically as their standard errors, while the coefficient of r is almost twice its standard error. The regression equation explains some 62 per cent of the variation in the new construction series. However, the Durbin-Watson statistic indicates that the true residuals are positively serially correlated.[34]

The elasticities of new construction, $E(h'_g)$, are shown in the first line below equation (10). They indicate that home-building is highly responsive indeed to changes in price or income. Either a 1 per cent fall in price or a 1 per cent increase in income leads to an increase in gross construction of about $5\frac{1}{2}$ per cent in the same year as the change in price or income. In the absence of further changes, of course, the annual rate of home-building would decline over time as the housing stock approaches the desired level. The response of new construction depends upon two things: the ultimate

[34] For twenty-five observations and four independent variables the bounds on this statistic are 1.04 and 1.77, respectively (see Durbin and Watson, *op. cit.*, pp. 173–74). Examination of the computed residuals reveals that equation (10) underestimates new construction during the period 1923 through 1929 and overestimates it from 1930 through 1937. While I have been unable to determine to my complete satisfaction the reasons for this, I believe it is largely due to three factors. First, because of the method by which the estimates of new construction were prepared, it seems likely that any errors of estimation in the 1920's affected the estimates for every year of the decade and that they overestimate new construction in the twenties relative to the thirties. Second, because I have been unable to find a suitable measure of property-tax rates, this variable has been excluded. While it would appear that there was no trend in tax rates during the period considered here, it would seem that they varied contracyclically— falling below the period average in the middle and late twenties and rising above the average in the early and middle thirties (see Colin D. Campbell, "Are Property-Tax Rates Increasing?" *Journal of Political Economy*, LIX [October, 1951], 434–42). (For further discussion of these two points see Appendix B.) And, third, Margaret G. Reid, "Capital Formation in Residential Real Estate," *Journal of Political Economy*, LXVI (April, 1958), 131–53, has argued that the Grebler, Blank, and Winnick stock data overestimate the housing stock in the twenties relative to the thirties. If this is the case, equation (10) would underestimate new construction in the twenties relative to the thirties, producing a time pattern of estimated residuals qualitatively similar to that actually observed.

One might think that taking first differences would tend to eliminate this serial correlation, but here it only makes matters worse. Taking first differences actually increases the serial correlation, $\delta = 0.628$, and results in a substantially worse fit, $R^2 = 0.425$. As shown in Appendix C, the presence of serially correlated residuals does not necessarily imply that the regression coefficients are biased, though the traditional least-squares estimators are not efficient. Likewise, the estimated standard errors shown here, which were computed on the assumption that the true residuals are serially uncorrelated, may be poor estimates of the variability of these coefficients in repeated samplings.

change in stock demand resulting from a given change in price or income and the rate of adjustment over time in the housing stock.[35]

The elasticities of desired stock demand, $E(h_d)$, are likewise shown below equation (10). These indicate that a 1 per cent fall in price or increase in income would lead to an eventual increase in stock of almost 1 per cent. These estimates indicate that housing demand is in fact considerably more responsive to price or income changes than is commonly believed. The estimate of income elasticity is almost twice as great as Morton and Winnick inferred from comparisons like that shown in Table 1. Even more striking is the estimate of price elasticity, -0.9 as compared with the Duesenberry-Kistin estimate of -0.08. Likewise, these estimates of price and income elasticity are almost twice as large numerically as those obtained in the preceding section, where it was assumed that the adjustment of the housing stock took place completely within a year's time. This result bears out the suggestion made in the last section that account of the dynamic lag of adjustment of the housing stock must be taken for a real understanding of the workings of the housing market.[36]

Further evidence on the dynamics of the adjustment of housing stock

[35] In estimating equation (10), a measure of the quantity of new construction was used. This is a measure of expenditures for new housing (price times quantity) adjusted for changes in the general level of prices and deflated by the index of relative price. There is, therefore, a possibility of a spurious correlation between measured quantity and price because of errors in the price series. If, however, we compare real expenditures with the independent variables of (10), the possibility of such spurious correlation is eliminated, and quantity elasticities can be obtained. Doing so, the elasticities of quantity obtained are almost identical with those obtained by using the measure of quantity directly, as in (10).

Likewise, if we compute the regression using the logarithms of the same variables as were used in equation (10), the coefficients of the independent variables are simply the elasticities of new construction. These, too, are virtually identical with the elasticity estimates obtained from the linear form of the regression in equation (10).

[36] The 95 per cent confidence limits on these elasticities are -0.421 and -1.80 for price and $+0.538$ and $+1.42$ for income. Thus the estimates obtained here are not necessarily inconsistent with numerically larger estimates obtained in some of the comparisons to be made in later sections of this study. The estimated elasticity with respect to the interest rate here is no larger than obtained in the previous section. On a priori grounds, we would expect it to be almost one-half of the price elasticity (see n. 10, above). One reason for this low value is the nature of the interest-rate series used. The bond-yield series might be interpreted as a close approximation to the pure rate of interest. The mortgage rate, in addition, includes provision for administrative costs and risk and, hence, is greater than the pure rate. If administrative costs and the risk premium were fixed rather than varying with the pure rate of interest, the unit increase in new construction and stock demand resulting from a change in the mortgage rate would be correctly estimated using the bond-yield series, but the elasticity of either new construction or stock demand would be underestimated.

is provided by the coefficient of h in equation (10). As equation (4) shows, the coefficient of h is equal to $-(d - k)$, where d is the coefficient of adjustment and k the rate of replacement. Now k is not known exactly, but it is probably about $3\frac{1}{2}$ per cent per year.[37] This, together with the coefficient of h in (10), suggests a value for d of 0.317. This means that individuals seek to add about one-third of the excess of desired over actual stock in any given year. If such were the case, of course, the actual stock of housing would never adjust completely but would come arbitrarily close to desired stock with the passage of time. For this value of d it would take almost exactly *six* years for the adjustment to be 90 per cent completed. Thus the ultimate change in the housing stock that would come about from a change in demand conditions is substantially greater than the change brought about in a single year.

Such are our basic estimates of housing demand. In the following paragraphs we shall consider the more important shortcomings to which they might be subject.

ERRORS OF MEASUREMENT

The estimates of equation (10) obtained above might be biased by errors in the statistical measures of the true variables to which our model relates. Such errors are of two kinds, random and systematic measurement errors.

One source of bias in the traditional least-squares estimators of the coefficients of a linear regression equation arises out of measurement errors in the observed values of variables being compared. The case where the measured values of the variables contain normally distributed "random"-error components—error components which are serially uncorrelated and are uncorrelated with the true values of the variables—has received some study. Koopmans has shown that maximum likelihood estimates may be obtained in this case, provided the covariances of the error components are known.[38] These estimates are termed "weighted-regression" estimates. He has also shown that the correctly weighted regression estimates are

---

[37] The rate of depreciation exclusive of maintenance and repair expenditures used by Grebler, Blank, and Winnick in obtaining their cumulated stock estimates is 2 per cent per year. To this should be added an allowance for maintenance and repair expenditures, which averaged about $1\frac{1}{2}$ per cent per year in the period studied here (for a discussion of the appropriate depreciation rate see Grebler, Blank, and Winnick, *op. cit.*, Appendix E, esp. pp. 377–82). While the exact value of the depreciation rate is of great importance in constructing stock estimates by cumulating and depreciating additions to stock, the conclusion reached in the text depends only upon its order of magnitude.

[38] Tjalling C. Koopmans, *Linear Regression Analysis of Economic Time Series* (Harlem: DeErven F. Bohn N.V., 1937).

bounded by those estimates obtained by computing all the "elementary" regressions—the regression in which it is assumed that only one variable is measured with error and which is simply the conventional least-squares regression with that variable taken as dependent—provided that the error components in the various measured variables are uncorrelated with each other. Thus, even if the covariances of the error components are unknown, it is possible to determine the limits within which the correctly weighted regression estimates would lie.

If four additional regression equations are computed, one for each of the four "independent" variables in equation (10), a set of five stock-demand elasticities for each variable can be obtained. The numerically smallest and largest stock elasticity estimates so obtained are -0.669 and -1.60 for price and $+0.652$ and $+1.17$ for income. Taking account of the possibility of random errors in the data would have but little effect on the stock-demand elasticity with respect to income but might lead to an estimate of price elasticity which is substantially larger numerically.

Actually, the most serious kind of error in the data with which we are faced is secular bias in the measures of price and stock used. The Boeckh index of residential costs, which was used to measure price, might be seriously biased for comparisons between widely separated years. This is because a fixed-weight index of material and labor costs would fail to reflect changes in the price of housing resulting from technological change or from substitution of inputs resulting from changes in relative factor prices. Such factors are likely to have operated more or less steadily over time, so that a large part of the possible error in the index can be "covered" by introducing a time trend into the regression equation.

In like manner, the most serious kind of error in the stock series used is likely to be a trend-wise bias. The Grebler-Blank-Winnick series used as a measure of housing stock was derived in the following way: an estimate of stock at the beginning of 1890 was prepared using data on mortgaged owner-occupied houses reported in the 1890 census. End-of-year stock for any year is the stock at the beginning plus gross capital formation during the year less capital consumption. Gross capital formation is the current dollar value of new housekeeping dwelling units and additions and alterations to existing dwellings deflated by the Boeckh index of residential construction costs. Capital consumption consists of a depreciation allowance, which is 2 per cent of the beginning-of-year stock plus 1 per cent of gross capital formation, plus an allowance for demolitions.[39] A trend-wise bias in their estimates would arise from such a bias in the construction-cost

---

[39] A full description of procedures used is given in Grebler, Blank, and Winnick, *op. cit.*, Appendix D. For a very detailed critical review of their work see Reid, *op. cit.*

index used as a deflator for gross capital formation or an incorrect depreciation rate. Such a bias would also arise if, as seems possible, annual estimates of the value of gross capital formation understate the true value. For these reasons, too, it might be argued that a time trend should be included in the regression analysis.

When a linear time trend, T, is included, the regression equation becomes

$$h'_g = -2.05p + 0.449y_p - 9.72r - 0.234h - 0.910T,$$
$$(0.718) \quad (0.0924) \quad (4.66) \quad (0.0830) \quad (0.855)$$

$$R^2 = 0.643, \tag{11}$$

$$E(h_d) \quad -0.870 + 1.05 \quad -0.179 \quad \ldots \quad \ldots \ldots$$

The coefficient of T in equation (11) is only slightly greater than its standard error, and it is significant only at about the 30 per cent level. Furthermore, introducing the time trend makes almost no difference in the estimated stock-demand elasticities. It is thus apparent that the possibility of a systematic secular bias in the price and stock variables can be dismissed as unimportant for our purposes. Likewise, including the time trend shows no evidence of any systematic change in consumer preferences or "tastes" for housing, as Winnick has alleged.[40]

EXPERIMENTS WITH THE INCOME VARIABLE

In all the comparisons presented so far, Friedman's expected-income series has been used. This series is a weighted average of the current disposable incomes of several recent periods, with the most recent period receiving the greatest weight. It is used in an attempt to measure the normal income level to which the housing stock is adjusted. Here we shall attempt to ascertain whether some other income variable gives us a better explanation of changes in the housing stock.

If, instead of Friedman's series, per capita current income, y_c, is used to measure income,[41] the least-squares regression corresponding to equation (10) is

[40] *Op. cit.* We shall return to a discussion of this point in the concluding section of this study.

[41] The series is from Raymond W. Goldsmith, *A Study of Saving in the United States* (Princeton, N.J.: Princeton University Press, 1956), III, 127, Table N-1, and is the series of current income upon which Friedman's series is based. Like Friedman's, it refers to all persons in the United States rather than to the non-farm population only. However, a current income series for the non-farm population was obtained by deducting estimates of the income of the farm population from total current income. This indicated that fluctuations in per capita current income of the non-farm population were al-

$$h'_v = -1.49p + 0.249y_c - 0.106r - 0.124h, \ R^2 = 0.607$$
$$(0.505) \ (0.0540) \quad (4.43) \quad (0.0621)$$

$$E(h'_v) \ -3.32 \ +2.98 \quad -0.0102 - 2.26$$
$$E(h_d) \ -1.02 \ +0.913 \quad -0.00313 \ \ldots .$$

(12)

According to equation (12), an increase of one dollar in current income was accompanied by an increase in new construction in the same year of only about twenty-five cents worth of housing. On the other hand, the coefficient of permanent income in equation (10) indicates an increase of about forty-four cents. This is just the sort of result we would expect if housing expenditures were geared to a consumer's normal income level. Housing demand reacts less to a change in current income precisely because a consumer's expectations of his normal income level change less rapidly than his current income. Note, too, that the coefficients of price and, especially, the rate of interest are much smaller when current income is used instead of Friedman's series.[42]

There is another reason besides the neglect of income expectations for believing that current income is a poor measure for the purposes of this analysis. In his study of automobile demand, Chow found that the rate of personal saving is a significant variable in explaining the purchase of new cars.[43] Now if consumption depends only upon permanent income, as Friedman's hypothesis suggests, then for a given level of permanent income a change in current income represents a change in saving. In particular, let

$$c = ay_p \text{ or } s = y_c - c = y_c - ay_p ,$$

(13)

where c is per capita real consumption, s is the per capita real saving, and a is the average propensity to consume, which, according to Friedman's hypothesis, is independent of the level of permanent income. Then, supposing that new construction depends upon personal saving in addition to

---

most identical with those for the whole population. While the mean value of per capita non-farm income was probably somewhat above that for the whole population in most of the period studied here, the effect of this difference on the estimated income elasticity is minor relative to sampling and other errors to which estimated income elasticity is subject.

[42] However, the price and income desired stock-demand elasticities inferred from equation (12) are quite similar to those from equation (10), despite the fact that the coefficients of the former are substantially smaller numerically. This is due to the smaller value of the coefficient of h in (12).

[43] Gregory C. Chow, *The Demand for Automobiles in the United States: A Study in Consumer Durables* (Amsterdam: North-Holland Publishing Co., 1957).

the excess of desired over actual stock, we have, using equations (3) and (13),

$$h'_g = dh_d - (d - k)h + es = db_0 + db_1p + (db_2 - ea)y_p \\ + db_3r - (d - k)h + ey_c \,. \tag{14}$$

Equation (14) suggests that the influence of personal saving on new construction can be estimated by including both current and permanent income in the regression analysis. If this is done, we find

$$h'_g = -2.13p + 0.266y_p - 4.97r - 0.220h + 0.110y_c, \\ (0.717)\ (0.216)\quad (5.88)\quad (0.0988)\ (0.125)\,, \tag{15}$$

$$R^2 = 0.637 \,.$$

Assuming an average propensity to consume of 0.9,[44] equation (15) can be rewritten as

$$h'_g = -2.13p + 0.366y_p - 4.97r - 0.220h + 0.110s \,. \\ (0.717)\ (0.124)\quad (5.88)\quad (0.0988)\ (0.125) \tag{16}$$

The coefficient of y_c in (15) or s in (16) is smaller than its standard error, while the coefficients of none of the other variables in (16) differ from the corresponding estimates in equation (10) by as much as one standard error. This indicates that the personal savings variable is not very important in determining the rate of new building. But the equations above indicate that if current rather than permanent income is used, as in (12), the income coefficient reflects the influence of saving as well as that of permanent income.

While it is apparent that current income is less satisfactory than Friedman's series for this analysis, might not some other weighted average of past current income be even better? Friedman himself comments:

> We have interpreted the exact meaning of permanent income in terms of the horizon of the consumer unit. Now there seems to be no reason why the horizon should be the same for all individual categories of consumption and some reasons why it should differ systematically. For example, it seems highly plausible that housing expenditures are planned in terms of a longer horizon, and so a different concept of permanent income, than expenditures on, say, food.[45]

Specifically, Friedman's expected-income series can be defined by

$$y_p(t) = (1 - e^{-\beta}) \sum_{j=0}^{\infty} e^{-\beta j} y_c(t - j) \,, \tag{17}$$

[44] See Friedman's estimate, *op. cit.*, Table 15, p. 147.

[45] *Ibid.*, pp. 207–8.

where the weight coefficient $\beta = 0.4$ and the symbol t stands for the year.[46] If housing expenditures are planned in terms of a longer horizon than all current consumption, the appropriate concept of permanent income would be a similar series but with a smaller weight coefficient, β. The effect of a smaller weight coefficient would be to give relatively smaller weight to current incomes of the immediate past and relatively more to those of the more distant past.

The hypothesis that the income horizon for housing expenditures is longer than for all current consumption can be tested by computing weighted averages similar to Friedman's but with different weight coefficients. The weighted average appropriate for our purposes is that which maximizes the correlation of new construction with income and the other

TABLE 3

HOUSING DEMAND FOR DIFFERENT
EXPECTED-INCOME MEASURES

β	Estimated $E(h_d, y_p)$	R^2
0.5	+0.869	0.563
0.4	+ .879	.621
0.3	+0.913	0.535

variables (see Appendix C). Table 3 summarizes the results of estimating the flow-demand equation for three values of the weight coefficient, β, in the neighborhood of 0.4. In this table the implied estimate of the income elasticity of stock demand and the coefficient of multiple determination for the regression of new construction on income and the other variables in (10) are shown for each of the three income series. The maximum value of R^2 is reached for β equal to 0.4, the weight coefficient for Friedman's series. The second column of Table 3 also shows that the implied income elasticity of desired stock-demand changes very little as the weight coefficient in the expected-income series is varied in the neighborhood of the maximum likelihood estimate, 0.4. Thus the admittedly very plausible hypothesis that consumers plan their housing expenditures in terms of an income horizon which is longer than that for all current consumption is not

[46] This is discussed at somewhat greater length in Appendix A. Actually, Friedman modifies this formulation to include a time trend. This need not be considered explicitly here, since it results only in the multiplication of the above by a constant. Iᵣ practice, the infinite summation indicated in (17) can be approximated by a weighted average of current disposable income for a finite number of time periods to any desired degree of accuracy.

consistent with our data. It would appear that Friedman's expected-income series is the appropriate one for studying housing demand.

In brief, the results of this section are:

1. The response of housing demand to price or income changes is much greater than is commonly believed. The estimates obtained in this section suggest that the elasticities of desired stock demand with respect to income and price are both about unity.
2. If the adjustment of the housing stock to changing demand conditions is to be properly understood, account must be taken of the dynamic lag of the adjustment of stock. This lag is substantial. Our estimates indicate that individuals seek to add about one-third the difference between desired and actual stock during a year, which implies that, for the adjustment of the actual housing stock to be 90 per cent completed, six years are required.
3. The rate of new home-building is highly responsive to price and income changes. The elasticities of new construction with respect to price and income are about 5.5, numerically.
4. Including a time trend in the regression analysis indicated that our estimates are not biased by secular bias in the measures of price and stock used. Likewise, it indicated that the demand for housing has not been influenced by a secular change in tastes.
5. Experiments with the income variable suggest that Friedman's expected-income series is indeed the appropriate one for studying housing demand.

VI. Ratio of Rent to Price as a Determinant of Construction

So far our attention has been concentrated upon estimating what I have called the "excess form" of the flow-demand function, because a primary aim of this study is to estimate the elasticities of housing demand. But we have seen that the rate of home-building can be related to the ratio of rent to price and the rate of interest. This follows because increases in the demand for housing cause rents to rise, since stock momentarily remains fixed. The rise in rent makes investment in new housing profitable. Since a more careful study of this mechanism gives new insight into the workings of the housing market, we shall consider it in some detail in this section.

Recall equation (6), which I called the "ratio form" of the flow-demand function; it states that the rate of new construction relative to the actual housing stock, (h'_a/h), depends upon the ratio of rent to price, (R/p), and the interest rate. Computing the regression for the period 1922–41, we find[47]

[47] Here the National Industrial Conference Board rent index is used to measure rent. The reasons for using this index are discussed in the next section. The comparison was restricted to the period 1922–41 because, for the comparison in equation (23), below, a weighted average of rent to price for several past periods as well is needed, and this rent index is available only for 1913 and following years.

$$(h'_{o}/h) = +0.255 \, (R/p) - 0.00608 \, r, \, R^2 = 0.714, \, \delta = 0.917 . \quad (18)$$
$$\phantom{(h'_{o}/h) = +0}(0.0455) (0.00451)$$

That new construction varied directly with the ratio of rent to price and inversely with the rate of interest is in accord with a priori expectation. The coefficient of the rent-price ratio exceeds its standard error by about four times, but the coefficient of the interest rate is not significant at the 5 per cent level. Together the two variables explain about seven-tenths of the variation of new construction in relation to actual stock, although, as judged by the Durbin-Watson statistic, there is a positive serial correlation in the true residuals.[48]

While the results of equation (18) are at least partly consistent with the model described in Section II, let us take a closer look at the rent-price ratio. Since housing is a very long-lived asset, we might expect that investment in housing depends not only upon the current profitability of housing, the ratio of rent to price, but also upon investor's expectations about its future profitability. Looking at this a little differently, the current ratio of rent to price is a measure of the position of the desired stock-demand schedule relative to the actual housing stock. It seems not unreasonable that investment in housing depends not only upon the current demand for housing but also on investor's expectations about housing demand in the future. If this hypothesis is correct, then, just as we needed a measure of consumer's expectations about their normal income in the previous section, now we need a measure of investor's expectations about the profitability of investment in housing.

I shall assume that the rate of change in the expected ratio of rent to price is proportional to the difference between the current ratio and the expected ratio.[49] This implies that the expected ratio of rent to price in year t is given by[50]

---

[48] For twenty observations and two independent variables the bounds on this statistic are 1.10 and 1.54 at the 5 per cent level (see Durbin and Watson, *op. cit.*, pp. 173–75).

[49] This hypothesis about the formation of expectations is due originally to Philip Cagan, "The Monetary Dynamics of Hyperinflation," in *Studies in the Quantity Theory of Money*, ed. Milton Friedman (Chicago: University of Chicago Press, 1956), pp. 25–117. It has also been employed by Friedman, *op. cit.*, and by Marc Nerlove, "Estimates of the Elasticities of Supply of Selected Agricultural Commodities," *Journal of Farm Economics*, XXXVIII (May, 1956), 492–509. Because this hypothesis has been found empirically to fit the formation of expectations about such diverse phenomena as future change in the general price level, future real incomes of consumers, and future relative prices of farm products, we might also expect the hypothesis to work for our purpose.

[50] See Appendix A.

$$(R/p)_e(t) = (1 - e^{-a}) \sum_{j=0}^{\infty} e^{-aj} (R/p)(t-j) \qquad (19)$$

where a is the weight coefficient. It therefore follows that

$$(R/p)_e(t) = g(R/p)(t) + (1 - g)(R/p)_e(t-1), \qquad (20)$$

where $g = 1 - e^{-a}$.

Given this assumption about the formation of expectations, there are two methods by which one might proceed, the iterative method and the recursive method. Proceeding by the iterative method, one selects a particular value for the weight coefficient and computes the expected ratio of rent to price using (19).[51] A regression similar to (18), but using the expected ratio of rent to price, is then calculated, and the whole process is repeated for various values of the weight coefficient. As shown in Appendix C, the maximum likelihood estimate of the weight coefficient is that value which results in the maximum correlation between new construction and the expected rent-price ratio and rate of interest. On the other hand, in the recursive method the effect of expectations is taken into account by including values of the interest rate and new construction relative to stock, both lagged one year, among the independent variables in a regression equation similar to (18). To see why this is so, rewrite equation (6) as follows:

$$(h'_g/h)(t) = c'_0 + c'_1(R/p)_e(t) + c'_2 r(t). \qquad (21)$$

Lagging equation (21) one year and substituting it along with (20) into (21) gives

$$\begin{aligned}(h'_g/h)(t) = g\,c'_0 + g\,c'_1(R/p)(t) + c'_2 r(t) \\ - c'_2(1-g)\,r(t-1) + (1-g)(h'_g/h)(t-1).\end{aligned} \qquad (22)$$

Hence, by the recursive method, the value of the weight coefficient can be estimated directly from the coefficient of lagged new construction. This variable, along with the lagged rate of interest, reflects the influence of the past profitability of housing on current new construction.

Estimating (21) by the iterative method, we find that an a equal to 0.8 maximizes R^2. The complete regression equation is

$$(h'_g/h)(t) = +0.356\,(R/p)_e(t) - 0.0113\,r(t), \quad R^2 = 0.851,$$
$$\quad\quad (0.0409) \quad\quad\quad\quad (0.00351) \qquad\qquad (23)$$

$$\delta = 0.869\,.$$

[51] In practice the infinite summation indicated by the right member of (19) is approximated by a finite sum, in this case for the smallest number of years such that the sum of the weights is at least equal to 0.98. Thus, for a weight coefficient of 0.5, the expected ratio of rent to price is a weighted average of the current ratio of rent to price for eight years, with the weights declining exponentially as we go back in time.

In (23) both coefficients are numerically larger than the corresponding coefficients in (18). Particularly striking is the effect on the coefficient of the rate of interest, which is nearly twice as large numerically when the expected rent-price ratio is used. The fact that the coefficient of the rent-price ratio in (18) is smaller than that in (23) is quite consistent with the hypothesis that expectations about the profitability of investment in housing depend only partly on the current profitability (here with a weight of about 0.5).[52] Testing whether the expected ratio of rent to price yields a better explanation of new construction than the current ratio is equivalent to testing whether the true value of the weight coefficient is greater than or equal to 4.0, in which case the expected ratio is equal to the current ratio. The latter can be tested by means of a likelihood ratio statistic, which in large samples is distributed as chi square with one degree of freedom. Here we find a chi square of 13.0, which is significant at the .001 level. Hence a better fit is clearly obtained in (23).

Estimating recursively, we find for (22)[53]

$$
\begin{aligned}
(h'_g / h)\,(t) = &+ 0.108\,(R/p)\,(t) - 0.0187\,r\,(t) \\
&\ \ (0.0287) \qquad\quad (0.00522)
\end{aligned}
$$

$$
+0.0136\,r\,(t-1) + 0.751\,(h'_g / h)\,(t-1),\ R^2 = 0.943,\ \delta = 1.27 .
$$
$$
\ \ (0.00510) \qquad\quad (0.0968)
$$

$$(24)$$

As in (23), the coefficient of $r(t)$ is substantially larger numerically than in (18). As seen from equation (22), the coefficient of the expected rent-price ratio in (21) can be determined from the coefficients of $(R/p)(t)$ and $(h'_g/h)(t - 1)$ in (24). These imply a value of $+.434$, which is also substantially larger than the coefficient corresponding to it in (18). Together the four independent variables explain 95 per cent of the variation of (h'_g/h).

Now, a skeptic might justifiably say, "Of course you get a high correlation because of including lagged new construction in (24). What about the joint significance of the other variables?" The answer is that the *F*-

---

[52] It should be noted here that the standard errors of the coefficients shown in (23) and the statistic δ are conditional on the value of the weight coefficient, 0.8. Since the latter is not known a priori but was estimated from the data, the standard errors are too small and the bounds on δ given in n. 48 are not exact. A test that is valid for large samples, the likelihood ratio test, indicates that the coefficient of the expected ratio of rent to price is significant at the .001 level, that of the interest rate at the .01 level. This test is described in Appendix C.

[53] This result, together with some of the other material of this section, was presented by me in a paper read at the Philadelphia meeting of the Econometric Society in December, 1957; an abstract of this paper is published under the title "Accelerator and Profit Principles in Investment Demand: New Housing," in *Econometrica*, XXVI (October, 1958), 616.

ratio is $F(3, 15) = 9.30$, significant at about the .01 level. Likewise, the F-ratio for testing the joint significanse of $r(t - 1)$ and $(h'_g/h)(t - 1)$, which measure the influence of past profit rates, is $F(2, 15) = 30.1$, significant at the .001 level. Note also that equation (22) implies that the coefficient of the lagged interest rate in (24) should be equal to the negative of the product of the coefficients of $r(t)$ and $(h'_g/h)(t - 1)$. In (24), where no such restriction was imposed upon the coefficients, we find this product to be $+.0140$ as compared with $+.0136$, the coefficient of $r(t - 1)$. This is a striking agreement with a priori expectation.

Thus, by either method of estimation, we find that taking account of expectations about the future profitability of housing explains a significantly larger fraction of the variation of new home-building. Both methods imply that new construction is considerably more responsive to changes in the expected rent-price ratio than the current ratio. Likewise, taking expectations into account increases the coefficient of the interest rate using either method. But the two methods do not yield completely identical results. The weight attached to the current rent-price ratio in forming the expected ratio is about 0.50 by the iterative method, while it is about 0.25 by the recursive method. Which of the two sets of estimates is preferable? Since the serial correlation in the residuals is less strong when estimating by the recursive method,[54] it is probably to be preferred in this case. The important point, however, is that the results obtained by either method are broadly consistent with our previous analysis.

How do these results contribute to our understanding of the workings of the housing market? First, they provide an additional check on the analysis of the second section of this study. In studying housing, we are fortunate, since it is one of the few consumer durables for which a price for its services is widely quoted on the market. Second, they give us an alternative way of estimating the elasticity of new construction with respect to the rate of interest. Equation (18) implies an elasticity of -0.400, while taking account of expectations raises this to -0.739 in (23) and to -1.22 in (24). But, more important, the examination of the rent-price ratio mechanism in this section suggests one additional reason for the dynamic lag in the adjustment of the housing stock to changing condi-

---

[54] While in (23) the Durbin-Watson statistic is inconsistent with the hypothesis that the true residuals are serially uncorrelated, in (24) this statistic sneaks into the region of indeterminacy. For twenty observations and four independent variables the bounds on at the 5 per cent level are 0.90 and 1.83, respectively. It should be noted, however, that one reason for the stronger serial correlation in (23) is serially correlated measurement errors in the expected rent-price ratio. Even if any errors in the current ratio are serially uncorrelated, weighted averages of these ratios will contain serially correlated errors because of the presence of common elements.

tions. This is the lag in the revision of the expectations of investors. To the extent that housing is owner-occupied, of course, this factor has been partly taken into account by considering income expectations, since the investor and the buyer of housing services are one and the same.[55] But a substantial fraction of the housing in this country is tenant-occupied, about one-half in the period considered here. The results of this section suggest that an increase in the demand for housing is not immediately viewed as permanent by investors in tenant-occupied housing. On this point it is interesting to note that during the twenties, while total home-building turned down in the middle of the decade, this downturn was largely accounted for by the downturn in single-family dwelling units, which are primarily owner-occupied. Building of apartment houses, on the other hand, continued to increase until later in the decade. Hence, in addition to the factors cited earlier, the lag in the housing stock behind changing demand conditions may result partly from the lag in adjustment of investor's expectations about the future profitability of housing.

VII. Further Evidence on Housing-Demand Elasticities

Our earlier results suggest that the income and price elasticities of housing demand are both about equal to 1.0 numerically. In this section we shall consider some additional evidence about the values of these elasticities which is provided by certain other comparisons. While it is not possible at this time to reconcile completely these results with those obtained earlier, on one point all the results obtained in this study are unanimous: housing demand is much more responsive to price and income changes than is commonly believed. The comparisons of this section are also important in that they indicate that our model is at least partly consistent with a wide range of phenomena, including the setting of rents in the market, the quality of newly built housing, and the variations in housing quality among cities.

THE DEMAND FOR SERVICES

The demand function for the services of housing is fundamental to our whole analysis of the housing market, and indeed it should be, since the sole purpose of housing is to provide consumer satisfaction. The demand for services depends upon their price per unit (i.e., rent) and real income—and, perhaps, other variables as well. But, since at any moment of time the flow of housing services on the market is fixed by the available stock of housing, this stock plus income determines the level of rent in the market.

---

[55] I say "partly" because other variables not explicitly considered here may influence the demand for housing services and, hence, the profitability of housing. Expectations about their future values might influence the investment decisions of owner-occupiers.

Hence the demand for services can be estimated directly and its price and income elasticities compared with the housing-demand elasticities obtained previously.

In using available measures of rent for this purpose, at least two difficulties must be faced. First, strictly speaking, available measures of rent refer only to tenant-occupied housing, since it is only for this kind of housing that market prices are available. While owner-occupiers are in effect considered here as landlords who sell housing services to themselves as tenants, these imputed rents are not covered by available rent indexes. But, so long as there was no systematic change in the quality of owner-occupied relative to tenant-occupied housing, this omission would cause no trouble. A second difficulty is that available measures of rent differ greatly as to their trend during the period we consider here. The rent component of the BLS Consumer Price Index fell about 21 per cent in real terms from 1915 to 1941. During the same period the National Industrial Conference Board rent index increased about 6 per cent. This is not a happy situation. The way out of this difficulty I have chosen is to use each in turn as a measure of rent and to evaluate the indexes in terms of the results.

First, using the BLS rent-component index, R', we find for the regression with rent as the dependent variable (non-war years, 1915–41)

$$R' = +0.0672h - 0.0461y_p, \quad R^2 = 0.0485 , \tag{25}$$
$$(0.0670) \quad (0.0690)$$

or, transformed,

$$h = +14.9R' + 0.688y_p , \tag{25'}$$
$$E(h_d) + 2.21 +0.464 .$$

In (25) the coefficient of neither variable is significantly different from zero. Further, the derived estimate of income elasticity is only about half as great as obtained earlier, and the estimated-price elasticity is *positive*. This hardly suggests that the BLS index is satisfactory for our purposes.[56] In contrast, if the NICB index, R, is used to measure rent, we find

$$R = -0.0875h + 0.121y_p, \quad R^2 = 0.302, \quad \delta = 0.937 , \tag{26}$$
$$(0.0414) \quad (0.0426)$$

which, transformed, is

$$h = -11.4R + 1.38y_p , \tag{26'}$$
$$E(h_d) -1.47 + 0.935 .$$

---

[56] In this regard it is interesting to note that the apparently erroneous Duesenberry-Kistin estimate noted in Sec. I also used BLS data on rents as a measure of price.

As would be expected, in equation (26) rent varies inversely with the per capita housing stock for a given level of per capita income. Both coefficients differ significantly from zero. The estimate of income elasticity implied by (26) is almost identical with the estimate obtained in Section V. The estimated-price elasticity of housing demand is more than half again as great numerically but is not necessarily inconsistent with the earlier estimate, as a rough judgment based upon the 95 per cent confidence limits of the latter would indicate.[57]

One possible difficulty with the above analysis is that rents may not adjust completely to changed conditions of demand for housing services in a year's time. Many dwelling units are rented on leases that may customarily run for a year or even longer. Hence, with an increase in market demand for the services of housing, average rents would gradually rise only as old leases expire. In addition, Blank and Winnick have argued that, when the demand for housing services is rising (falling), landlords prefer to maintain rents at old levels, at least for a time, and passively accept increases (decreases) in occupancy.[58] If this hypothesis is correct, it would provide an additional reason for sluggishness of rents.

Now, if the lag in adjustment of rents were a significant feature of the housing market insofar as annual data are concerned, we would expect that actual rents would be below average rents for given stock and income in years when rents are rising and conversely when rents are falling. In other words, the estimated residual from equation (26) for any year would be opposite in sign to the change in rent. If, however, we compare the residuals from (26) with the change in rents by year, we find that in only eleven of twenty-five cases are the signs different.[59] This comparison would seem to contradict the hypothesis that market rents lag behind short-run equilibrium rents.

Further evidence on this point can be obtained by comparing rents with occupancy ratios.[60] If rents were sluggish, we would expect below-average occupancy ratios when actual rents are above average rents for given stock and income and conversely. But, if the estimated residuals from (26) are compared with occupancy ratios for the years 1930 through 1938, the over-all relationship is, if anything, positive rather than negative.

[57] The upper limit as noted earlier is -1.80 for price elasticity.

[58] David M. Blank and Louis Winnick, "The Structure of the Housing Market," *Quarterly Journal of Economics*, LXVII (May, 1953), 181–208.

[59] If we use money instead of real rents for the comparison, the signs are different in twelve of twenty-four cases, there being no change in money rents in one year.

[60] Occupancy ratios for the United States for the years 1930–38 are given by Blank and Winnick (*ibid.*).

While falling occupancy ratios were associated with increasing residuals from 1930 to 1932, from 1934 through 1938 both the estimated residuals from (26) and the occupancy ratios were increasing.

Thus equation (26) provides some evidence that rents are set in the market by the available housing stock in relation to the level of income. Except perhaps for the early 1930's, the comparisons made here reveal no evidence of a lag in market rents so far as annual data are concerned. The estimate of income elasticity obtained here is quite consistent with the earlier estimate obtained from equation (10), although equation (26) suggests that the price elasticity of housing demand may be nearer to -1.5 than to -1.0.

THE QUALITY OF NEW DWELLINGS

Earlier we have repeatedly emphasized the lag in the adjustment of the housing stock to changing conditions, and earlier empirical results suggest that this lag is indeed substantial. Now, while the total stock of housing may not adjust immediately, it seems highly likely that changes in price and income would be reflected in the average quality of newly built dwelling units soon after the change. If an increase in what consumers expect to be their normal income level were to take place, we would expect that, on the average, bigger and better (hence more costly) housing units would be built soon thereafter, even though conditions that we have stressed earlier might prevent the total housing stock from changing immediately to the extent ultimately desired. In this section, therefore, we shall consider the changes in the quality of new dwellings that result from price and income changes.

We are tempted to identify the elasticities of the quality of newly built dwelling units with desired stock-demand elasticities, but we must step carefully here. The total stock of housing at any time, in addition to once new but now depreciated dwelling units accumulated from the past, also includes depreciated past expenditures for additions and alterations to existing dwellings. The variable, H_n, therefore, which measures the average quality of new dwelling units,[61] is only one source of enlargement of the housing stock. In addition, existing houses can be, and are, enlarged and improved. Hence there is no reason to expect that the elasticities of the average quality of new dwelling units would be the same as the elasticities

---

[61] This variable is measured here by the average current dollar value of new housekeeping dwelling units from David M. Blank, *The Volume of Residential Construction, 1889–1950* (New York: National Bureau of Economic Research, 1954), Appendix A, Table 22, deflated by the Boeckh index of residential construction costs. The value data for years prior to 1921 are estimates made by Blank; for 1921 and later years they are based on data published by the Department of Commerce, *op. cit.*

of desired stock demand. Indeed, we might well expect that the income elasticity of average quality would be higher, just as the income elasticity of prime beefsteak is probably higher than that of stewing beef.

Comparing the average quality of new dwelling units, H_n, with price, expected income *per household*, Y_p, the interest rate, and the average size of households, P,[62] we find

$$H_n = -59.1p + 4.09Y_p - 510r + 385P, \quad R^2 = 0.723 ,$$
$$(17.7) \quad (0.621) \quad (146) \quad (802) \tag{27}$$

$$E(H_n) \quad -1.21 + 1.87 \quad -0.452 \quad \dots .$$

The three determinants of desired stock which we have considered—price, income, and the interest rate—explain about seven-tenths of the variation in the quality of new dwelling units. The coefficient of the average size of household, however, does not differ significantly from zero. The estimated elasticities show that quality is highly responsive to changes in conditions of demand. The price elasticity is about the same order of magnitude as that for desired stock, but the income elasticity is twice as large as the income elasticity of desired stock estimated earlier. While there is no reason to expect the two income elasticities to be the same, this comparison indicates that the income elasticity of desired stock demand may be somewhat higher than the estimates obtained earlier would suggest. Likewise, the elasticity with respect to the rate of interest seems more plausible in its relation to price elasticity than the estimate obtained earlier.[63] This comparison, too, strengthens my contention that the response of housing demand to changes in price and income is much greater than is realized.

VARIATIONS IN HOUSING QUALITY AMONG CITIES

Further evidence on housing demand is provided by considering variations in housing quality from city to city. Examination of these differences is particularly desirable for two reasons. First, the data used for this purpose are not likely to be subject to the same kind of biases as the time-series data used earlier, namely, the possibility of secular bias in the price

---

[62] Expected income per household is simply per capita expected income multiplied by persons per household, P. The latter was obtained by straight-line interpolation of data for census years published in the *Statistical Abstracts*. As such, it is probably a good measure of the trend of this variable, but it may miss year-to-year fluctuations. It was included to make the estimates here more comparable with earlier estimates, which relate to per capita magnitudes.

[63] As has been argued above, we would expect the interest-rate elasticity to be about one-half as large numerically as the price elasticity. Here it is about three-eighths as large, as compared with only one-seventh for the elasticities of desired stock demand obtained in Sec. V.

and stock measures used. A second reason, on the technical statistical side, is that the comparisons among different cities are unlikely to be affected by correlations of the true residuals or by the joint determination of several variables included in the regression analysis.

But, while the comparisons among cities are free from some of the limitations inherent in the time-series comparisons, they are also subject to certain limitations of their own. The first of these arises from the fact that the stock data refer to actual rather than desired stock. However, there is no way out of this difficulty, since, to my knowledge, there are no data on new construction in the various cities from which to infer stock-demand elasticities, as was done in Section V. We must therefore be content with a comparison based on actual stock figures. There are many reasons, of course, why actual stock might differ from desired stock in the different cities. But these would lead to bias in the stock-demand elasticities obtained only if the difference between desired and actual housing stock—part of the residual term—were correlated with one of the independent variables in the regression equation. It is only for this reason that the time-series comparison assuming complete adjustment in Section IV gave biased estimates of the demand elasticities. One such source of bias might arise in the following way: it is shown in Appendix A that, if desired stock grows at a constant rate, actual stock will tend to grow at this same rate, and the ratio of desired to actual stock will tend to a constant which varies directly with the rate of growth in desired stock and inversely with the adjustment parameter, d. Now if, for example, income grows at different rates and grows more rapidly where incomes are relatively low, a comparison of actual stock with income and other variables would overestimate the income elasticity of desired stock demand.

A second limitation of the comparison among various cities arises from the coverage of the stock variable used. The stock variable is based upon the value of owner-occupied dwelling units in one-unit detached structures as reported by the 1950 census.[64] As such it refers only to part of the housing stock in any city and, contrary to the other stock data examined in

[64] More precisely, the stock variable, H_0, is the average current dollar value of this class of dwelling for 1949 deflated by the Boeckh city index of residential construction costs; hence it is a measure of stock per dwelling unit rather than per capita. The value data are from U.S. Department of Commerce, Bureau of the Census, *1950 Census of Housing* (Washington, D.C.: Government Printing Office, 1953), Vol. V, Table 1. The data refer to vacant non-seasonal, not dilapidated, units for sale as well as to occupied units. The Boeckh city index of residential construction costs is used as a measure of price. I wish to thank the compiler, Mr. E. H. Boeckh, of Washington, D.C., for making these unpublished data available to me. Only those cities for which both stock and price data are available were included in the comparison.

this study, includes land as well as structures. It is readily apparent that estimates based upon such a stock variable are not wholly comparable with the preceding ones. In the first place, the data refer only to one-unit detached structures rather than to all structures. The former are typically inhabited by the higher-income groups, and it seems quite possible that the income elasticity of demand for this type of dwelling might exceed that for multi-unit structures. Second, the data include the value of land as well as structures, and there is no reason to expect that the income elasticity of demand for housing including land should be the same as that for structures only and, indeed, some reason for thinking that it might be higher. It seems quite possible that, as income increases, relatively more of a consumer's expenditure for housing, defined to include land, would be channeled toward securing a desirable location as compared with structural features. For these two reasons the elasticity estimates obtained in this comparison do not necessarily refer to the same kind of housing demand as our previous estimates.

Still another difficulty arises in connection with the comparisons among cities. It has been argued here that the influence of income on housing demand is best appraised by using a measure of the normal income level of the consumer unit. However, the best available income data for the comparison among cities are measures of the average current income of the inhabitants of the class dwellings to which the stock data refer.[65] While it is possible that average permanent income may differ from average current income in a given city, it would seem likely that the fraction of the variation in average current income accounted for by variation in permanent income is substantially greater as among different places at the same time than in time-series comparisons. For example, Friedman's expected-income series fell only one-half as much in real terms between 1929 and 1933 as current income, but the per capita income of Georgia was only about one-third that in New York State whether we make the comparison for 1929 or 1933. One reason, however, why the difference between average current and permanent income might differ in different cities is unemployment. The year 1949, to which the comparisons here refer, was one of some unemployment, and the different cities included differed substantially in unemployment in that year. Since an above-average incidence in unemployment would imply an above-average difference between per-

---

[65] This is the average income of primary families and individuals in owner-occupied dwelling units in one-unit structures. It was calculated from the distributions published in U.S. Department of Commerce, Bureau of the Census, *1950 Census of Housing* (Washington, D.C.: Government Printing Office, 1953), Vol. II, Table 7, using $500 and $20,000 for the mean values of the lower and upper open-end classes, respectively.

manent and current income, a measure of unemployment in 1949 is included in one comparison below as a check on the current income variable.[66]

Let us turn now to the comparison of stock per dwelling unit, H_0, in different cities in 1949. In addition to the price and income variables discussed above, two others are included in the analysis. These are persons per household, P, and the percentage of all dwelling units in the city which are in one-unit detached structures, D.[67] The least-squares regression equation is

$$H_0 = -150p + 3.22Y - 1,630P - 11.7D, R^2 = 0.797 ,$$
$$\quad (29.5) \quad (0.271) \quad (738) \quad (9.16) \tag{28}$$
$$E(H_0) - 1.59 + 1.68 \quad \cdots \quad \cdots \cdot$$

These variables explain about 80 per cent of the variation of the stock variable among cities, although the D variable contributes little to this explanation. Stock varies directly with income and inversely with price, as would be expected, and the estimated stock elasticities are both substantially greater than 1.0, numerically.[68] Furthermore, if the unemployment variable is included in the analysis, there is virtually no change in the results:

[66] Unemployment is measured by the percentage of the male labor force reporting work in 1949 who reported twenty-six weeks or less work. The data used are for the Standard Metropolitan Area in which the city is located and were obtained from the U.S. Department of Commerce, Bureau of the Census, *1950 Census of Population* (Washington, D.C.: Government Printing Office, 1952), Vol. II, Table 72. The population census of 1950 did not tabulate data relating to unemployment in 1949 for cities. Since the incidence of unemployment need not have been the same throughout a Standard Metropolitan Area, the data used might contain an error of unknown magnitude.

[67] Persons per household is included for comparability with the previous estimates, which are in per capita terms. It is measured by data from *1950 Census of Housing*, Vol. II, Table 1. Total persons in households in owner-occupied one-unit dwelling units was calculated by assuming a mean value of nine for the open-end class in the tabulated distributions. The variable D was included in an attempt, perhaps unsuccessful, to remove the effects of differences in land values in different cities. Where land is relatively expensive, it is relatively cheaper to provide housing in the form of apartment buildings or other multi-unit dwellings than with one-unit detached structures. We would therefore expect that the price of land and the percentage of dwelling units in one-unit detached structures would be negatively related. The latter was calculated from data from *ibid.*, Table 6.

[68] The estimated elasticities presented here differ from those presented by me in "The Demand for Non-Farm Housing" (abstract), *Econometrica*, XXV (April, 1957), 365–66, primarily because a different income variable was used.

$$H_0 = -149p + 3.26\,Y - 1{,}670P - 11.2\,D + 64.1\,U,$$
$$(29.7)\quad(0.282)\quad(746)\quad(9.23)\,(168.0)$$
$$R^2 = 0.800 \,. \tag{29}$$

As would be expected, the sign of the unemployment variable is positive, since the greater the level of unemployment, the farther below permanent income is current income. However, the coefficient of U is much smaller than its standard error and could quite possibly result from chance association.

It is not too surprising that these elasticity estimates turn out to be larger numerically than those obtained in some of the previous comparisons. This follows from the fact that the stock variable includes the value of land and refers only to one-unit detached structures. Since there are more substitutes for one-unit detached structures than for all housing, the estimated-price elasticity should be larger. Likewise, we have indicated several reasons why the income elasticity obtained from this comparison might be greater than that for all structures. Still, these results indicate that the price and income elasticities of housing demand might be somewhat greater than those inferred from the time-series comparisons in Section V would indicate.

To recapitulate, the additional evidence considered in this section all indicates that housing-demand elasticities are considerably greater than previous estimates would lead us to believe. While reasons have been given why higher elasticities might be obtained from the comparisons involving the quality of new dwellings over time or the quality of one-unit detached structures in different cities, these estimates indicate that the price and income elasticities might exceed unity. The comparisons made in this section also indicate that the analysis developed earlier in this study is broadly consistent with a wide range of housing phenomena. This fact serves to increase our confidence in the elasticity estimates which this analysis suggests.

VIII. Summary and Concluding Observations

This study has been concerned both with the ultimate response of housing demand to changes in price and income and with the rate at which adjustments of the actual housing stock take place. A considerable amount of empirical evidence bearing on these two questions has been marshaled in the preceding sections. This evidence is summarized in the present section, and some of its implications for questions not considered earlier are noted.

HOUSING-DEMAND ELASTICITIES

All the evidence on the elasticities of housing demand gathered here suggests that they are much greater than is commonly believed. The previously published estimates discussed in the introductory section are -0.08 for price and $+0.5$ for income. The evidence gathered here suggests that both are at least equal to about unity and may even be numerically larger.

The elasticities obtained in this study are summarized in Table 4. The numerically smallest of these are the desired stock elasticities obtained

TABLE 4

SUMMARY OF HOUSING-DEMAND ELASTICITIES

ELASTICITY OF:	WITH RESPECT TO:	
	Price	Income
Desired stock demand:		
From flow demand, equation (10)...	-0.904	$+0.879$
95 per cent confidence limits.....	$-0.421, -1.80$	$+0.538, +1.42$
Limits from different regressions..	$-0.669, -1.60$	$+0.652, +1.17$
From demand for services, equation (26)......................	-1.47	$+0.935$
Quality of new dwellings, equation (27)	-1.21	$+1.87$
Quality of dwellings in various cities,* equation (28).................	-1.59	$+1.68$

* In one-unit, detached structures.

from estimates of the excess form of the flow-demand function from time-series data. Both the price and the income elasticities estimated from this comparison are about 1.0 in absolute value. While these are numerically smaller than the other elasticity estimates shown in Table 4, the confidence limits on each suggest that the true values might be considerably greater. Stock-demand elasticities were also estimated by comparing rent with stock and income (eq. [26]). The estimate of income elasticity so obtained was almost identical with that obtained from equation (10), but the estimated-price elasticity was nearer -1.5 than -1.0. The comparison based on rent, however, is rather unsatisfactory, both because of the uncertainty in the true movement of rents over time and because of the rather low correlation obtained.

Evidence on the variation of the quality of new dwellings over time and variations in quality among cities in 1949 was also considered. While the elasticities so obtained are not wholly comparable with the desired stock-demand elasticities estimated earlier, both sets of estimates reinforce the conclusion that housing demand is highly responsive to changes in income and price. Because both sets of estimates were greater than 1.0, the price and income elasticities might be even greater numerically than the estimates from equation (10) indicate. However, additions to stock in the form of new dwelling units are only part of total additions, since additions and alterations to existing dwellings are not included, and the stock variable for the comparisons among cities covered only housing in one-unit, detached dwellings and included land in addition to structures. Since for either definition of housing there are more substitutes than for all housing taken together, it is not surprising that the estimated-price elasticities should turn out to be greater. Likewise, it is quite possible that the true income elasticities on either definition of housing are different from that for all housing. The latter two sets of estimates, therefore, are not necessarily inconsistent with the estimated desired stock-demand elasticities.

That the price and income elasticities of housing demand are much greater than is commonly believed has an important bearing upon two questions about housing recently discussed in the literature. The first of these relates to Winnick's alleged downward shift in consumer preferences for housing. Because the Grebler-Blank-Winnick stock estimates indicate that the housing stock has not increased as rapidly since around 1910 as the elasticity estimates discussed in the first chapter would imply, Winnick concluded that such a shift in tastes has occurred.[69] However, the failure of measured stock to increase more rapidly during the first half of this century may be partly due to underestimation of stock for the post–World War II period. As was pointed out earlier, the Grebler-Blank-Winnick stock estimate for 1950 is about 22 per cent less than an estimate based on 1950 census data. Allowing for this underestimation, their data show some increase in per capita stock from 1910 to 1950, but one which is much smaller than would be expected if housing-demand elasticities were −0.08 for price and +0.5 for income, as Winnick appears to believe.

But, even if the Grebler-Blank-Winnick stock estimates were to describe correctly the secular trend in the stock of housing, is there any need to assume a change in tastes to explain this trend? As judged by the Boeckh index of residential construction costs, the same measure Winnick himself used, the real price of housing has increased by a little over one-half since 1910. Now if the price elasticity of housing demand were almost zero, as the Duesenberry-Kistin estimate indicates and Winnick

[69] *Op. cit.*, p. 87.

believed, such a price increase would have but little effect upon the quantity of housing demanded. However, if the price elasticity is −1.0 or even larger numerically, as the estimates obtained here would suggest, the increase in the real price of housing would have a substantial effect indeed. In fact, in a subsequent discussion of his thesis Winnick admits that "if the price elasticity with respect to housing is higher than income elasticity there is no need to introduce a change in taste argument."[70] Our estimates suggest that the price elasticity for housing is about the same as the income elasticity. This, together with the uncertainty of the secular trend in the housing stock, suggests that it is by no means certain that consumer's preferences toward housing have changed.[71] In fact, had there been a systematic change in tastes during the past half-century, we would expect the trend variable in equation (11) to reflect this fact. Actually, its coefficient did not differ significantly from zero.

A second question about housing upon which the elasticity estimates provided by this study throw some light is the alleged regressivity of property taxation. In his recent study, *Housing Taxation*, Morton has concluded that this tax is regressive.[72] His conclusion was based partly on an estimated-income elasticity of +0.5, which was derived by comparing expenditures for housing with current income by income level for the whole nation at a given time. It has been emphasized earlier that such a comparison is likely to underestimate the elasticity of housing demand with respect to permanent income, the relevant elasticity for appraising the effects of a tax on housing. Since the latter elasticity is at least equal to 1.0, as judged from the estimates obtained here, the tax on housing is at least proportional, and perhaps even progressive. Morton also based his conclusion on a comparison of property taxes with current income level for consumers in the same city. This showed that the ratio of

---

[70] See Jack Guttentag, "Winnick's Case for a Changing Attitude toward Housing: Comment," and Louis Winnick, "Reply," *Quarterly Journal of Economics*, LXX (May, 1956), 320.

[71] The Grebler-Blank-Winnick estimates show a fall in the per capita constant dollar housing stock of 11.2 per cent from 1910 to 1950. Adjusting their estimate for 1950 upward by 22.4 per cent—as suggested by their comparison with the estimate derived from the 1950 housing census—converts this change to an *increase* of 8.6 per cent. Over the period 1910–50 the real price of housing increased by 56 per cent, as judged by the Boeckh index, and Friedman's expected-income series increased by 71.4 per cent. Elasticities of −0.08 and +0.5 for price and income, respectively, thus imply an expected increase in per capita stock of 31.2 per cent from 1910 to 1950. However, the elasticities in the first line of Table 4 imply an expected increase in stock of only 12.2 per cent.

[72] *Op. cit.*

property taxes paid to current income declines with the level of income. But this comparison is faulty for the same reason that the comparison of housing expenditures with current income is.

THE RATE OF NEW CONSTRUCTION

In this study new construction is viewed as the means by which the actual stock of housing is adjusted to the stock ultimately desired. The latter has been shown to depend upon the relative price of housing, real income, the interest rate, and population, though it may depend upon additional variables as well. The time path of new construction depends upon that of desired stock or upon those of its determinants. The model analyzed here is capable of generating many different time patterns of new construction, including asymptotic adjustment to a once-and-for-all change in desired stock, a constant rate of growth of new construction in response to a constant rate of growth of desired stock, or cyclical fluctuations in new construction in response to cyclical fluctuations in desired stock or in its determinants.

When the excess form of the flow-demand function was fitted to data for the period 1915–41, not quite two-thirds of the variation in measured new construction was explained as induced by changes in price, income, the interest rate, and the actual housing stock. The fact that about one-third of the variation of new construction in this period is unexplained, together with the serial correlation in the residuals from equation (10), suggests the possibility of a sizable independent cyclical component in new construction. It was argued, however, that his unexplained component of measured new construction might be due in part to two factors, serially correlated errors in the estimates of new construction and of the housing stock and a contracyclical fluctuation in property-tax rates, which could not be included in the analysis. When new construction was related to the expected rent-price ratio in Section VI, between 85 and 95 per cent of the variation from 1922 to 1941 was explained.[73] The latter comparison, in particular, suggests that there is little need to suppose that new construction is influenced by independent cycles of replacement demand or to appeal to such currently popular devices as non-linearity or ceilings or floors to explain the construction cycle in the interwar period.

The evidence provided by equation (10) indicates that new construction is highly responsive indeed to changes in income or in the price of housing. It indicates that the elasticities of new construction with respect

---

[73] If equation (10) is refitted to data for 1922–41, an R^2 of about 0.8 is found. Thus part of the explanation for the relatively low correlation obtained including the earlier years might lie in poorer data for these years.

to price and income are about equal to 5.5 numerically. Likewise, the estimated elasticity of new construction with respect to the interest rate was about −0.8, and it was indicated that this is likely to underestimate the true elasticity. But, even though new construction is highly responsive to changes in demand conditions for housing, we have seen that the lag in the adjustment of the actual housing stock to the level ultimately desired is also quite substantial. We estimated that individuals seek to add about one-third of the difference between actual and desired stock to the housing stock in any year. This, in turn, implies that, for a given adjustment to be 90 per cent completed, about six years are required. Several reasons for this lag have been suggested. Because housing decisions are carefully considered and moving to new quarters is often made to coincide with other events such as children starting school, consumers do not respond immediately to changes in demand conditions. Second, in the short run the price of housing or the cost of mortgage funds might rise above their normal levels as new resources move into the home-building industry. And, finally, the examination of the rent-price ratio mechanism in Section V suggests that investors in tenant-occupied housing might not react immediately to changes in the current profitability of housing.

In addition to the lag of adjustment of actual to desired stock, another lag must be considered if we are to understand the nature of short-run fluctuations in home-building. This is the lag in the revision of expectations of their normal income level by consumers. It has been shown that a measure of normal income level, such as Friedman's expected-income series is, provides a better explanation of new construction than a measure of current income. According to his series, expected income changes only one-third as much as current income in any given year. Since desired stock demand depends upon permanent income, fluctuations in desired stock lag behind fluctuations in current income.

The effect of these two lags—the lag of adjustment of actual to desired stock and the lag of adjustment of desired stock to current income—is most easily seen by considering the comparatively simple case of the adjustment of actual stock to a once-and-for-all change in income.[74] This is illustrated in Figures 4 and 5. It is assumed that initially actual stock is equal to desired stock and that current income increases by such an amount that, if maintained indefinitely, desired stock would increase by one unit. If the increase in current income is immediately believed to be permanent, desired stock immediately increases by one unit to this new level. Furthermore, if the actual stock of housing were adjusted to the

[74] The differential equations which describe the time paths of adjustment shown graphically here are derived in Appendix A.

new desired level in, say, a year, the dashed line in Figure 4 would show the housing stock for Year 1 and for each moment in time thereafter. If, however, the assumption that stock adjusts immediately is dropped, and it is assumed instead that the annual net rate of increase in stock is one-third the difference between actual and desired stock, the time path of the housing stock is that indicated by the line labeled *A* in Figure 4. Here, actual stock increases at a decreasing rate and approaches arbitrarily close to the new desired stock as time passes. The time path of new construction corresponding to this case is that shown by the line labeled *A* in Figure 5. In this figure the zero point on the ordinate is the new level of replacement demand—*k* times desired stock. New construction jumps initially from the old level of replacement demand (−0.035 here) at time

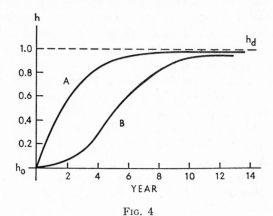

Fig. 4

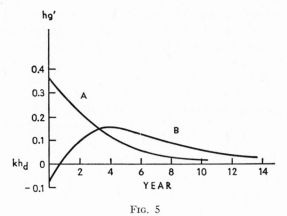

Fig. 5

zero and then declines, approaching the new level of replacement demand asymptotically.

To introduce the second lag, drop the assumption that consumers expect the increase to be permanent immediately, assuming instead that income expectations are revised in the manner indicated by Friedman's series. In this case, permanent income and desired stock increase in a manner similar to that indicated by line *A* in Figure 4. Still assuming that the annual rate of increase in stock is one-third the difference between actual and desired stock, the housing stock grows as indicated by the line labeled *B* in Figure 4, slowly at first and then more rapidly, again approaching the new desired stock as time goes by. Gross construction in this case, indicated by line *B* in Figure 5, increases to a peak at about three years from the initial increase in income and then gradually declines. Each of the lags has the effect of spreading new construction out over a period longer than a year and reducing the amplitude of the fluctuations in new construction. When both are considered, it is easily seen that the peak in new construction lags behind the change in current income.[75] Both lags act as built-in stabilizers in the housing market, moderating fluctuations in new home-building and in the housing stock.

In this study, new construction has been treated as induced by changes in desired stock and the actual housing stock. The influence of new construction upon fluctuations in over-all economic activity has been neglected. Such an influence, suggested by the currently popular theory of income and employment, has often been pointed to as partly responsible for the depression of the 1930's. Now new construction reached a peak in 1925 when it equaled about $72 (1935–39 = 100) per capita. By 1929 it had fallen to about $48, or by about one-third (the fall in net investment over the same period was about one-half). Yet current income grew at only a slightly slower rate following 1925 than in the early twenties in real per capita terms. Only after 1929, or four years following the downturn in residential construction, did current income begin to fall. If other forms of expenditure were able to take up the slack created by the fall in residential construction following 1925, it would seem that the answer to "Why the Great Depression?" is to be found in why they did not continue to do so following 1929 rather than in why the downturn in residential construction resulted in a fall in current income four years later. This is not to argue that, under conditions of less than full employment, a fall in residential building could not lead to a fall in current income.

[75] In the case where new construction fluctuates cyclically, it can be shown that, with the introduction of either lag, the housing stock lags behind current income as does new construction. Also, either lag may reduce the amplitude of fluctuations in both the housing stock and new construction.

Rather it is to suggest that the strategic factors in the onset of the Great Depression are to found elsewhere.

Closely related to the argument that the fall in new construction in the late twenties was partly responsible for the depression following 1929 is the argument advanced by some that there was "overbuilding" of housing during the 1920's. Gordon, in particular, has argued that the stock of housing was too large relative to the demand for housing during the latter part of this decade.[76] But estimates of desired stock obtained from equation (10) assuming a depreciation rate of $3\frac{1}{2}$ per cent per year indicate that Gordon's contention is incorrect. These estimates are shown in Table 5, together with new construction and the end-of-year housing

TABLE 5

NEW CONSTRUCTION, ACTUAL STOCK, AND
ESTIMATED DESIRED STOCK, SELECTED
YEARS, 1925–35

(1935–39 Dollars per Capita)

Year	New Construction	End-of-Year Actual Stock	Estimated Desired Stock
1925.........	71.9	744	828
1927.........	67.0	786	864
1929.........	48.7	810	852
1931.........	27.6	794	835
1932.........	17.7	783	807
1933.........	15.4	774	748
1935.........	22.6	745	771

stock. They indicate that desired stock exceeded the actual stock of housing throughout the late 1920's and, in fact, until 1932. Desired stock grew less rapidly following 1925 than before, both because permanent income grew at a slightly slower rate and because the price of housing, as indicated by the Boeckh index, increased between 1925 and 1929. The fall in new construction in the late twenties occurred because of the decline in the rate of growth of desired stock, not because housing was overbuilt.

Gordon cites the fall in rent from 1925 to 1929, during which time current income was increasing, as evidence of this alleged overbuilding.[77]

[76] Robert A. Gordon, "Population Growth, Housing, and the Capital Coefficient," *American Economic Review*, XLVI (June, 1956), esp. 312 and 321, and his earlier "Cyclical Experience in the Interwar Period: The Investment Boom of the 'Twenties,' " in *Conference on Business Cycles* (New York: National Bureau of Economic Research, 1951), pp. 204–5.

[77] "Cyclical Experience in the Interwar Period: The Investment Boom of the 'Twenties,' " *op. cit.*

But the level of rent varies with the excess of desired over actual stock. While the estimates shown in Table 5 indicate that desired stock exceeded the actual housing stock until 1932, they indicate that the excess over actual stock did decline following 1925. The fall in rents that took place in the late twenties is thus consistent with the estimates of desired stock shown above and does not imply that housing was overbuilt. Rather the fall in rent indicates that housing was becoming less "underbuilt." Gordon's contention is plainly inconsistent with the evidence assembled here.

APPENDIX A
TWO MATHEMATICAL NOTES
SOME DYNAMIC IMPLICATIONS OF THE FLOW-DEMAND EQUATION

In this comment the response of the actual stock of housing and new construction to certain changes in desired stock is analyzed. First to be considered is the response to a once-and-for-all change in desired stock; second, the response to a once-and-for-all change in current income. These two cases are described in the example in Section VIII. Also considered below is the case of a constant rate of growth of permanent income. While not considered explicitly, the case where desired stock fluctuates cyclically could be analyzed by the same methods used here.

Consider first the case of a once-and-for-all change in desired stock from an initial position of long-run equilibrium with stock h_0 to the new level h_d. The flow-demand equation implies

$$h = h_d - (h_d - h_0) e^{-dt} \qquad (30)$$

$$h_g' = (d - k)(h_d - h_0) e^{-dt} + k h_d , \qquad (31)$$

where the symbol t refers to time from the initial change.[78] Thus actual stock increases exponentially, approaching the new desired stock asymptotically, and gross construction declines exponentially and approaches the level of replacement demand corresponding to the new desired stock as time passes.

Suppose now that from an initial position of long-run equilibrium with stock equal to h_0 and both permanent and current income equal to y_0, current income increases by an amount y' and remains constant there-

---

[78] Here the symbol d is an instantaneous annual rate of change rather than an annual average rate of change as in the text. The latter is equal to $(1 - e^{-d})$; so, for an annual average rate of change equal to 0.317, the instantaneous annual rate is about 0.381. The two differ by not more than $d^2/2$. Likewise, in this appendix, k is an instantaneous annual rate of depreciation.

after. It is assumed, however, that expectations as to permanent income are revised in the manner indicated by Friedman's series, so that desired stock, which is assumed to depend upon permanent income, does not increase immediately. Permanent income is then described by (see below)

$$y_p = y_0 e^{-\beta t} + \beta \int_0^t e^{-\beta(t-v)} (y_0 + y') \, dv$$

$$= y_0 + y' (1 - e^{-\beta t}) .$$

(32)

Permanent income, therefore, tends to $y_0 + y'$ as t increases without limit. Desired stock, to a linear approximation, and actual stock are

$$h_d = h_0 + b_2 y' (1 - e^{-\beta t})$$

$$h = h_0 + \int_0^t h'(v) \, dv .$$

(33)

Differentiating equations (33) and the flow-demand equation,

$$h'' = d h'_d - d h' = d \beta b_2 y' e^{-\beta t} - d h' .$$

Solving for h', we have

$$h' = \frac{d \beta b_2 y'}{(d - \beta)} (e^{-\beta t} - e^{-dt}), \quad d \neq \beta .$$

Therefore, we find that

$$h = h_0 + b_2 y' + \frac{b_2 y'}{(d - \beta)} [\beta e^{-dt} - d e^{-\beta t}] ,$$

(34)

$$h'_g = k (h_0 + b_2 y') + \frac{b_2 y'}{(d - \beta)} [d (\beta - k) e^{-\beta t} - \beta (d - k) e^{-dt}] .$$

Hence, as t increases without limit, actual stock approaches the limiting value of desired stock and gross construction approaches a level k times this limiting desired stock. If h, as given by (34), and its first three derivatives are analyzed, we see that actual stock grows first at an increasing rate, then at a decreasing rate, and that the net rate of construction reaches a maximum at some time t greater than zero. This behavior differs from the case of a once-and-for-all increase in desired stock discussed above; in the latter stock grows at a decreasing rate throughout, and the peak in net new construction occurs at time t equal to zero, which coincides with the change in desired stock. If $d = \beta$, the expressions for h and h'_g are somewhat different from equations (34), but the qualitative behavior of both actual stock and gross construction is the same as that for which $d \neq \beta$.

Finally, let us consider the case where permanent income grows at a constant rate, γ, so that $y_p = y_0 e^{\gamma t}$. To a linear approximation

$$h_d = b + b_2 y_0 e^{\gamma t}, \quad h_d'/h_d \approx \gamma . \tag{35}$$

(Where u and v are functions of time, the expression $u \approx v$ means that the ratio of u to v approaches 1 as t increases without limit.) In the limit desired stock grows at a constant rate equal to the rate of growth of income. Since

$$h = h_0 + \int_0^t h'(v) \, dv , \tag{36}$$

differentiating equations (35) and (36) and the flow-demand equation gives

$$h'' = d h_d' - d h' = d\gamma b_2 y_0 e^{\gamma t} - d h' .$$

The solution to this differential equation, assuming $h_d(0) = h_0$, is

$$h' = \frac{d\gamma b_2 y_0}{(d+\gamma)} (e^{\gamma t} - e^{-dt}) \approx \frac{d\gamma b_2 y_0}{(d+\gamma)} e^{\gamma t}.$$

Solving for h and h_g', we have

$$h = (h_0 - b_2 y_0) + \frac{b_2 y_0}{(d+\gamma)} (d e^{\gamma t} + \gamma e^{-dt}) \approx \frac{d b_2 y_0}{(d+\gamma)} e^{\gamma t}$$

$$h_g' = k (h_0 - b_2 y_0) + \frac{b_2 y_0}{(d+\gamma)} [d (\gamma + k) e^{\gamma t} \tag{37}$$

$$- \gamma (d - k) e^{-dt}] \approx \frac{d (\gamma + k) b_2 y_0}{(d+\gamma)} e^{\gamma t}.$$

Note here that it is assumed that the process begins from a position of long-run equilibrium at time zero, so h_0 is equal to $(b + b_2 y_0)$. Comparing h' with h, we note that actual stock also grows at the rate γ asymptotically, while the ratio of gross construction to actual stock approaches a constant equal to the rate of growth of income plus the rate of depreciation, k. Likewise, comparing (35) with (37), we see that the ratio of desired stock to actual stock approaches $(1 + \gamma/d)$ as t approaches infinity. Therefore, where income grows at some constant rate, the higher the rate of growth of income, the greater the ratio of desired to actual stock for d constant.

DERIVATION OF THE EXPECTATIONS FUNCTION

Let

$$x'(t) = a [y(t) - x(t)] , \, t \geq 0, \, x(0) = x_0 , \tag{38}$$

where $x(t)$ is the value of the expectations variable x at time t, $y(t)$ is the value of the variable upon which expectations are based, and a is a constant.

The solution to this differential equation is

$$x(t) = x_0 e^{-at} + a \int_0^t e^{-a(t-v)} y(v) \, dv \cong a \int_0^t e^{-a(t-v)} y(v) \, dv, \quad (39)$$

for t large enough. If in the interval $t - (j+1)$, $t - j$, for $j = 0, 1, 2, \ldots$, $y(v)$ is a constant equal to $y(t - j)$,

$$
\begin{aligned}
x(t) &= \sum_{j=0}^{\infty} y(t-j) \int_{t-(j+1)}^{t-j} a e^{-a(t-v)} \, dv \\
&= (1 - e^{-a}) \sum_{j=0}^{\infty} e^{-aj} y(t-j).
\end{aligned}
\quad (40)
$$

In the case of Friedman's expected-income series, x above is expected income, y is current income, and the constant a is equal to the weight coefficient. Similarly, in the case of the expected ratio of rent to price, x is this expected ratio, and y is the ratio of current rent to price.

APPENDIX B

FURTHER NOTES ON DATA USED

All data used for the time-series demand comparisons made in the text are displayed in Table B1. The sources and principal characteristics of these data have already been noted. Some further comments which are helpful in interpreting the empirical results of this study are presented in this appendix.

THE BOECKH INDEX OF CONSTRUCTION COSTS

There is no series available which directly measures the market value of a unit of non-farm housing for the whole nation for a period of time that is long enough for the purposes of this study. Therefore, an index of residential construction costs has been used as a measure of price. The Boeckh index, selected for this purpose, is a fixed-weight index of the prices of labor and material inputs. The national index is an average of indexes separately compiled for residential structures in twenty given cities throughout the country, with each city having the same weight. Each city index includes current local prices for brick, lumber, cement, and structural steel, local wages for common labor, masons, carpenters, and plasterers, and such items as heating and plumbing equipment, paint,

TABLE B1

DATA USED FOR TIME-SERIES COMPARISONS

Year	h_g'	h_f	y_p	y_c	p	R' (BLS)	R (NICB)	r	H_n	Y_p	P
1914.....	......	728	.....	.....	......	......	......	.....	......	......	......
1915.....	43.7	731	423	410	80.0	128.1	97.5	4.31	4,747	1,876	4.43
1916.....	44.1	733	435	436	79.5	120.7	92.2	4.05	4,640	1,919	4.41
1917.....	......	......	.....	.....	78.6	......	81.1	.....	......	......	......
1918.....	......	708	.....	.....	80.2	......	77.4	.....	......	......	......
1919.....	33.3	692	478	497	80.9	83.0	73.9	4.97	3,986	2,080	4.35
1920.....	27.4	678	475	446	90.2	84.2	76.3	5.43	3,821	2,057	4.33
1921.....	34.7	671	462	413	81.9	108.5	93.7	5.73	3,822	1,986	4.30
1922.....	54.4	686	461	436	80.3	119.2	98.2	5.06	4,294	1,973	4.28
1923.....	59.6	698	479	491	88.2	120.1	100.5	4.80	4,229	2,037	4.25
1924.....	66.8	716	492	493	87.0	124.1	106.6	4.80	4,819	2,082	4.23
1925.....	71.9	744	501	491	84.1	121.4	101.8	4.50	4,967	2,102	4.20
1926.....	71.7	769	514	514	84.0	119.2	98.2	4.40	5,457	2,148	4.18
1927.....	67.0	786	525	520	84.6	119.6	96.7	4.30	5,343	2,179	4.15
1928.....	62.4	804	529	512	85.8	118.1	93.6	4.05	5,296	2,187	4.13
1929.....	48.7	810	547	554	89.1	115.4	92.0	4.57	5,474	2,243	4.10
1930.....	32.3	800	544	509	89.4	115.2	91.9	4.40	4,459	2,217	4.08
1931.....	27.6	794	531	480	90.2	119.9	92.9	4.03	5,303	2,145	4.04
1932.....	17.7	783	497	406	85.4	119.8	90.9	4.70	4,339	1,986	4.00
1933.....	15.4	774	470	395	90.6	109.0	84.6	4.00	3,725	1,862	3.96
1934.....	17.0	757	463	424	95.8	98.6	83.0	3.70	3,289	1,818	3.93
1935.....	22.6	745	471	464	91.2	96.0	87.9	3.00	3,673	1,837	3.90
1936.....	29.5	737	497	522	93.3	97.3	96.4	2.64	4,303	1,918	3.86
1937.....	30.1	730	518	533	100.3	98.2	103.2	2.38	4,314	1,983	3.83
1938.....	29.0	724	519	496	105.8	103.3	105.8	2.60	3,809	1,972	3.80
1939.....	35.4	724	532	531	109.0	104.9	106.4	2.18	4,576	2,002	3.76
1940.....	37.5	724	552	561	111.2	104.4	106.3	1.95	4,336	2,057	3.73
1941.....	39.4	727	594	647	113.7	101.1	103.1	1.88	4,099	2,181	3.67

DEFINITIONS OF SYMBOLS

In all cases monetary magnitudes are adjusted for changes in the general level of prices, the base period being 1935–39. Where deflation was necessary, I used the BLS index of consumer prices.

h_g' Per capita gross rate of non-farm residential construction in constant dollars. The current dollar value of new dwellings, additions and alterations to existing units, and maintenance and repair expenditures deflated by the Boeckh index and the non-farm population of the continental United States.

h_f End-of-year per capita non-farm housing stock in constant dollars. Grebler, Blank, and Winnick estimates of the non-farm housing stock deflated by the non-farm population of the continental United States.

y_p Friedman's per capita expected real income series.

y_c Per capita current real income.

p Boeckh index of residential construction costs in real terms.

R' BLS rent component index in real terms.

R NICB rent index in real terms.

r Durand's basic yield of ten-year corporate bonds.

H_n Average quality of new dwellings. The average current dollar value of new housekeeping dwelling units deflated by the Boeckh index.

Y_p Expected real income per household, $y_p \times P$.

P Average size of household.

glass, and hardware. The compiler claims that wage rates are adjusted to reflect the efficiency of local labor.[79]

The only alternative to using a construction-cost index to measure housing prices is a rent index. But we have already indicated that a measure of rent—the price of housing services rather than of houses—is not likely to be well suited to our purposes. In the first place, in the short run, rents fluctuate with the excess of desired over actual housing stock even if the price per unit of stock remains fixed. And, second, in the long run, rents might vary with changes in interest rates and taxes even if housing prices remain unchanged.

While the construction-cost index is the only satisfactory measure of the price of housing stocks available to us, it has one serious shortcoming. This is the possibility of secular bias. If over time there have been important changes in the efficiency of utilization of a given collection of inputs or substitution of inputs in response to technological change or changes in relative factor prices, the secular trend in a fixed-weight construction-cost index would overstate the trend in house prices. We have already tested for this possibility by including a time trend in the analysis in Section V. The fact that doing so did not lead to significantly different results strongly suggests that the Boeckh index is not biased by secular changes. Two other comparisons made here lead us to exactly the same conclusion.

The first of these is a comparison of the Boeckh index with Blank's index of house prices, shown in Table B2.[80] Blank's index was derived from data on owner estimates of the value of housing in 1934 and market value in the year of acquisition by the owner in 1934, which are contained in the 1934 *Financial Survey of Urban Housing*. Value in year of acquisition relative to value in 1934 was calculated for one-family owner-occupied units in each city. The median of these twenty-two ratios for each year was then adjusted for depreciation to obtain the price index. The most striking comparison shown in Table B2 is the lack of any trend of the ratio of house prices to construction cost, such as would be expected if the latter were biased for long-run comparisons. Blank concluded that "the long run movement of the two indexes is remarkably similar . . . the almost identical movement of the two series over four and a half decades argues strongly that the construction cost index measures with quite

---

[79] Actually, indexes for several types of residential structures are available. They exhibited virtually identical movements over the period studied here. The index actually used is for brick residential structures.

[80] *Op. cit.*

TABLE B2

HOUSE PRICES AND BUILDING COSTS, 1896–1934

Year	Deflated Blank Index (1929 = 100)* (1)	Deflated Boeckh Index (1929 = 100)† (2)	Ratio (1)/(2) (3)
1896.......	76.2	78.0	0.977
1897.......	81.6	78.2	1.043
1898.......	88.0	81.6	1.078
1899.......	78.1	80.2	0.974
1900.......	87.0	81.2	1.071
1901.......	74.0	80.2	0.923
1902.......	83.1	81.4	1.021
1903.......	87.5	82.7	1.058
1904.......	94.7	83.3	1.137
1905.......	82.5	85.6	0.964
1906.......	92.1	87.3	1.055
1907.......	97.8	86.6	1.129
1908.......	96.0	90.0	1.067
1909.......	93.4	91.8	1.017
1910.......	97.1	90.2	1.076
1911.......	94.5	87.5	1.080
1912.......	93.3	84.1	1.109
1913.......	94.5	81.1	1.165
1914.......	99.5	81.6	1.219
1915.......	91.0	82.3	1.106
1916.......	91.3	79.1	1.154
1917.......	78.2	76.5	1.022
1918.......	74.8	80.8	0.926
1919.......	74.3	83.7	0.888
1920.......	72.6	95.0	0.764
1921.......	85.7	90.8	0.944
1922.......	93.4	88.6	1.054
1923.......	93.3	96.4	0.968
1924.......	95.7	95.9	0.998
1925.......	101.1	94.3	1.072
1926.......	97.5	94.1	1.036
1927.......	97.9	95.6	1.024
1928.......	99.7	94.9	1.051
1929.......	100.0	100.0	1.000
1930.......	101.0	101.5	0.995
1931.......	103.9	103.3	1.006
1932.......	105.1	97.6	1.077
1933.......	106.7	101.6	1.050
1934.......	99.1	104.9	0.945

* David M. Blank, *The Volume of Residential Construction, 1889–1950* (New York: National Bureau of Economic Research, 1954), Table 3, p. 75, deflated by GNP deflator from Raymond W. Goldsmith, *A Study of Saving in the United States* (Princeton, N.J.: Princeton University Press, 1955), I, 377, Table T-16.

† Blank, *op. cit.*, Table 4, p. 76, deflated by Goldsmith's GNP deflator.

reasonable accuracy the secular movement in house prices."[81] There are, however, at least two possible shortcomings in this comparison. First, the ratios of value in year of acquisition to value in 1934 are based only upon those dwelling units acquired in a given year which survived until 1934. And, second, the ratio of Blank's index to the Boeckh index depends upon the rate of depreciation assumed in obtaining the former. Thus, while the comparison might be faulty, it provides no evidence that the Boeckh index is secularly biased.

Another piece of evidence on the long-run behavior of construction-cost indexes is provided by Colean and Newcomb.[82] They compare an average of cost indexes of four large construction firms with the *Engineering News-Record* building-cost index for the period 1913–51 (neither of these refer specifically to residential construction). The latter is a fixed-weight index of factor prices like the Boeckh index, while the former is based upon actual cost estimates of the four firms for building comparable structures in different years. Thus, in principle, the contractor index would allow for reductions in cost due either to technological change or to changes in relative factor prices. The two indexes are compared in Table B3. If the fixed-weight construction-cost index were biased for long-run comparisons, we would expect that the ratio of the contractor index to the Boeckh index would decline over time. However, column (3) of Table B3 indicates that there is no long-run divergence between the two indexes. While this comparison is based upon the estimates of a few firms only and does not refer specifically to residential construction, it does not suggest that construction-cost indexes are biased for long-run comparisons of price.

In Section III we referred to the comparison of the Department of Commerce GNP deflator for residential construction with the Boeckh index of construction costs. The former is derived by multiplying the latter by a price-cost ratio to correct for the fact that the Boeckh index covers only materials and labor costs. The numerator of this ratio is the total market value of all construction, while the denominator is the numerator minus corporate profits before taxes, net interest paid, depreciation, and the incomes of unincorporated construction firms. Such an adjustment, in principle, would reflect changes in interest and depreciation charges as well as profits in the accounting sense. The data for this adjustment are not available for years prior to 1929, nor are separate data available for residential and non-residential construction.

Table B4 suggests that this adjustment has little effect on the Boeckh

[81] *Ibid.*, p. 78.

[82] *Op. cit.*, pp. 69 ff. and Appendix Q, pp. 247–48.

index. The ratio of the adjusted to the unadjusted Boeckh index falls about 7 per cent from 1929 to 1933 (while new construction fell by over one-half) and rises about 5 per cent from 1933 to 1941. However, in the post–World War II period the ratio falls steadily and does not appear to be related to the level of new construction.

TABLE B3*

COMPARISON OF CONTRACTOR AND BUILDING-COST
INDEXES, 1913–51

Year	Deflated Contractor Index (1935–39 = 100) (1)	Deflated *Engineering News-Record* Building Cost Index (1935–39 = 100) (2)	Ratio (1)/(2) (3)
1913	79.3	76.2	1.040
1914	79.6	69.0	1.153
1915	87.4	70.6	1.237
1916	92.1	90.6	1.017
1917	92.4	98.2	0.941
1918	91.8	79.7	1.152
1919	83.3	69.2	1.204
1920	90.8	77.8	1.166
1921	82.1	70.0	1.172
1922	81.5	69.8	1.168
1923	90.1	82.2	1.096
1924	90.8	82.0	1.108
1925	89.0	78.6	1.131
1926	88.7	78.9	1.125
1927	88.1	80.8	1.091
1928	88.2	82.6	1.068
1929	87.8	84.0	1.046
1930	85.4	83.5	1.023
1931	84.1	83.8	1.003
1932	84.4	77.8	1.085
1933	89.8	86.3	1.040
1934	95.5	94.0	1.015
1935	93.1	91.2	1.021
1936	95.6	93.5	1.022
1937	103.2	102.8	1.003
1938	104.0	105.3	0.988
1939	103.8	106.8	0.972
1940	106.8	109.2	0.979
1941	111.9	108.1	1.035
1946	117.3	101.2	1.160
1947	121.5	105.7	1.150
1948	122.3	108.1	1.131
1949	122.2	111.4	1.096
1950	123.6	117.5	1.051
1951	124.7	116.4	1.071

* Source: Data from Miles L. Colean and Robinson Newcomb, *Stabilizing Construction* (New York: McGraw-Hill Book Co., 1952), Appendix Q, pp. 247–48, converted to 1935–39 = 100 and deflated by the Consumer Price Index, 1935–39 = 100.

The implication of this comparison for the profits of construction firms is not entirely clear. Fluctuations in the ratio of the adjusted to the unadjusted Boeckh index could arise from changes in interest and depreciation charges as well as from changes in profits, but the former two items tend to be fixed over short periods of time. The data on which the adjustment is based refer to all construction firms, not residential alone. Likewise, the fall in profits from 1929 to 1933 and the subsequent increase were experienced by most industries, not just the construction industry. But on the basis of this comparison it seems unlikely that fluctuations in profits accompanying those in new construction resulted in significant fluctuations in house prices.

TABLE B4

COMPARISON OF COMMERCE CONSTRUCTION COMPO-
NENT GNP DEFLATOR AND BOECKH INDEX, 1929–53

Year	Deflated GNP Deflator (1935–39 = 100)* (1)	Deflated Boeckh Index (1935–39 = 100)† (2)	Ratio (1)/(2) (3)
1929......	93.0	89.1	1.044
1930......	93.0	89.4	1.041
1931......	93.0	90.2	1.031
1932......	83.6	85.4	0.978
1933......	87.9	90.6	0.970
1934......	94.4	95.8	0.985
1935......	90.7	91.2	0.994
1936......	94.3	93.3	1.010
1937......	100.3	100.3	1.000
1938......	105.7	105.8	1.000
1939......	108.7	109.0	0.998
1940......	111.3	111.2	1.001
1941......	115.9	113.7	1.019
1946......	129.4	120.4	1.075
1947......	135.7	126.8	1.070
1948......	141.0	132.3	1.065
1949......	138.9	131.4	1.057
1950......	143.3	137.1	1.046
1951......	141.8	136.8	1.036
1952......	142.1	137.6	1.033
1953......	143.5	139.3	1.030

* From U.S. Department of Commerce, Office of Business Economics, *National Income, 1954 Edition* (Washington, D.C.: Government Printing Office, 1954), Table 41, pp. 216–17, converted to 1935–39 = 100 and deflated by the Consumer Price Index, 1935–39 = 100.

† Boeckh index, residential (brick), deflated by the Consumer Price Index, both 1935–39 = 100.

NEW CONSTRUCTION ESTIMATES

The annual rate of new construction is measured here by the current dollar value of gross construction deflated by the Boeckh index of residential construction costs. The current dollar estimates of gross construction used are those published by the Department of Commerce.[83] Included in the gross construction estimates are the value of new dwelling units, additions and alterations in existing units, and maintenance and repair expenditures.[84] Only private residential construction is included.

The construction estimates published by the Department of Commerce are based principally upon building-permit data. But permit valuation is less than the total value in permit-requiring areas for two reasons. Permit valuation omits certain costs which should be included in the total value of construction, and some construction is performed for which no permits are obtained. Hence, in preparing estimates of the value of construction, adjustments are made to correct for these sources of undervaluation. In addition, separate estimates of construction activity in areas not requiring building permits must be made. It is possible that these adjustments of permit valuation fail to correct for the difference between it and the total value of construction, so that the latter is underestimated.

The Department of Commerce estimates of the current dollar value of gross construction in the decade 1920–29 might also be in error because of the way in which estimates of the value of new dwelling units were prepared for areas for which building-permit information was not reported. The estimates for the twenties are based upon estimates made by Wickens.[85] He first computed the ratio of new dwelling units to the increase in

[83] These estimates, prepared jointly by the Office of Business Economics and the Bureau of Labor Statistics, are published in *Construction and Building Materials, Statistical Supplement, May, 1954.* Information about the estimates of construction is also contained in Department of Labor, Bureau of Labor Statistics, *Estimating National Housing Volume* ("Techniques of Preparing Major BLS Statistical Series" [BLS Bull. 1168] [Washington, D.C.: Government Printing Office, 1945]) and in Blank, *op. cit.*

[84] The estimates of gross construction used here include the value of non-housekeeping dwelling units. The latter are not included in the stock estimates of Grebler, Blank, and Winnick and, it might be argued, should be excluded from the estimates of gross construction as well. But the value of non-housekeeping dwelling units represented a significant part of the total value of construction only in the twenties and even then was less than 10 per cent of the total. Excluding non-housekeeping dwelling units from gross construction also leads to no essential difference in the estimates of equation (10).

[85] David L. Wickens, *Residential Real Estate* (New York: National Bureau of Economic Research, 1941), pp. 41–76. This volume contains a detailed description of procedures Wickens used.

the number of families in permit-reporting cities for the decade 1920–29. Dwelling units built during the decade were then estimated for non-reporting areas by applying a ratio based upon reporting cities of a similar character in the same region to the increase in the number of families. The number of dwelling units estimated for non-reporting areas were approximately half the national total for this decade. Annual estimates were prepared by assuming that the proportion of the decade total built in any single year was the same for non-reporting as for reporting cities. Wickens estimated the value of new construction by multiplying the estimates of the number of dwelling units so obtained by estimates of costs per dwelling unit. The latter were based upon permit data for reporting cities, and the sample of reporting cities contained a larger proportion of cities in the northeastern part of the country than the population of all cities in the country. While Wickens adjusted the estimated average cost ratios of non-reporting cities for differences in the proportions of one-family, two-family, and multifamily structures in cities of different size classes, he made no allowance for regional differences in cost even though "costs in northeastern states [averaged] nearly double those in the South."[86]

Thus it seems likely that Wickens' procedure led to an overestimate of the value of new dwelling units for the decade 1920–29 relative to that for later years, for which building-permit information is available for a larger number of cities. In any case, it seems likely that any errors in his procedure, in estimating either the number of dwelling units built or the value per dwelling unit built, would affect the data for every year in the decade 1920–29, so that errors in the measure of gross construction used here are serially correlated. The possibility of errors in the Department of Commerce estimates of gross construction discussed in this section would be reflected in the cumulated stock estimates of Grebler, Blank, and Winnick, since the measure of gross construction they used is based upon these same Department of Commerce estimates for 1921 and later years.

THE PROPERTY-TAX RATE

Our analysis in Section II indicated that a measure of property taxes should be included in the empirical analysis of housing demand. But data on property taxes are scanty, and, to the writer's knowledge, no satisfactory time series covering the period 1915–41 is available. The most complete series is that computed by Campbell for the period since 1921 from reports of the Bureau of Governmental Research.[87] These estimates,

---

[86] *Ibid.*, p. 51.   [87] Campbell, *op. cit.*

which are partially reproduced in Table B5, are official rates per assessed valuation multiplied by estimates of the ratio of assessed to true valuation, averaged for reporting large cities. Campbell notes that these estimates probably overstate true tax rates in the late thirties because the

TABLE B5

PROPERTY-TAX RATES, SELECTED YEARS, 1923–39

YEAR	RATE PER $1,000 OF TRUE VALUE IN LARGE CITIES*	CITIES HAVING 100,000 OR MORE POPULATION†		
		No. of Cities	Ratio of Property Taxes to:	
			Assessed Value ($ per 1,000)	Expenditures
1923........	23.59	76	25.38	0.682
1927........	22.82	88	25.56	.651
1931........	24.34	94	26.33	.692
1935........	25.57	94	31.21	.765
1939........	27.61	94	31.60	0.647

*Colin D. Campbell, "Are Property-Tax Rates Increasing?" *Journal of Political Economy*, LIX (October, 1951), 434–42, Table 2.

† Computed from data for city areas (city corporations and overlying local governments) in U.S. Department of Commerce, Bureau of the Census, *Historical Review of State and Local Government Finances* (Washington, D.C.: Government Printing Office, 1948), Tables 14 and 15.

TABLE B6

INDEXES OF PROPERTY-TAX RATES
SELECTED YEARS, 1929–39
(1931=100)

Year	Estimated by State and Local Property Taxes*	Estimated by Property Taxes in 94 City Areas†
1929........	90.2	....
1932........	116.5	109.4
1936........	99.6	102.4
1939........	88.5	90.0

* Index of state and local property taxes computed from data in *National Income, 1954 Edition*, Table 8, divided by index of value of non-farm residential structures, both in current dollars.

† Index of property taxes in 94 large cities, 100,000 or more population, computed from data in U.S. Department of Commerce, Bureau of the Census, *Historical Review of State and Local Government Finances*, Table 14, divided by index of value of non-farm residential structures, both in current dollars.

ratios of assessed to true value were probably overestimated. His conjecture is borne out by data on the ratio of property taxes to assessed value in column (4) of Table B5, whose movement in the thirties is similar to Campbell's data in column (2).

Two alternative estimates of property-tax rates are shown in Table B6. Both are indexes of property taxes divided by an index of the current dollar value of non-farm residential housing computed from the estimates of Grebler, Blank, and Winnick. While these estimates are admittedly very crude, they verify Campbell's suggestion that the data of the Bureau of Governmental Research overestimate tax rates in the late thirties relative to earlier years. Together, the data in Tables B5 and B6 suggest that property-tax rates remained roughly unchanged from 1920 to 1940 but that they were about 10 per cent below the period average in the middle twenties and about 20 per cent above it in the early thirties. Therefore, the omission of property taxes from the empirical analysis of housing demand is not likely to lead to any secular bias; however, because this variable is serially correlated, its omission is likely to lead to a serial correlation of the residuals in the demand regression equations presented in the text.

APPENDIX C

COMMENTS ON STATISTICAL METHODS USED

THE PROBLEM OF JOINT DETERMINATION

In recent years the method of least squares in estimating economic parameters from time-series data has been subject to rather severe criticism. In particular, the possibility of bias in the parameter estimates obtained by this method due to the simultaneous determination of several variables in the regression equation has received much attention. Now the demand regressions in the text classified three variables as "independent" which might in fact be jointly determined with new construction: price, income, and the interest rate. However, the evidence presented in Section III suggests that the construction-cost index used to measure price is not likely to be affected by changes in new construction. This is because it would appear that labor and material prices are fixed to the residential construction industry and that, in the long run, resources are freely mobile into the industry. Likewise, the interest-rate variable included is to be interpreted as the long-run equilibrium pure rate of interest on mortgages, and it is not obvious that this variable will change with short-run fluctuations in new construction. To the extent, however, that fluctuations in new construction lead to fluctuations in current income, which enters into Friedman's permanent income series, the estimates might contain an unknown bias due to joint determination.[88]

SERIAL CORRELATION

This comment discusses some of the implications for the "usual" least-squares estimators in the case where the true residuals are serially correlated. Let

$$Y = Xb + \eta , \qquad (41)$$

where Y and η are column vectors of T components, and η is uncorrelated with X; b is the column vector of the n unknown slope parameters; X, the T-by-n matrix of the independent variables, assumed to be fixed in repeated samples; the y's and x's have zero means; and the variance of η_t is σ^2. The "usual" least-squares estimator of b is

$$\hat{b} = (X'X)^{-1}(X'Y) , \qquad (42)$$

provided that X is of rank n; thus

$$(\hat{b} - b) = (X'X)^{-1}(X'\eta) . \qquad (43)$$

The bias in $\hat{b}$ is

$$E(\hat{b} - b) = (X'X)^{-1}(X'E\eta) , \qquad (44)$$

which is equal to zero, since $E\eta$ is zero. Hence serial correlation of the true residuals does not necessarily bias the estimator (42). The variance of $\hat{b}$ is given by

$$
\begin{aligned}
V(\hat{b}) &= E(\hat{b} - b)(\hat{b} - b)' \\
&= E[(X'X)^{-1}(X'\eta)][(X'X)^{-1}(X'\eta)]' \qquad (45) \\
&= (X'X)^{-1}X'E(\eta\eta')X(X'X)^{-1} .
\end{aligned}
$$

If the η's are serially uncorrelated, $E(\eta\eta')$ is equal to $\sigma^2 I$, and

$$V(\hat{b}) = \sigma^2(X'X)^{-1} . \qquad (46)$$

All the standard errors shown in this study were computed using equation (46). But if $E(\eta\eta') \neq \sigma^2 I$, then $V(\hat{b})$ is not correctly given by (46), so

---

[88] Recent discussion of methods of estimating economic parameters suggests that the question of whether the method of least squares or the limited-information method, which takes into account joint determination, yields "better" estimates is still unresolved (see Karl A. Fox, "Econometric Models of the U.S. Economy," *Journal of Political Economy*, LXIV [April, 1956], 128–42, and Carl F. Christ, "Aggregate Econometric Models," *American Economic Review*, XLVI [June, 1956], 385–408).

that the standard errors of the b's shown in the text and the t and F tests based upon them are not correct. Nor are the "usual" least-squares estimates efficient.

MAXIMUM LIKELIHOOD ESTIMATES FOR EXPECTATIONS VARIABLES

Consider the equation

$$y = b_0 + b_1 x_1 (a) + b_2 x_2 + u , \tag{47}$$

where the expectations variable x_1 depends upon the unknown parameter a, the weight coefficient in Friedman's permanent income series, for example. To find the maximum likelihood estimate of a and the b's in (47), where the u's are independently and identically normally distributed with zero mean and variance σ^2, consider the logarithm of the likelihood function

$$L (b, a, \sigma^2) = \log F (u) = - (n/2) \log 2\pi - (n/2)$$
$$\log \sigma^2 - (1/2\sigma^2) \Sigma (y - b_0 - b_1 x_1 [a] - b_2 x_2)^2 . \tag{48}$$

Here the symbol u refers to the vector of the u_t, while b is the vector (b_0, b_1, b_2).

The maximization can be performed "stepwise," that is, for each value of a find

$$L (a) = \max_{b, \sigma^2} L (b, a, \sigma^2) = - (n/2) (\log 2\pi + 1)$$
$$- (n/2) \log \hat{\sigma}^2 (a) , \tag{49}$$

where $\hat{\sigma}^2(a)$ is the maximum likelihood estimate for the given value of a. Now

$$\max_{a, b, \sigma^2} L (b, a, \sigma^2) = \max_a L (a) = - (n/2) (\log 2\pi + 1)$$
$$- (n/2) \log \min_a \hat{\sigma}^2 (a) . \tag{50}$$

But

$$R^2 (a) = 1 - \frac{\hat{\sigma}^2 (a)}{\sigma_y^2} ,$$

or

$$R^2 (\hat{a}) = 1 - \frac{\min_a \hat{\sigma}^2 (a)}{\sigma_y^2} = \max_a R^2(a) . \tag{51}$$

Thus the maximum likelihood estimate of a is that value of a which, together with $\hat{b}(\hat{a})$ and $\hat{\sigma}^2(\hat{a})$, maximizes the multiple correlation coefficient.

To test the null hypothesis that $a = a_0$, form the logarithm of the likelihood function

$$\log \lambda = \log \max_{b,\,\sigma^2} L\,(b,\,a_0,\,\sigma^2) \; - \log \max_{a,\,b,\,\sigma^2} L\,(b,\,a,\,\sigma^2)$$

$$= (n/2)\log \frac{\hat{\sigma}^2\,(\hat{a})}{\hat{\sigma}^2\,(a_0)}\,. \tag{52}$$

As is well known, in large samples the quantity $-2\log \lambda$ is distributed as chi square with 1 degree of freedom.[89] Hence, to test the null hypothesis $a = a_0$ at the p per cent level, reject if

$$-\,n\,\log \frac{\hat{\sigma}^2\,(\hat{a})}{\hat{\sigma}^2\,(a_0)} \geq \chi_p^2\,(1)\,. \tag{53}$$

A similar test is applicable to test the hypothesis that is, say, $b_1 = b_{1,0}$.

[89] See S. S. Wilks, *Mathematical Statistics* (Princeton, N.J.: Princeton University Press, 1950), pp. 151–52. Wilks states the regularity conditions under which this holds true.

III

The Demand for Household Refrigeration in the United States

M. L. BURSTEIN

The Demand for Household Refrigeration in the United States

I. Introduction and Summary

Wнат are the price and income elasticities of demand for household refrigeration in the United States? The conclusions of this study are that the price elasticity is between −1.0 and −2.0 and, somewhat less conclusively, that the income elasticity is between 1.0 and 2.0. The principal problems faced in the study—problems giving it a somewhat different character from that of most demand studies—are:

1. Refrigerators and freezers are durable goods. An estimate of the rate of consumption of refrigeration services is necessary for each year considered. This, it must be noted, is definitely not the same problem as estimating the rate of output of new machines.
2. Marked changes in quality have occurred over the period of the study, 1931–55.
3. Pronounced trends appear in the price and quantity series as well as in the income series, giving rise to the problem of multicollinearity to a greater degree than is typically encountered in demand analyses.

In order to cope with the quality problem, the concept of a unit of refrigeration service is introduced. Such a unit might conceivably be measured in terms of a physical characteristic, such as cubic content, but it was considered preferable to allow also for other changes in the typical refrigerator. This is accomplished by the device of measuring the "amount of refrigeration" contained in different models at any one time by their relative prices. A price index for refrigeration service links consecutive years by measuring the change in the cost of "this year's" model mix between "last year" and "this year." The index of manufacturers' sales of refrigerators is obtained by deflating annual sales in current dollars by the price index for refrigeration service. The index of the stock of household refrigeration is obtained by cumulating annual (deflated) sales, with allowance for the depreciation of the stock carried into any year.[1]

The transition from the stock of refrigeration to its service yield is closely tied to the assumptions made about depreciation in order to compute the stock variable itself. In one formulation the service yield is

---

[1] Practically all computations include freezers.

assumed to be proportional to the (constant dollar) value of the stock; any one machine is assumed to yield less service in each succeeding year of its life. This formulation assumes that the depreciation of the machines (and accordingly the reduction in their service yield) is at a constant rate per annum against a declining balance. Three alternative rates were used: 10 per cent, 20 per cent, and 25 per cent.

In another formulation it was assumed that refrigerators yielded the same service each year for a finite length of time and then ceased to yield any service at all, an assumption corresponding to straight-line depreciation. However, the two formulations do not differ merely in terms of the way in which they measure depreciation. Rather, in the one case (declining-balance method), the service yield can be assumed proportional to the value of the stock, while in the other (straight-line method) it cannot. The straight-line depreciation formulation in turn employed alternative assumptions as to the life of the machines: ten-year life and fifteen-year life.

Not only in the case of depreciation methods was it found desirable to make alternative assumptions rather than to rely on a single, perhaps arbitrary choice. Alternative price series are used. Two income variables, the Department of Commerce's disposable-income series and the "expected-income" series based on Milton Friedman's "permanent income" concept, are used. Other instances of alternative assumptions will be mentioned later.

If we formed the naïve autoregressive equation

$$S_t^* = a + \beta S_{t-1}^* + u_t ,\tag{1}$$

where S_t^* is the per capita rate of consumption of refrigeration services at time t (under declining-balance depreciation assumption) and u_t is a disturbance term, the resulting regression line would fit the observations with an R^2 (squared correlation coefficient) in excess of .98. In other words, the consumption-of-services variable can be explained by trend alone without resort to economic theory. The reason for this is readily seen if two arrays of zero-order squared correlation coefficients are put down, Array A not including 1942–44 in contrast to Array B which does.[2]

The price and income variables are themselves strongly correlated

---

[2] The notation is as follows: S^* = per capita consumption of services under the declining-balance depreciation assumption, P^* = relative price of refrigeration services, Y_d and Y_e = per capita disposable and expected income, respectively, and T = trend variable. All variables were cast into logs for regression purposes.

with the trend variable.[3] It follows that, if the price and income variables explain the data, the trend variable alone will almost inevitably give a good fit. In fact, both arrays reveal strong correlation among "independent" variables, suggesting that it might be difficult to separate out the "true" influence of either price or income. The crucial problem of *multicollinearity* emerges. As it happens, the multicollinearity problem becomes serious only with respect to the influence of the trend variable, but it enters into almost all the subsequent discussion of time-series

ARRAY A

	S^*	P^*	Y_e	T	
S^*1		0.98	0.89	0.99	(Signs show direc-
		–	+	+	tion of simple
P^*		1	0.82	0.97	correlation)
			–	–	
Y_e			1	0.91	
				+	
T				1	

ARRAY B (INCLUDING 1942–44)

	S^*	P^*	Y_e	T
S^*1		0.92	0.87	0.97
		–	+	+
P^*		1	0.68	0.82
			–	–
Y_e			1	0.92
				+
T				1

studies. The influence of trend is treated in a variety of ways, ranging from regressions excluding it altogether to others imposing trends and analyzing the residual variation of the consumption-of-services variable. It is concluded that, despite the multicollinearity problem, the influence of the price and income variables can be separated out and narrowly defined and that these conventional variables serve to explain the data within the framework of traditional economic theory.

The study does not confine itself to time-series data. There are cross-sectional estimates based on data organized both by states and by families. Unfortunately, the limitations of these data require that the cross-

[3] The trend variable was constructed as follows: subtract 12 from the last two digits of the year in question and take the log of the difference. Thus, $T_{1954} = \log 42$. The first differences of the logs are, of course, progressively smaller, since log (43/42), for example, is less than log (20/19).

sectional estimates be confined to the income parameter. These regressions also posed problems of such difficulty that numerous alternative assumptions were relied on rather than single arbitrary choices.

II. CONSTRUCTION OF THE TIME SERIES

The price series should meet at least two standards: (1) reflection of actual prices paid as against "suggested" prices and (2) measurement of the cost of refrigeration service as against the cost of a refrigerator. Consequently, a key decision was the choice of Sears, Roebuck mail-order catalogue quotations as being representative of actual prices paid. Sears has been a substantial force in the refrigeration market from the outset of the period of the study and has maintained a stable market position. The fact that Sears mail-order sales are not negotiated and do not involve trade-ins means that these are real as against "suggested" prices. The *Consumers Research Bulletin* for October, 1956, confirms this choice in the course of a rather colorful comment:

> It will be noted that [non-mail-order refrigerators] have list prices of $500 or more while a mail order house sells the equivalent for about $300 including freight. . . . Big mail order houses do not accept trade-ins and consequently prices are actual, not packed. Allowances of $100 and $200 . . . are not uncommon and $200 television sets are being offered [with purchase of a non-mail-order refrigerator].

The computation of the price index involves the following steps:

1. The percentage, h_i, of total production devoted to the ith size category in year t can be obtained from national model-mix data.

2. Once the Sears price, p_i, for each size category has been ascertained, a chain-lined (Paasche) index can be computed. If 1931 is taken as 100, that for 1932 is

$$P_{32} = \frac{\Sigma p_i(32) \, h_i(32)}{\Sigma p_i(31) \, h_i(32)} \times 100. \tag{2}$$

Correspondingly,

$$P_{33} = \frac{p_i(33) \, h_i(33)}{p_i(32) \, h_i(33)} \times P_{32}. \tag{3}$$

A judgment point typically arises in selecting a representative model for the ith size category for year t. In general, the representative model in year t is superior in quality to that for year $t - 1$. Consequently, in computing the Paasche index, in asking the question, "What would this year's model mix have cost last year?" the price of a standard model in t must frequently be compared with that of a luxury model (although both models are in the same *size* category) in $t - 1$.

Three problems arose in constructing the price series which were considered important enough to warrant alternative possibilities being tested separately. Accordingly, two alternative price series, each embodying one of the two possible decisions at the following three crossroads, were constructed.[4]

1. *The index number for 1932.*—Straightforward application of the computational instructions (Series II) would result in but a 3.9 per cent fall in the price index, whereas suggested list prices of other companies fell about 24 per cent in that period. In view of business conditions of that time, the disparity is disturbing but is possibly explained by Sears having introduced its 1931 line at low prices in order to break into the market picture.[5] Alternatively, it is possible that suggested list prices of other companies for 1932 were reduced as a selling gambit, although actual prices changed much less because of large discounts having been offered from 1931 suggested prices.

2. *Linkage of 1948 to 1941.*—Sears mail-order sales of refrigerators were resumed only in 1948, having been suspended in 1942. Accordingly, it was necessary to link 1948 to 1941. The model mix changed greatly between 1941 and 1948, and it is difficult to find refrigerators of comparable specifications. Depending upon the choice of models to be compared within the two size categories that could be compared, the undeflated price of refrigeration increases 50 per cent (P_I) or 60 per cent (P_{II}) from 1941 to 1948.

3. *Major model changes in 1953.*—Again depending upon the choice of models to be compared within each size category, either a 2 per cent (P_I) or an 8 per cent (P_{II}) fall in the undeflated price of refrigeration is measured between 1952 and 1953.

The real price series[6] were obtained by deflating the price indexes by the Implicit Gross National Product Deflator, a deflator considered least biased by such problems as unenforced price-ceiling regulations.[7]

The formula for manufacturers' sales in year t is

$$q_t r_t / P_t = x_t = \text{Index for Manufacturers' Sales},\qquad(4)$$

where q_t is the total number of machines sold by all manufacturers in year t, and r_t is the average Sears's realization. The sales series, then, is a

[4] All computation problems involving the 1942–44 period are treated at the end of this chapter. These are best understood after the general picture is before the reader.

[5] Sears first introduced electric refrigerators in 1931.

[6] Appendix, Table A7.

[7] It might be argued that a price index such as the Bureau of Labor Statistics' Consumer Price Index is more appropriate. The squared correlation coefficient of the CPI and GNP deflator series for the years 1931–44, 1948–55 is .9929.

deflated value index, reflecting the rate of production of "stored" refrigeration service rather than merely enumerating machines. As we have seen, the latter procedure leads to gross inaccuracy where quality has changed as drastically as has been the case with refrigeration.

How good an approximation is r_t to industry realizations or at least how well do changes in r_t reflect changes in the "true" average realization? If we are satisfied that Sears prices well represent industry prices, the answer depends upon whether or not the Sears model mix is typical. Assurances by Sears executives to this effect—note well that r_t is based on all Sears sales, not just mail-order sales—is bolstered by the following statement: "The most striking characteristic of the comparison of sizes purchased by buyers of nationally advertised brands and mail-order brands of mechanical refrigerators is the similarity of the two tabulations."[8]

This calculating procedure might bias the estimated-price elasticity toward -1.0, insofar as the sales index is built into the consumption-of-services index. Thus, if P_t is measured with an error of 1 per cent, x_t will be in error, on this account, by 1 per cent in the opposite direction since x_t varies inversely with P_t.[9]

Underlying the alternative consumption-of-services indexes discussed earlier are two concepts of service yield and/or depreciation: (1) a refrigerator yields less service per year as it grows older (declining-balance assumption); (2) it yields the same service per year as it grows older (straight-line depreciation). Under either alternative there emerges the question, "What is the appropriate rate?" In neither case is there a categorical answer.[10]

On the declining-balance assumption, service yield is proportional to the constant-dollar value of the stock of refrigerators which in turn is a cumulant of past sales (in terms of depreciated units of refrigeration).

[8] *Refrigeration Survey* (Philadelphia: Curtis Publishing Co., 1941), p. 16.

[9] Refrigerator sales are taken net of exports. Freezer sales include exports, but these are seen to be miniscule (Appendix, Table A11).

[10] The direct measurement of the depreciation rate is impossible here because of the paucity of data on transactions in used machines together with absence of data on rental transactions. Of course, various interest rates will result in divergent comparative valuations where alternative depreciation assumptions are made, *ceteris paribus*.

Once the constant dollar value of the initial stock has been estimated,[11] the series is generated by the equation

$$S_t = (1 - k) S_{t-1} + x_t ,\qquad(5)$$

where S_t = stock at time t, x_t = quantity of newly produced refrigeration sold at t, and k = rate of depreciation.

On the straight-line assumption service yield is proportional to the cumulated sales of refrigeration units over the last L years, where L is the length of life assumed for refrigerators.

There seems to be strong evidence that the range 0.10–0.25 encompasses the upper and lower limits for the depreciation rates. Chow has shown that a rate of depreciation on declining balances of 0.25 gives an excellent fit for automobiles in the United States.[12] Casual observation indicates that refrigerators are a more durable good than automobiles. Hence 0.25 seems a safe upper limit. On the other hand, a rate of 0.10 implies that, even allowing for scrappage, 20 per cent of the "embodied service units" of sales of year t remains at the end of year $t + 15$, although the engineering life of a refrigerator is variously estimated as being from twelve to fifteen years. Thus 0.10 is a safe lower limit. Inspection of Chart I shows that the plots of the logs of stock series computed on the assumption of 0.10, 0.20, and 0.25 rates are very similar. The writer must confess to a strong heuristic preference for the 0.10 rate. Examination of the calculated stock series (cf. Appendix) indicates that a rate of 0.20 or 0.25 results in a 1945 stock—the nadir of the post-1939 period—which is so much lower than the 1941 stock as to defy common sense. Correspondingly, the fifteen-year "straight-line" assumption seems preferable to the ten-year assumption.

An important conclusion of the study is that the main orders of magnitude of the parameter estimates are not affected by the choice of alternative depreciation rates or by alternative service yield assumptions.

Both the Department of Commerce's disposable personal income per capita and Milton Friedman's expected-income variable are employed in

[11] The problems underlying calculation of the stock of refrigeration for 1931 are discussed in the Appendix.

[12] Gregory Chow, *The Demand for Automobiles in the United States* (Amsterdam: North-Holland Press, 1957).

the study.[13] The latter is obtained by applying exponentially declining weights to current real disposable income and that for eight preceding years.[14] In general, the alternative income series do not much affect the parameter estimates. However, it is true that the expected-income parameter is more stable as between "original" and first-difference equations than is the disposable-income parameter. This is precisely the result that would be expected under the permanent-income hypothesis, since the transitory component of income will be much larger relative to first dif-

CHART I

GROSS STOCK WITH ALTERNATIVE DEPRECIATION RATES

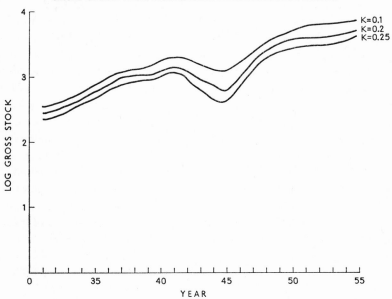

ferences of disposable income than to disposable income itself for any given period.[15] Consequently, the implicit error in the disposable-income measure becomes especially important in the first-difference form.

The war years are of considerable interest for this study, since the stock and price variables here depart from their upward and downward

[13] Milton Friedman, *A Theory of the Consumption Function* (Princeton, N.J.: Princeton University Press, 1957).

[14] The Appendix gives the details of construction of the income variables.

[15] For discussion of the transitory component, etc., see Friedman, *op. cit.*, pp. 25 ff. Expected income is an empirical approximation to Friedman's permanent-income concept.

trends, a fact that is of importance in connection with the multicollinearity problem. On the other hand, since the production of household refrigerators practically ceased in 1942 and since list prices in 1946–47 were not market-clearing prices, it becomes evident that the source for price data for 1942–47 must be quotations on used machines. It was found that the only reasonably reliable source for such data was newspaper quotations, and more than a hundred and fifty man-hours were spent searching the want ads of the *Chicago Tribune*, the *Chicago Sun*, the *Evanston Review*, and the *New York Times* over the 1942–47 period. The net result was that it became possible to construct index numbers for 1942, 1943, and 1944, the procedure being as follows:[16]

1. Collect want-ad offers—there were practically no demand prices, only supply prices—specifying the models and ages of the refrigerators being offered. Since the previous approaches have been based on the comparison of machines in equivalent units, it is evident that knowledge of at least the size and age of used machines is necessary if the data are to be usable.

2. Construct the price index number for 1942, according to the following formula,

$$P_{42} = \frac{\Sigma r_i (42)}{\Sigma r_i (41) [1 - k]}, \tag{6}$$

where r_i (1942) stands for a deflated individual price quotation for 1942, r_i (1941) is the 1941 Sears price for a comparable model, also deflated by the general price level, and where k is, as before, the assumed depreciation rate. The index for 1943 is, correspondingly,[17]

$$P_{43} = \frac{r_i (43)}{r_i (41) (1 - k)^2}. \tag{7}$$

Since the stock variable is estimated as of December 31 of Year t, observations would ideally be confined to prices of that date. However, despite the fact that hundreds of observations were made on the war years, relatively few were amenable to our procedure: 14 second-half observations for 1942; 21 second-half observations for 1943; and 17 observations for the entire calendar year 1944.

The choice of depreciation rate enters directly into computation of

[16] The 1942–44 index numbers appear in the Appendix.

[17] Since the actual transactions probably took place at lower prices than those quoted by the offerers (sellers), this procedure tends to bias the price-index numbers for 1942–44 upward. As a result, a bias toward lower estimated price elasticity of demand is introduced, since the bias makes it appear that a larger price increase was necessary to ration supply than was in fact the case.

these price-index numbers. Note, however, that, while choice of a higher depreciation rate leads to higher price-index numbers for the 1942–44 period,[18] it also means that the estimated stock is correspondingly lower, the influence one tending toward lower estimates of price elasticity, the other toward higher estimates. It happens, however, that these are not substantial effects.

The computations described above have been made on the assumption that the Sears realized prices were identical with the industry's, but the key consideration is not the absolute level of the Sears prices but rather their accuracy as a reflection of the movement in industry prices. Therefore, a second set of computations was undertaken on the assumption that a 1.18 factor, the ratio of suggested list prices to Sears prices in 1941, was accurate and maintained throughout the war period. Although skeptical of this assumption, we follow it through on grounds of completeness.[19] The first procedure is called "Assumption I"; the second, "Assumption II."

III. THE TIME-SERIES REGRESSIONS

The model employed throughout is a single equation, a demand equation of the form

$$S^* = aP^{*\beta_1} Y^{\beta_2} (10)^u , \qquad (8)$$

where $S^* =$ per capita consumption of services, $P^* =$ real price, and $Y =$ real income per capita. This is, of course, equivalent to the log-linear form

$$\log S^* = a' + \beta_1 \log (P^*) + \beta_2 \log (Y) + u . \qquad (9)$$

β_1 and β_2, then, are demand elasticities.[20] The estimating procedure is that of least-squares regression.

The problem of identification might arise in the case of demand equations excluding trend—this despite the great changes in the conditions of production causing large shifts in the supply curve—if the trend-induced shifts of the demand equation are highly correlated with those of the supply relation. But, as is suggested in the next paragraph, the "true" price elasticity of demand can readily be bracketed so as to avoid the identification problem on even a priori grounds.

[18] The "anticipated" price is, of course, lower for a higher depreciation rate. The actual price is obviously independent of the selected depreciation rate.

[19] The effect of the second assumption is to "predict" higher prices than under the first. Hence the calculated price-index numbers will be lower and an upward push given to the price-elasticity estimates.

[20] It is true that the cost of holding a durable good includes interest, but variations in the interest rate were slight compared to those of price and income over the 1931–55 period, particularly over 1948–55.

In the time-series regressions whose results are presented in detail, the consumption-of-services variable is treated as dependent.[21] However, an alternative estimate of the price elasticity is given in each case, this being based on the regression of price on consumption of services, income, and (where relevant) trend. Whatever bias may be introduced by the use of the least-squares estimator in the presence of a positively sloped supply equation is presumptively upward in the alternative regression and downward in the original regression; the two price-elasticity estimates therefore tend to bracket the "true" elasticity.[22] Also the two estimates provide for the alternative extreme possibilities that the consumption variable is measured with error, while the price variable is exact, and vice versa.

The analysis begins with straightforward regressions of consumption of services on price, income, and trend. The problem of collinearity emerges at once, particularly with respect to the income variable. In some cases in econometric work, we feel sufficiently confident to rule out the possibility of an independent trend in demand—numerous regressions are shown below which do precisely that—but the extraordinary extent to which the consumption, price, and income variables exhibit trendwise variation requires, at least for the sake of completeness, that the trend (multicollinearity) issue be faced. This is done through two devices: (*a*) use of first-difference forms and (*b*) the imposition of fitted trends. Two further refinements of the time-series analysis are made: (*a*) regressions are computed including the period 1942–44, the price variable being calculated from newspaper want-ad quotations, and (*b*) the assumption of instantaneous adjustment of actual to desired refrigeration holdings is relaxed, the result being somewhat inconclusive but suggestively similar to those obtained in related studies of demand for consumer durables.

Regressions I and II are of the form:[23]

$$\log S^* = a + \beta_1 \log (P^*) + \beta_2 \log (Y) + \beta_3 T + u . \qquad (10)$$

[21] The shifting of the supply curve over time as a result of technological change supports treating consumption as the dependent variable.

[22] Cf. Arnold C. Harberger, "A Structural Approach to the Problem of Import Demand," *American Economic Review, Papers and Proceedings*, Vol. XLIII, No. 2 (May, 1953).

[23] The "style" of the regressions should be explained. The numbers immediately below the calculated coefficients are the standard errors of estimate. The third element of the price column gives the estimated upper limit of the price elasticity. The r^2 entries give the squared partial correlation coefficients. R^2 is the square of the multiple correlation coefficient; k is the rate of depreciation.

$$
\begin{array}{cccc}
r_p^2 & r_y^2 & r_t^2 & R^2
\end{array}
$$

I. $(K = 0.1)S^* = a - 1.172P_I^* + 0.825Y_d + 1.246T + u$

$$
\begin{array}{ccccccc}
& 0.195 & & 0.212 & & 0.380 & \\
& -1.605 & & & & &
\end{array}
\qquad 0.73 \;\; 0.53 \;\; 0.44 \;\; 0.997
$$

II. $(K = 0.1)S^* = a - 1.180P_I^* + 0.400Y_e + 1.628T + u$

$$
\begin{array}{ccccccc}
& 0.156 & & 0.495 & & 0.867 & \\
& -3.025 & & & & &
\end{array}
\qquad\qquad\; 0.38 \qquad\qquad 0.994
$$

Regressions I and II omit 1942–44. Regression III is of the same form but includes these years:

$$
\begin{array}{ccc}
r_p^2 & r_t^2 & R^2
\end{array}
$$

III. $(K = 0.1)S^* = a - 0.953P_{II} + 0.273Y_e + 1.875T + u$

$$
\begin{array}{ccccccc}
& 0.122 & & 0.322 & & 0.297 & \\
& -1.217 & & & & &
\end{array}
\qquad 0.78 \qquad\quad 0.70 \;\; 0.993
$$

The tremendous collinearity between the trend variable and the price and income variables suggests that the surprising thing is not the fate of Regressions II and III (and incidentally that of the expected-income variable) but rather the survival of Regression I. The "freely estimated" trend terms of II and III seem to defy common sense. Thus the trend coefficient estimated for II implies that in 1931—approximately ten years after the introduction of electrical refrigeration in the United States—a trend alone, assuming no change in price and income, would result in an 8 per cent increase in per capita consumption of refrigeration service and, more suspiciously, that as late as 1955 its influence would account for a 4 per cent increase in consumption. The corresponding implications for III are 9.50 per cent and 4.75 per cent. For that matter, the estimated trend in Regression I is very large, suggesting a 6.25 per cent increase in consumption in 1931, *ceteris paribus*, and a 3.10 per cent increase in 1955, *ceteris paribus*. The trend coefficient, 1.246, estimated for I implies that, if relative price and real income per capita had remained unchanged from 1931 to 1944, per capita consumption of services would have increased by almost 300 per cent![24]

It becomes important at this point to focus the discussion. The evidence already presented makes clear that a non-first-difference model cannot sharply separate out the influence of price and income when the

[24] Of course, there had been a considerable increase in the availability (and/or reduction in the price) of such strong complements to household refrigeration as frozen foods. To some extent, the increase in the availability of cheap complements can be seen as part of the full (long-run) adjustment to lower prices of refrigeration service. But, from the standpoint of an instantaneous-adjustment model, the complementary developments serve to accentuate the influence of trend and to increase interest in regressions, including trend.

trend variable is included and its parameter "freely" estimated. Clear-cut alternatives immediately present themselves. We can abruptly turn aside from trend, arguing that the conventional price and income variables explain the data perfectly well and that the correlation of the dependent variable and trend is spurious, induced by the trendwise movements of price and income. Regressions based on this view are presented immediately below. On the other hand, the collinearity issue can be met head-on, either by transforming the data (here, into first differences) or by imposing trends and analyzing the residual variance of the dependent variable. If these efforts were to meet with success, it could be asserted that the influences of price and income can be separated out, that precise estimates of partial price and income elasticities can be made, even if it is assumed that the influence of trend has been substantial. This also is done. We first turn to a series of regressions excluding trend, regressions which in addition provide evidence that such issues as alternative depreciation, price-series, and income-variable assumptions do not result in meaningful differences in parameter estimates.

The following regressions are of the form

$$\log (S^*) = c + \beta_1 \log (P^*) + \beta_2 \log (Y) + u.^{[25]} \qquad (11)$$

The results are quite uniform. Estimated price elasticities range from -1.585 to -1.893; income elasticities, from 1.229 to 1.638. The higher estimates as against those emerging from regressions including the trend variable are not surprising, since the price and income variables are here permitted to "carry" all the variance of the consumption variable without interference from the powerfully collinear trend variable. The narrow range of variation within this set suggests that widely different assumptions in conjunction with construction of regression variables have little effect on the resulting estimates.

The effects of alternative depreciation rates can be shown through nine regressions, five from this series and four from regressions including 1942–44, here introduced only in connection with the effects of alternative depreciation rates on declining balances.

					r_p^2	r_y^2	R^2
IV.[26] $K = 0.1$	$S^* = c - 1.823 P_{II}^* + 1.458 Y_e + u$						
		0.17	0.29		0.88	0.63	0.987
		$- 2.064$					

[25] Excluding 1942–44.

[26] S^* = stock per capita; P^* = real price; Y = real income per capita; T = trend variable. Regressions IX–XII include the war years 1942–44. Regressions IX–X are based on Price Index II, Assumption I; XI–XII on Price Index II, Assumption II.

V. $K = 0.2$ $S^* = c - 1.640P_{II}^* + 1.568Y_e + u$
           0.165   0.28   0.87   0.68   0.987
           $- 1.888$

VI. $K = 0.25$ $S^* = c - 1.585P_{II}^* + 1.638Y_e + u$
            0.166   0.28   0.86   0.69   0.986
            $- 1.847$

VII.[27] $K = 0.1$ $S^* = c - 1.893P_I^* + 1.229Y_e + u$
             0.12   0.24   0.94   0.63   0.994
             $- 2.000$

VIII. $K = 0.25$ $S^* = c - 1.705P_I^* + 1.385Y_e + u$
              0.12   0.26   0.93   0.66   0.992

IX. $K = 0.1$ $S^* = c - 1.134P_{II}^* + 2.542Y_e + u$
            0.178   0.331   0.69   0.76   0.960
            $- 1.643$

X. $K = 0.2$ $S^* = c - 1.076P_{II}^* + 2.425Y_e + u$
           0.117   0.237   0.83   0.85   0.972
           $- 1.305$

XI. $K = 0.2$ $S^* = c - 1.210P_{II}^* + 2.228Y_e + u$
            0.113   0.219   0.86   0.85   0.978
            $- 1.399$

XII. $K = 0.1$ $S^* = c - 1.455P_{II}^* + 2.034Y_e + u$
             0.165   0.289   0.81   0.73   0.976
             $- 1.791$

Regressions VII and IV and VI and VIII give the opportunity to compare the effects of the two indexes, *ceteris paribus*. The paired estimates of price and income elasticities are within 1 standard error of each other.

No significant difference in income-elasticity estimates emerges when the expected-income variable is substituted for the disposable-income variable. Witness Regressions XIII and XIV:

                                                    r_p^2 r_y^2 R^2
XIII. $K = 0.1$ $S^* = a - 1.744P_I^* + 1.300Y_d + u$
              0.23   0.40   0.80   0.41   0.994
              $- 2.194$

XIV. $K = 0.1$ $S^* = a - 1.893P_I^* + 1.229Y_e + u$
             0.12   0.24   0.94   0.63   0.994
             $- 2.000$

What happens to the estimates when the assumption that service yield is proportional to stock is dropped in favor of the assumption that a machine yields services at a constant rate over a finite lifetime, alterna-

[27] Regressions VII and VII use Price Index I.

tively assumed to be ten and fifteen years? Regressions based on this assumption and otherwise comparable to IV–VIII are XV and XVI.[28]

			r_p^2	r_y^2	R^2
XV. 15 years	$C = a - 2.067P_I^* + 1.007Y_e + u$				
	0.15	0.31	0.93	0.41	0.990
	-2.223				
XVI. 10 years	$C = a - 2.014P_I^* + 0.819Y_e + u^{29}$				0.991

Here the estimates of price elasticity are above the -1.893 upper end of the IV–VIII range. The income elasticity estimates are lower than 1.229, the lower end of that range.[30]

The seven regressions, IV–VIII, XIII, and XV, all excluding 1942–44, all in "original" as against first-difference form, and all excluding trend, present a range of price-elasticity estimates of from -1.585 to -2.067, that for income elasticity being 1.007–1.638.[31]

---

[28] C is the log of the index number for consumption of services, this being based on straight-line depreciation assumptions.

[29] Both coefficients are significant at the .05 level.

[30] Of course, the estimated-income elasticity for XVI is 0.819. But the ten-year life assumption is extreme. Even the 25 per cent depreciation rate on declining balances assumes more than 6 per cent remains after ten years, the point at which the machine "dies" under the ten-year assumption.

[31] The calculated residuals show serial correlation. This gives rise to the query whether the residuals (predicted minus actual) are characteristically negative in the early years of the study and positive in the later years. This would indicate that factors contributing to the influence of trend were not properly being accounted for. We are especially interested in the behavior of the residuals of regressions excluding trend.

Special calculations were made for Regressions I, IV, IX, XVII, and XXVIII. The residuals for I and XXVIII (adjustment coefficient without trend) definitely show no tendency toward consistent overprediction in the later years. On the other hand, those for XVII (first-difference equation with arithmetic trend) do. This led to the following experiment, suggested by Robert H. Strotz, of Northwestern University: Construct a polynomial trend term of the form

$$a_0 + a_1t + a_2t^2 + \dots,$$

where t is the first difference of the logs of the trend variable described in n. 3. (Recall that a_0, the constant term of the first difference regression, estimates a log-linear trend—cf. n. 32.)

Higher-order trend terms should subject the "economic" variables to more strenuous tests. However, at the first stage of the experiment, the coefficient for the first-order term of the trend expression ($a_0 + a_1t$) proved insignificant. The price coefficient fell to $-.67$, within a standard error of that for XVII, but remained highly significant. The income coefficient fell to .81 but was significant. The R^2 went to 0.68 and was higher than that for XVII (0.63) after adjustment for loss of a degree of freedom. When the results of this experiment are taken together with the failure of the residuals of the trendless regressions, IV, IX, and XXVIII, to indicate consistent overprediction in the later years, it seems clear that the path to success is not to be found in the construction of more and more complex trend terms.

The first of the head-on attacks on the multicollinearity issue, here expressed as the problem of obtaining price- and income-elasticity estimates in the presence of a trend variable, is based on casting the data into first differences. The first-difference regressions are in first differences of logs, it being recalled that the "original" time-series regressions are also in logs. As is shown in Array C, the analogue to Arrays A and B, the use of first differences tremendously reduces collinearity.

ARRAY C: FIRST DIFFERENCES OF
LOGS EXCLUDING 1942–44

	S^*	P^*	Y_d
S^*	1.0	0.16	0.20
P^*		1.0	0.06
Y_d			1.0

CHART II

REGRESSION I

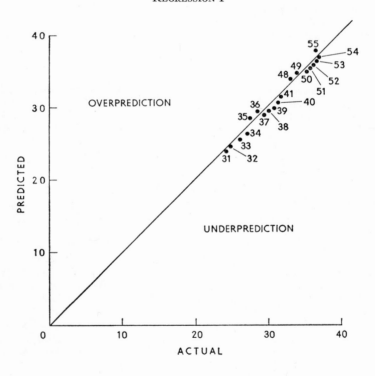

The influence of trend is expressed in the constant term of the first-difference regressions.[32] The algebraic identity of the parameters of the first-difference regressions and the "original" regressions can be seen from the following simple operations which also indicate the way in which trend is expressed in first-difference forms (through the constant term):[33]

[32] The trend variable implicitly operating in the first-difference regressions implies a constant rate of growth in consumption, *ceteris paribus*, in contrast to the earlier trend variable which implies a diminishing growth rate, *ceteris paribus*.

[33] Of course, the estimated coefficients of the "original" and first-difference regressions might differ substantially due to such factors as random errors of measurement being greater relative to first differences of observations than to the observations themselves, different degrees of collinearity, etc. Furthermore, if serial correlation is present in the "true" disturbances in the equation, it can be shown that, the larger is the serial correlation of these disturbances, the smaller will be the computed correlation coefficient of the first-difference regressions. (I am indebted to Marc Nerlove, of the University of Minnesota, for this point.) While we do not know the serial correlation of the true disturbances, we do know that significant positive serial correlation prevails in the computed disturbances of the regressions. This may provide a partial explanation for the relatively low correlation coefficients found for the first-difference regressions.

CHART III

Regression IV

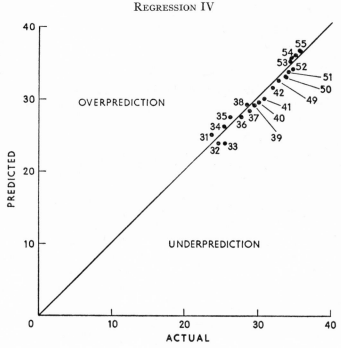

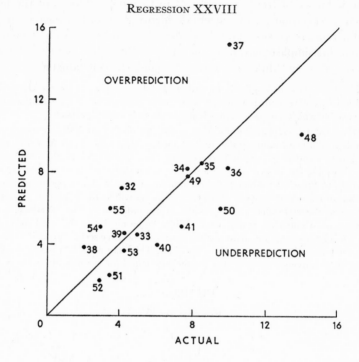

CHART IV
Regression XXVIII

OVERPREDICTION

UNDERPREDICTION

PREDICTED

ACTUAL

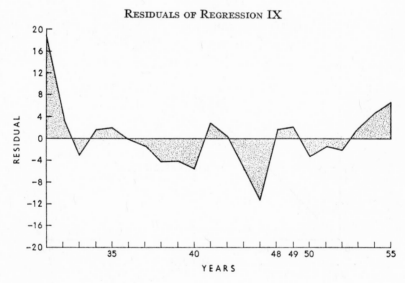

CHART V
Residuals of Regression IX

RESIDUAL

YEARS

1. Form the equation for per capita stock as a function of relative price, per capita income, and trend for years t and $t - 1$. Note that the first three variables are in log form.

$$S^*_{t-1} = a + \beta_1 P^*_{t-1} + \beta_2 Y_{t-1} + \beta_3 T_{t-1} + u_{t-1}, \qquad (12)$$

$$S^*_t = a + \beta_1 P^*_t + \beta_2 Y_t + \beta_3 T_t + u_t. \qquad (13)$$

2. Subtract (12) from (13). The constant term, a, falls out. Since it is assumed $T_t - T_{t-1} = 1$, β_3 is simply multiplied by 1 in the first-difference equation

$$\Delta S^* = \beta_3 + \beta_1 \Delta P^* + \beta_2 \Delta Y + v, \qquad (14)$$

where ΔS^*, for example, $= S^*_t - S^*_{t-1}$.

Regressions XVII, XVIII, and XIX are in first-difference form and include constant terms. They exclude the 1942–44 period.

CHART VI

REGRESSION XVII

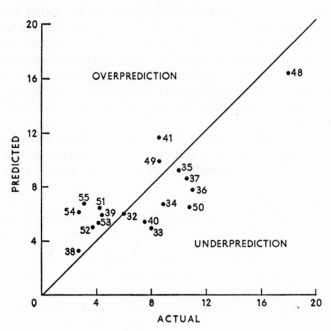

			r_p^2	r_y^2	R^2

XVII. $K = 0.1$ $S^* = 0.031 - 0.871P_I^* + 1.271Y_e + u$

      0.27   0.30   0.42   0.56   0.629

      $- 2.085$

XVIII. $K = 0.1$ $S^* = 0.034 - 0.894P_I^* + 0.704Y_d + u$

       0.31   0.21   0.36   0.47   0.520

       $- 2.514$

XIX. $K = 0.1$ $C = 0.043 - 0.726P_I^* + 0.972Y_e + u$

      0.286   0.311   0.30   0.39   0.489

      $- 2.421$

The constant terms of these regressions are large; the implicit influence of trend is substantial. For example, the constant term for XVII implies that 70 per cent of the 220 per cent increase in per capita stock from 1948 to 1955 could be accounted for by the influence of trend alone if real price and per capita income had remained constant! Thus, while statistical procedures do not permit the assertion that the influence of trend is not so great as that implied in Regressions XVII–XIX, common sense tells us that -0.726 represents a lower bound for the "true" price parameter. The lower bound for the price parameter becomes -0.871 if we confine ourselves to the declining-balance depreciation assumption; that for the income parameter, 0.704. However, it should be noted that this lower bound is for the *disposable* income variable, and it has already been shown[34] that the disposable income variable is particularly apt to be weak in first-difference formulations. Large inroads, then, have been made into the collinearity problem in that, despite the allowance for very large trend terms in first-difference formulations, meaningful estimates have been made, establishing lower bounds for the price and income parameters.[35]

The second attack on multicollinearity is through fitted trends. In this section substantial trend coefficients are imposed, and the residual variation of the consumption variable is analyzed in an attempt to establish

[34] Cf. p. 106 above.

[35] Regressions XX and XXI are in first-difference form but are forced through the origin so as to exclude trend. As a result they are on all fours with VII and XIII.

			R^2

XX. $K = 0.1$ $S^* = -1.446P_I^* + 1.603Y_e + u$ 0.491

XXI. $K = 0.1$ $S^* = -1.546P_I^* + 0.961Y_d + u$ 0.431

The corresponding parameters of VII (vis-à-vis XX) and XIII (vis-à-vis XXI) are -1.744, 1.300 and -1.893, 1.229. The price parameter is slightly lower, while the effect on the income parameter depends upon whether expected or disposable income is used.

upper and lower bounds for the parameters.[36] Three of the basic regressions (not in first differences)—Regressions I, II, and XII—were recomputed with trend coefficients of 1.0 and .5 imposed. The 1.0 coefficient for the basic (logarithmic) trend variable implies that, if relative price and per capita income had remained constant from 1931 to 1932, consumption of services would have increased by 5 per cent and that consumption would have increased 2.4 per cent from 1954 to 1955, *ceteris paribus*. The .5 coefficient, of course, implies changes of 2.5 and 1.2 per cent. That the 1.0 coefficient implies a "high" trend is obvious when it is realized that, under this assumption, per capita consumption of refrigeration service would have been 323 per cent higher in 1955 than in 1931 even if relative price and per capita income had remained unchanged over that twenty-four-year interval, this for a product that has been on the market since at least 1922. The corresponding percentage increase for the .5 coefficient is 181. Regressions XXII, XXIII, and XXIV impose a trend coefficient of 1.0. Regressions XXV, XXVI, and XXVII, .5. Regressions XXII and XXV are counterparts of Regressions II and VII; XXIII and XXVI of I and XIII; XXIV and XXVII of III and XII.[37]

		r_p^2	r_y^2	R^2
XXII.	$S^{*\prime} = a - 1.455P_I^* + 0.719Y_e + u$			
	0.10　　　　0.21	0.92	0.44	0.990
	-1.58			
XXIII.	$S^{*\prime} = a - 1.28P_I^* + 0.92Y_d + u$			
	0.13　　　　0.21	0.84	0.55	0.995
	-1.53			
XXIV.	$S^{*\prime} = a - 1.19P_{II}^* + 1.10Y_e + u$			
	0.14　　　　0.38	0.77	0.49	0.978
	-1.55			
XXV.	$S^{*\prime} = a - 1.67P_I^* + 0.97Y_e + u$			
	0.12　　　　0.22			
	-1.81	0.93	0.55	0.992
XXVI.	$S^{*\prime} = a - 1.51P_I^* + 1.11Y_d + u$			
	0.14　　　　0.26	0.86	0.54	0.994
	-1.74			
XXVII.	$S^{*\prime} = a - 1.32P_{II}^* + 1.57Y_e + u$			
	0.17　　　　0.46	0.77	0.39	0.978
	-1.71			

[36] Regression XII is discussed on pp. 121 ff. It includes 1942–44.

[37] The dependent variable, S^*, for Regressions XXII–XXVII is based on adjustment of the consumption variable for the implicit influence of trend. In other words,

The results, presented in tabular form, are:

	No Trend	$\beta_3 = 0.5$	$\beta_3 = 1.0$
II–VII formulation			
Price elasticity..............	−1.89	−1.67	−1.46
Income elasticity............	1.23	0.97	0.72
I–XIII formulation			
Price elasticity..............	−1.74	−1.51	−1.28
Income elasticity............	1.30	1.11	0.92
III–XII formulation			
Price elasticity..............	−1.46	−1.32	−1.19
Income elasticity............	2.04	1.57	1.10

The results are generally consistent with previously established upper and lower bounds, although the expected-income parameter, when "faced" with $R_3 = 1.0$, is considerably lower (0.72 versus 1.27) than that of the first-difference formulation, XVII, a regression also including a "high" implicit trend (0.72). However, when the twelve estimates of XXII–XXVII are taken as a whole, the experiment must be considered a success. The first twenty-seven regressions are consistent with the conclusion stated at the outset of the paper that "the price elasticity is between −1.0 and −2.0 and, somewhat less conclusively, . . . the income elasticity is between 1.0 and 2.0."[38]

The decision to compute regressions taking account of the 1942–44 period was originally based on the hope that the fact that these years saw breaks in the monotonous trends in the stock and price series would permit an independent avenue of attack on the collinearity problem. Unfortunately, however, as comparison of Array B with Array A (p. 101) shows, despite some reduction in collinearity, the main aspects of the problem remained unchanged. This is confirmed by Regression III (p. 110), which includes the 1942–44 observations; the income parameter is insignificant. In short, this attack failed. On the other hand, it is felt that Regressions IX–XII are of sufficient interest to be included in this paper. After all, there were major movements in the stock, price, and income

the normal equations for XXII–XXVII are of the form

$$\begin{bmatrix} m_{s*p*} - \beta_3 m_{p*t*} \\ [m_{s*y} - \beta_3 m_{yt}] \end{bmatrix} = \begin{bmatrix} m_{p*p*} & m_{p*y} \\ m_{p*y} & m_{yy} \end{bmatrix} \begin{bmatrix} \beta_1 \\ \beta_2 \end{bmatrix},$$

where β_3 is equal to 1.0 or 0.5 as the case may be. The m's are moments about the respective means.

[38] See p. 99 above.

variables over the 1942–44 period, and, as has been shown, it is possible to construct meaningful price series for the war period through resort to newspaper quotations.

The elasticity estimates of IX–XII are as follows:

	Price Elasticity	Income Elasticity
IX	−1.13	2.54
X	−1.08	2.43
XI	−1.21	2.23
XII	−1.46	2.03

Regressions IX and X were based on Assumption I, Regressions XI and XII on Assumption II. As against the comparable Regressions IV–VIII (excluding 1942–44), it is seen that in IX–XII the range of price-elasticity estimates is lower—1.07–1.46 as against 1.58–1.89. On the other hand, the range of income-elasticity estimates is higher, 2.03–2.54 as against 1.23–1.64.[39]

These results are not altogether clear cut. The price-index numbers for 1942–44 are particularly subject to errors of measurement, while the errors of measurement of the stock series for this period are no greater than in any other, since there was practically no production in 1942–44. As is seen on pages 126–27, the argument for taking price as the independent variable becomes stronger in these circumstances,[40] If price is taken as the dependent variable in IX–XII, the resulting estimates of price elasticity are much closer to those of IV and V[41] (with price independent). On this basis the comparable estimates for IV and IX are −1.823 and −1.643; that for IV and XII, −1.823 and −1.791.

As for income-elasticity estimates, the covariance of the estimates of the price and income elasticities for IX–XII is positive. This means that, if it is correct to assume that using stock as the dependent variable introduced downward (*algebraically* upward) bias into the price-elasticity estimates in IX–XII, the income-elasticity estimates were correspondingly biased upward.

Up to this point it has been assumed that consumers *instantaneously* adjust their rates of consumption of refrigeration service (or, in the declining-balance formulation, their stocks) to the levels called for by the

[39] When XXIV is compared to XXII or XXVII to XXV, it is again seen that the price-elasticity estimate is lower and the income elasticity higher when the 1942–44 period is included, *ceteris paribus*.

[40] From an economic standpoint it is clear that the dependent variable for the 1942–44 period was price, since the community was unable to much change its stock position; the stock was rationed by the price of refrigeration.

[41] Regressions IV and V are on all fours with IX–XII.

various price-income constellations. But the time path of adjustment need not collapse into a point.

In order to estimate the adjustment coefficient, the following model was set up: since the stock held at the end of year $t - 1$ is known, it follows that the equilibrium stock position at the end of year t can be expressed as a ratio of S_t^* (actual per capita stock) to S_{t-1}^*. The form of the demand function has been expressed as

$$S_t^* = \alpha P_t^{*\beta_1} Y_e^{\beta_2} (10)^u .^{42} \tag{15}$$

Up to now, adjustment of actual to desired positions has been assumed to be instantaneous so that we could have written

$$\log S_t^* - \log S_{t-1}^* = \alpha + \beta_1 \log P_t^* + \beta_2 \log Y_{e_t} - \log S_{t-1}^* \tag{16}$$

as equivalent to (15). However, if it is assumed that only a fraction, B, of the adjustment will be accomplished within a year, it can no longer be expected to observe equilibrium stock S^* but rather actual stock S^{**}.[43] The implied stochastic relation would be[44]

$$\log (S_t^{**}/S_{t-1}^{**}) = \alpha' + B\beta_1 \log P_t^* + B\beta_2 \log Y_{e_t} - B \log S_{t-1}^{**} + u . \tag{17}$$

This is the form of Regression XXVIII, a regression not including 1942–44, based on Price Index II, and not including trend[45]

[42] Regression XXVIII, below, does not include trend.

[43] The values here inserted for S^{**} are precisely those hitherto inserted for desired stock, S^*. Since a declining-balance model is being employed, "stock" is used instead of the more cumbersome, but equivalent, "consumption-of-services" term.

[44] Equation (16) states that $S_t^{**}/S_{t-1}^{**} = (S_t^*/S_{t-1}^*)^B$, where B is a fraction between 0 and 1.0. Thus, if the left-hand side were 1.21 and $B = 0.5$, the right-hand side would be equal to 1.1. Or, if the left-hand side were 0.81 and $B = 0.5$, the ratio of actual to desired stock at t would be 0.9. The reader should be careful not to confuse this model with one expressed in arithmetic units.

[45] The significance of the R^2 (0.6866) can be tested by using the ratio $R^2/(1 - R)^2$ (Helen M. Walker and Joseph Lev, *Statistical Inference* [New York: Henry Holt & Co., 1952], p. 324). The statistic is distributed as F with $n_1 = 3$, $n_2 = 14$ and has the value 10.2236. $F_{0.95} = 3.34$, $F_{0.99} = 5.56$. The R^2 is then highly significant.

The form of regression XXVIII is such that it "explains" the variance of first differences of the logs of the dependent variable. It is equivalent to a regression of the form

$$\log S_t^{**} = \alpha' + B\beta_1 \log P_t^* + B\beta_2 \log Y_{e_t} + (1-B) \log S_{t-1}^{**} + u . \tag{16'}$$

When put in this form, the R^2 is 0.997. This explains 99.7 per cent of the variance of $\log S_t^{**}$. The analogous Regression IV—identical except for the assumption that $B = 1.0$—has an R^2 of 0.987.

When XXVIII is cast into first differences, permitting allowance for trend, the

XXVIII.	$B\beta_1$	$B\beta_2$	B	$r^2_{B\beta_1}$	$r^2_{B\beta_2}$	r^2_B	R^2	β_1	β_2	B
	−0.682	0.884	0.461	0.45	0.48	0.55	0.687			
	0.192	0.245	0.112					−1.419	1.917	0.461

The estimates of the equivalent Regression IV were −1.823 and 1.458 (vis-à-vis −1.419 and 1.917 of XXVIII) The magnitudes of the esti-mates remain stable, and the adjustment coefficient itself is interesting in its rough correspondence with the findings of Chow and Muth for automobiles and housing.[46]

IV. THE CROSS-SECTION REGRESSIONS

Limitations of data force the cross-sectional studies to be confined to estimation of the income parameter. Obviously, cross-sectional stock and income variables must be constructed. But the simple correlations of in-come and stock are very low; income alone cannot begin to explain be-tween-state variations in stock. It is necessary to use such variables as urbanization and temperature to filter out the other sources of variation before a significant relationship between stock (consumption of services) and income can be established.

The cross-sectional regressions reflect four basic approaches to the problem of measuring consumption of refrigeration services: (*a*) data based on cumulated sales; (*b*) census data; (*c*) survey data on holdings according to income group; and (*d*) survey data on average expenditure on new machines purchased organized by income group.

The details of the procedures used to construct cross-sectional variables are provided in the Appendix, but the over-all picture should be described at this point. The consumption-of-services variables used in Regressions XXIX–XXX (since declining-balance depreciation assumptions are em-ployed here, consumption of services and stock are proportional) are built up from sales data. Limitations of these data prevent determination of *values* of sales by states;[47] we know only the *numbers* of refrigerators

---

adjustment coefficient goes to .73 and the price and income parameters are estimated as −0.68 and 1.48. The constant term is 0.028 ($R^2 = 0.69$). All the parameters are significant at least at the .05 level. The estimates of the equivalent XVII are −0.87 and 1.27.

[46] Chow, *op. cit.*; Richard Muth, chap. ii, above.

If disposable income is substituted for expected income in Regression XXVIII, the resulting equation is

XXVIIIa.	$B\beta_1$	$B\beta_2$	B	$r^2_{B\beta_1}$	$r^2_{B\beta_2}$	r^2_B	R^2	β_1	β_2	B
	−0.133	1.069	0.358		0.79	0.76	0.831			
	0.118	0.145	0.053					−0.372	2.986	0.358

[47] Nor do we have data as to interstate transfers of used machines.

and freezers sold in the various states as far back as 1939. We are forced to assume that the average per unit sales price is the same in all states, an assumption that obviously biases the cross-sectional income elasticity estimates downward. Given these limitations, it is possible to construct a stock index for a given year, 1954 in this case, reasonably consistent with the time-series-data criteria by converting the raw sales data into "real" sales data, the adjusted data taking account of quality changes over time. The adjusted sales data can then be summed for each state in the same manner employed earlier for obtaining United States stock in the time-series estimates. After deflating by a size factor, in this case civilian population, we have per capita stock by state for 1954.

The freezer stock variable used in Regressions XXXI and XXXII was computed by summing state sales (in "number of units sold" terms) over the 1947–54 period and deflating by state civilian population.[48] The stock variable for Regressions XXXIII and XXXIV is based upon a census source, namely, percentage of dwelling units with refrigerators in 1940 and 1950. Freezers do not appear in these regressions.

The Survey Research Center of the University of Michigan has provided exceptionally useful material showing refrigerator holdings by year of purchase and by income category for the year 1952.[49] These data have been weighted by the present writer so as to account for depreciation of refrigerator holdings and for the improved quality of more recent purchases. However, these data do not indicate the relation between income status and prices paid for new machines purchased. The resulting relation accordingly makes no allowance for the effects of income on the quality of purchases, but, fortunately, it has been possible to collect Bureau of Labor Statistics data which permit an estimate of the income-average expenditure parameter. The details are shown in the Appendix.

The income variable used in Regressions XXIV–XXXII is a weighted average of real personal income (by states) analogous to the expected-income variable of the time-series regressions.[50] On the other hand, the income variable for Regressions XXXIII–XXXIV is merely personal income for 1940 and for 1950.

Mean temperature by state was used in some regressions. This, along with the more important urbanization variable, was employed in order

[48] This becomes equivalent to assuming straight-line depreciation.

[49] I am greatly indebted to James N. Morgan, of the University of Michigan, in this connection and to Charles M. Tiebout, of the University of California at Los Angeles. The details are found in the Appendix.

[50] See Appendix for details.

to separate out that part of the variance of the cross-section stock variable accounted for by non-income regional differences. As for urbanization, it is evident that the convenience yield of refrigeration, especially that of a home freezer, for a consumer fifteen miles from the nearest grocery store is, *ceteris paribus*, greater than for a resident of Manhattan, the latter being able to obtain a great variety of foods at almost a moment's notice and facing much higher rentals for storage area. The urbanization variable, the percentage of urban total population, is especially powerful in Regressions **XXXI** and **XXXII**, the regressions considering only freezers; there, the simple correlation coefficient for income is weak and negative, but the partial correlation coefficient for income is significant and the partial-elasticity estimate substantial.

For regression purposes the cross-sectional data are cast into logs except for the census-based Regressions **XXXIII** and **XXXIV**, in which the data are in "percentage-change" form. The extent of intercorrelation is much less than is the case for the time-series variables. This is demonstrated by Array D, an array of simple squared correlation coefficients for stock (S), income (Y), and urbanization (Z) for the forty-eight-state cross-sectional regressions:

ARRAY D

	S	Y	Z
S	1	0.03	0.02
Y		1	0.42
Z			1

Regressions **XXIX–XXX** are based on a forty-eight-state cross-section with the stock variable being compiled from cumulated manufacturers' sales data, including refrigerators and freezers. (H is the temperature variable.) Regression **XXIX** treats S^* as the dependent variable, while **XXX** treats income as dependent. Regression **XXX** is then transformed into a form comparable to **XXIX**. While all the coefficients in both equations are highly significant, there is a wide range between the parameter estimates of **XXIX** and those of **XXX**. Such results are common in cases where the variables are subject to substantial errors of measurement.

XXIX. $S^* = a + 0.428Y_e - 0.273Z + 0.33H + u$
$\quad\quad\quad\quad\quad 0.143 \quad\quad 0.102 \quad\quad 0.182 \quad\quad\quad R^2 = 0.184$[51]

XXX. $Y_e = a + 0.512Z - 0.661H + 0.394S^* + u$
$\quad\quad\quad\quad 0.072 \quad\quad 0.150 \quad\quad 0.131 \quad\quad\quad R^2 = 0.640$

$\quad\quad S^* = a' + 2.537Y_e - 1.299Z + 1.677H$

[51] The R^2 is significant at least at the 5 per cent level, the calculated F ratio being 3.30, while $F_{0.05}$ ($n_1 = 3$, $n_2 = 44$) = 2.59.

Regressions **XXX***a* and **XXX***b* are "weighted" in an attempt to cope with the problem of measurement errors. Regression **XXX***a* is based on the assumption that the error of measurement is equally distributed among the stock, income and urbanization variables, while **XXX***b* assumes that the error of measurement is equally distributed among the stock and income variables but that urbanization is measured without error. Neither includes the temperature variable. The estimated-income elasticity for **XXX***a* is 0.958; that for **XXX***b*, 0.733.[52]

Regressions **XXXI** and **XXXII** are based on freezers only.

XXXI. $S_f^* = a + 1.271 Y_e - 1.362 Z + u.$
$\qquad\qquad\; 0.326 \qquad 0.257 \qquad\quad R^2 = 0.443^{53} \; r_y^2 = 0.33, r_z^2 = 0.26$

Regression **XXXII** takes income as the dependent variable, the resulting estimate of income elasticity of demand being 5.737.

Regressions **XXXIII** and **XXXIV** use a census-based stock variable which excludes freezers. The variables are defined as follows:

$$S' = (S_{1950} - S_{1940}) / S_{1940}, \; Y' = (Y_{1950} - Y_{1940}) / Y_{1940},$$

where S' and Y' are computed for each of the forty-eight states. Thus we are regressing relative change in stock with relative change in income. The squared correlation coefficient for these regressions (**XXXIII** and **XXXIV**) is .608. Regression **XXXIII** takes the stock variable as dependent, while **XXXIV** takes the income variable as dependent. The respective estimates of income elasticity are 2.161 and 3.552.

Interpretation of Regressions **XXIX–XXXIV** is difficult; it is obvious that we are faced with extremely poor identification of the income parameter, the estimates of which are spread over a large range. Consider Regressions **XXIX** and **XXX**, regressions differing only in the choice of the dependent variable. "The question arises, therefore, which of the two regressions—that of price on quantity or that of quantity on price—is

---

[52] I am greatly indebted to D. L. Harris, Department of Astronomy, Northwestern University, for setting up the computational procedures for Regressions **XXX***a* and **XXX***b*. For a discussion of weighted regression see Lawrence R. Klein, *A Textbook of Econometrics* (Evanston, Ill.: Row, Peterson & Co., 1953), pp. 289–300. Note that, insofar as temperature variable is significant, its omission biases the income parameter estimate downward, since income and temperature are negatively correlated. Therefore, the "truncated" regression will be influenced by the fact that it does not account for the effect of temperature in "causing" the stock to be lower than would otherwise be the case where income is higher.

[53] The value of the appropriate F statistic at the .01 level is 4.26, whereas the calculated value of the statistic in this case is 11.60. The calculated R^2 is then highly significant.

to be taken as the demand curve?"[54] The answer is usually given within the context of an "errors-in-the-variables" model.[55] Taking a two-variable case, if x is measured with a non-systematic error while y is measured exactly, the estimate of the regression coefficient would be biased if x is chosen as the independent variable, since the "true" disturbance is correlated with x. It follows that x should be regressed on y. What does this criterion suggest with respect to Regressions XXIX–XXX?

The income data were obtained from United States Department of Commerce sources.[56] The procedures followed by the USDC in forming the data and by the present writer in converting them into "expected income by state" were not ideal, largely because the preferable basic data, per capita disposable income for 1954 and the eight preceding years, are not available. The difficulties faced by the Department of Commerce in constructing the data published in 1955, per capita personal income by state, are well described in he article cited in note 56.

The stock data were derived from sales data reported by the vast bulk of the industry to the National Electrical Manufacturers Association and published in *Electrical Merchandising* marketing issues. In order to obtain estimates of stock by state, these data were adjusted for quality changes and depreciation. In other words, the basic data—the sales data—are measured with the accuracy of practically complete enumeration, while the adjustments are subject to considerable error.

Regressions taking stock as the dependent variable assume that income is measured with complete accuracy and vice versa. Obviously, neither assumption can be justified, but the matter is of great importance when the parameter estimates are as disparate as the 0.43 and 2.5 estimates of Regressions XXIX and XXX. It follows that Regressions XXX*a* and XXX*b* have special significance, modifying, as they do, the obviously extreme assumptions of the alternative "conventional" treatments and resulting, as they do, in estimates for the income parameter within the range of the time-series regressions.

Inspection of Regressions XXXIII and XXXIV, the census-based regressions, shows similar dispersion in the stock-dependent and income-dependent estimates, 2.1 and 3.5. Furthermore, these estimates lie outside the range of all the time-series regressions except for IX–XII,

[54] Henry Schultz, *The Theory and Measurement of Demand* (Chicago: University of Chicago Press, 1938), p. 147. Cf. Schultz's discussion of the general issue, *ibid.*, pp. 146–49.

[55] Cf. Klein, *op. cit.*, pp. 282 ff., for a discussion of this and related matters. The literature abounds with discussion of this issue.

[56] Cf. *Survey of Current Business*, September, 1955, pp. 12 ff.

regressions including 1942–44. (But it has already been seen that there are reasons to believe that the income-elasticity estimates of **IX–XII** are biased upward.)[57] It should be noted that the "high" income-elasticity estimates of **XXXIII** and **XXXIV** cannot be accounted for by trend, since these regressions are concerned with deviations of percentage changes in stock and income from 1940 to 1950 in the various states from the *mean* percentage change in stock and the *mean* percentage change in income.

Regressions **XXXV–XXXVIII** are based on data organized according to family income. Charts VIII and IX in the Appendix provide a visual version of these regressions. Regressions **XXXV** and **XXXVI** relate income and average price paid for new machines where new machines are purchased, while **XXXVII** and **XXXVIII** relate family income and refrigerator stocks.[58]

	Income Elasticity	R^2	
XXXV.	0.223	0.895	Expenditure (average price paid) dependent
XXXVI.	0.250		Income dependent
XXXVII.	0.466	0.975	Stock dependent
XXXVIII.	0.477		Income dependent

The close fits of Regressions **XXV–XXXVIII** makes unimportant the issue of "income-dependent versus income-independent" regressions; the estimates are not much affected by the direction of the regression. On the other hand, the interpretation of these regressions is not obvious. Consider Regression **XXXVII**. Two sources of downward bias are apparent:[59] (*a*) freezers are omitted and (*b*) no account is taken of the possibility that those in higher-income brackets bought more expensive machines than those in lower-income brackets.[60] Regressions **XXXV** and **XXXVI**, relating income status and price paid for new machines purchased, permit partial compensation for downward bias introduced by (*b*). They indicate that a 1 per cent difference in income is associated with a 0.22–0.25 per cent difference in expenditure on new machines (in the same direction), *considering only those actually purchasing new machines*. It follows that the

[57] Cf. p. 121 above.

[58] All four regressions exclude freezers. There are but three degrees of freedom for **XXXVII** and **XXXVIII**, and five for **XXXV** and **XXXVI**.

[59] Another source of downward bias of the estimate of the income elasticity is the failure of the Michigan data to discriminate between urban and rural families within regions.

[60] The quality adjustment made by this writer with respect to the Michigan data is intertemporal, not intratemporal.

0.46–0.48 income-elasticity estimates of **XXXV** and **XXXVI** should be adjusted upward by 0.22–0.25, resulting in a total estimated income elasticity of demand for refrigerators of 0.68–0.73 on the basis of budget data.

But the data underlying Regressions **XXXV–XXXVIII** omit freezers. Regressions **XXXI** and **XXXII** indicate that income elasticity of demand for freezers is substantially greater than that for refrigerators, a not un expected result. As the general level of income has risen, we would expect less variability between income groups with respect to now-standard sources of refrigeration than with respect to more luxurious forms such as freezers. Thus it is reasonably certain that the 0.68–0.73 estimate is biased downward, especially when it is realized that about 20 per cent of total refrigeration stock today is accounted for by freezers.[61] It follows that the results of Regressions **XXXV–XXXVIII**, when taken in conjunction with Regressions **XXXV** and **XXXVI**, suggest an estimated income elasticity of demand for *all* household refrigeration within the range of the time-series estimates.

APPENDIX

THE UNDERLYING DATA: THE DEVELOPMENT OF THE REGRESSION VARIABLES

I. THE TIME-SERIES VARIABLES

a) THE PRICE SERIES

1. *The model-mix data.*—Table A1 shows the percentage of United States production devoted in the years shown to various categories of refrigerators. Table A2 shows home freezer sales and values for the years 1946–55.

2. *Price quotation data.*—Before presenting Table A3, "Sears Mail-Order Price Quotations in Current Dollars," a few comments are in order. First, the source:

The source is the spring and fall Sears general mail-order catalogues. The Chicago catalogue was used after it became apparent that no significant difference existed with respect to quotations in other catalogues. Prices are f.o.b. shipping point. Where spring and fall quotations differed, these differences are interpolated, keeping in mind that the catalogues were issued ahead of the actual seasons. Thus, where quoted prices were rising, as in 1940–41, more weight was placed on the later quotations. In other words, it was assumed that there was a slight time lag in the Sears response to market changes when market

---

[61] Cf. Tables A3 and A8 in the Appendix.

conditions were being changed by such exogenous disturbances as war in Europe, etc. The possible error introduced by faulty interpolation is much reduced by the annual linkage procedure.

Second, for obvious commercial reasons, the designation of a given model was often changed from year to year. It was possible to spot changes in labeling of practically identical machines by checking such specifications as shipping weight, capacity, etc. The dashed line under 1953 in Table A3 is to aid the reader in observing the marked and continuous decrease in price through the years. Two of the models used for comparison were changed in 1954 in connection with automatic defrosting. However, the 1954/1953 linkage was maintained through the use of comparable models.

3. *The indexes.*—The indexes are presented in Table A4. The sources of the disparities between indexes were discussed in Section II. Owing to the chain linkage, a difference between indexes for 1932, for example, is

TABLE A1*

PERCENTAGE MODEL-MIX DATA, UNITED STATES

YEAR	MODEL						
	4 Cu. Ft.	5 Cu. Ft.	6–7 Cu. Ft.	8 Cu. Ft. and More	8 Cu. Ft. or Less	9–10 Cu. Ft.	Greater than 10 Cu. Ft.
1931	45	45	7	3			
1932	45	45	7	3			
1933	40	40	17	3			
1934	35	24	36	5			
1935	31	30	34	5			
1936	18	29	49	4			
1937	16	27	52	5			
1938	17	23	54	6			
1939	13	19	61	7			
1940	6	5	80	9			
1941	5	1	84	10			
1946	3		89	8			
1947	1		65	34			
1948					71	26	3
1949					69	27	4
1950					58	30	12
1951					53	29	18
1952					45	34	21
1953					35	39	26
1954					33	34	33
1955					24	28	48

* Source: National Electrical Manufacturers Association and Sears, Roebuck and Company.

maintained throughout the remaining years in the series employed, 1931=100. Table A5 shows that the series are really much more alike than seems to be the case with a 1931 base. This is shown by simply using a 1939 base, there obviously being no substantive difference as a consequence of shifting the base year.

We now wish to obtain a real price index by deflating the indexes of Table A4 by the implicit Gross National Product Deflator, a deflator considered least biased by such problems as unenforced price-ceiling regulations. The results appear in Table A6.

b) THE MANUFACTURERS' SALES SERIES

The formula $x_t = q_t r_t / P_t$, where q_t = number of units sold, r_t = Sears average realization, P_t, the "refrigerator-cost-of-living" index number (P_{I} or P_{II}), and x_t = manufacturers' real sales prior to indexing established the procedure for deriving the sales index. Two other facts should be noted:

1. Starting with 1946, the value of freezer output at Sears average prices was added to the value of refrigerator output.

TABLE A2*

FREEZER SALES AND TOTAL VALUE, SEARS AVERAGE
REALIZED PRICES†

Year (1)	No. Freezers Sold, United States (2)	Sears Average Price (3)	Value at Sears Average Price (4)
1946............	210,000	$355	$ 74,550,000
1947............	607,000	343	208,201,000
1948............	690,000	341	235,290,000
1949............	485,000	320	155,200,000
1950............	890,000	280	249,200,000
1951............	1,050,000	296	310,800,000
1952............	1,141,000	322	367,402,000
1953............	1,090,000	395	430,550,000
1954............	975,000	332	323,700,000
1955............	1,100,000	305	335,500,000

* Sources: National Electrical Manufacturers Association; *Electrical Merchandising*, annual marketing issues; and Sears, Roebuck and Company.

† The refrigerator price index includes adjustment for quality changes. This average price statistic is misleading, since the proportion of freezers 11 cubic feet and over rose from 33.4 per cent in 1948 to 91.2 per cent in 1955. However, since the catalogue source is not so precise as might be desired, column (4) was deflated by the price index computed for refrigerators. This appears to lead to little or no distortion, since the real price of freezers, without adjustment for changes in quality, in 1955 was 83 per cent of the 1948 real price, while that for refrigerators was 62 per cent. The 21 percentage-point difference is readily accounted for by the increasing size of the machines as time passed. It might be noted that, to the extent that freezer prices did not fall as rapidly as refrigerator prices, the price elasticity was biased downward.

2. Although the price data for 1946 and 1947 cannot be derived with enough accuracy to permit these years to be included in the regressions, some approximation is necessary for purposes of computation of the stock series which, of course, is a weighted average of past sales. We do know the Sears average realizations for 1946–47 as well as the number of machines produced in the United States. The problem narrows down to the choice of the best deflators. The Sears average realizations were $193, $264, and $276 in the years 1946, 1947, and 1948, with Price Index II standing at 95.6 in 1948. Since the 1947 and 1948 model mixes were not far apart while the 1946 mix showed a substantially larger fraction devoted to smaller models, it was decided to use a divisor of 95.0 in deflating the value series for 1946 and 1947. In other words, the slightly smaller average realization in 1947 as against 1948 with similar model mixes was considered equivalent to a slightly lower price of refrigeration. On the other hand, the lower average realization for 1946 was considered offset by the model mix stressing smaller models. Remember, there were no catalogue quotations for 1946 and 1947.

TABLE A3

SEARS MAIL-ORDER PRICE QUOTATIONS IN CURRENT DOLLARS

YEAR	MODEL						
	4 Cu. Ft.	5 Cu. Ft.	6–7 Cu. Ft.	8 Cu. Ft. and More	8 Cu. Ft. or Less	9–10 Cu. Ft.	Greater than 10 Cu. Ft.
1931	137.50	159.50	179.50	205.00	....	....	....
1932	124.75	154.75	174.95	200.00	....	....	....
1933	111.75	148.75	170.00	190.00	....	....	....
1934	94.50	124.50	180.00	*	....	....	....
1935	92.50	97.00	134.50	184.50	....	....	....
1936	89.95	96.50	129.50	169.50	....	....	....
1937	79.50	94.85	129.50	152.50	....	....	....
1938	79.50	91.85	128.50	147.75	....	....	....
1939	76.50	90.00	128.50	139.50	....	....	....
1940	77.50	89.50	128.50	149.50	....	....	....
1941	....	....	142.00†	166.00†	....	....	....
1948	....	....	....	....	214.95	288.95	289.95
1949	....	....	....	....	174.00	230.75	256.75
1950	....	....	....	....	174.00	226.00	280.00
1951	....	....	....	....	176.00	240.30	263.00
1952	....	....	....	....	181.00	244.75	294.00
1953	....	....	....	....	184.00	200.00	317.00
1954	....	....	....	....	155.00	300.00‡	385.00‡
1955	....	....	....	....	150.00	300.00	350.00

* Unavailable, weights adjusted.
  † Elaborate models used for comparison with comparable standard 1948 models.
  ‡ Model change.

TABLE A4

PRICE INDEXES I AND II

Year	Price Index I	Price Index II
1931............	100.0	100.0
1932............	75.6	96.1
1933............	65.0	90.6
1934............	62.6	77.4
1935............	54.5	68.0
1936............	53.5	66.3
1937............	50.0	61.6
1938............	49.3	60.1
1939............	47.4	57.7
1940............	47.8	58.2
1941............	45.0	60.5
1948............	68.5	95.6
1949............	57.8	85.2
1950............	55.9	83.4
1951............	56.3	84.3
1952............	55.6	83.8
1953............	54.6	77.6
1954............	51.7	72.6
1955............	49.0	68.8

TABLE A5

TABLE A6 TRANSFORMED TO A 1939 BASE
(1939 = 100)

Year	Price Index I	Price Index II
1931............	211.1	173.1
1932............	159.6	166.3
1933............	139.1	156.8
1934............	132.1	134.0
1935............	115.0	117.7
1936............	112.9	114.8
1937............	105.5	106.7
1938............	104.0	104.1
1939............	100.0	100.0
1940............	100.8	100.9
1941............	96.8	104.9
1948............	144.5	165.8
1949............	121.9	147.8
1950............	117.9	144.7
1951............	118.7	146.3
1952............	117.2	145.4
1953............	115.1	134.6
1954............	109.0	125.9
1955............	103.3	119.3

The freezer value series is found in Table A2. We are now in a position to deflate the elements of column (4) (total value) (remembering that these include the corresponding freezer values from Table A2), by the undeflated "refrigerator cost-of-living index" of Table A4. When the resulting numbers are indexed, Table A8 is derived.

TABLE A6*

IMPLICIT GNP DEFLATOR AND PRICE INDEXES I AND
II, DEFLATED†

Year	GNP Deflator	Price Index I, Deflated	Price Index II, Deflated
1931........	101.9	98.1	98.1
1932........	91.7	82.4	104.8
1933........	91.2	72.3	99.5
1934........	96.8	64.7	80.0
1935........	95.8	56.9	70.5
1936........	98.1	54.6	67.5
1937........	100.0	50.0	61.6
1938........	98.6	50.0	61.0
1939........	97.8	48.4	59.0
1940........	99.0	48.3	59.0
1941........	107.3	42.8	56.5
1948........	178.2	38.5	53.5
1949........	180.1	32.1	47.4
1950........	181.9	30.8	45.7
1951........	195.9	28.8	43.0
1952........	198.6	28.0	42.0
1953........	201.0	27.5	38.7
1954........	202.6	25.9	35.4
1955........	205.1	23.9	33.6

* Sources: Sears mail-order catalogues; *Electrical Merchandising* market issues; National Electrical Manufacturers Association; *National Income Supplement to the Survey of Current Business, 1954; Economic Report of the President, 1957;* and Sears, Roebuck and Company.

† The Bureau of Labor Statistics has computed a price index for refrigerators over the period 1935–52 (Bull. 1165), June, 1954. I have extended this index to cover 1954 with the aid of Bull. 1182, June, 1955. As shown in Chart VII, there is close correspondence between this index and my own. There follows comparison of the BLS Index with P I P II, all undeflated.

Year	BLS Index (1935–39 = 100)	Price Index I (1939 = 100)	Price Index II (1939 = 100)
1935.....	97.0	115.0	117.1
1939.....	101.8	100.0	100.0
1941.....	89.3	96.8	104.9
1948.....	150.6	144.5	165.8
1949.....	145.9	121.9	147.8
1950.....	142.7	117.9	144.7
1951.....	150.2	118.7	146.3
1952.....	144.9	117.2	145.4
1953.....	144.0	115.1	134.6
1954.....	130.0	109.0	125.9

Originally, the BLS priced a 6–7 cubic foot box. Some time before June 1952, it priced a box of 8–9.7 cubic feet with an across-the-top freezer.

CHART VII

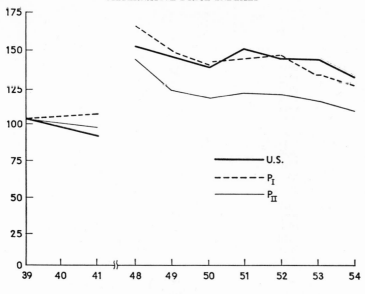

TABLE A7*

NUMBER OF REFRIGERATORS SOLD, SEARS AVERAGE PRICE (REFRIGERATORS), AND VALUE OF MANUFACTURERS' SALES FOR REFRIGERATORS AND FREEZERS†

Year	No. of Refrigerators Sold	Sears Average Price (Refrigerators)	Total Value of Sales of Refrigerators and Freezers
1931...........	949,000	$200.00	$ 189,800,000
1932...........	770,000	151.00	116,270,000
1933...........	1,065,000	132.00	140,580,000
1934...........	1,373,000	133.00	182,609,000
1935...........	1,590,000	125.00	198,750,000
1936...........	2,080,000	129.00	268,320,000
1937...........	2,369,000	132.00	312,708,000
1938...........	1,279,000	135.00	172,665,000
1939...........	1,800,000	129.00	232,200,000
1940...........	2,600,000	124.00	322,400,000
1941...........	3,373,000	131.00	441,863,000
1946...........	2,100,000	193.00	479,850,000
1947...........	3,400,000	264.00	1,105,802,000
1948...........	4,495,000	276.00	1,475,910,000
1949...........	4,284,000	238.00	1,174,792,000
1950...........	6,020,000	222.00	1,585,640,000
1951...........	3,731,000	226.00	1,154,006,000
1952...........	3,195,000	248.00	1,159,762,000
1953...........	3,650,000	265.00	1,397,800,000
1954...........	3,425,000	252.00	1,186,800,000
1955...........	3,825,000	250.00	1,291,750,000

* Sources: *Electrical Merchandising* and Sears, Roebuck and Company.

† The Sears average prices for 1931–34 had to be approximated. A factor of 0.78 was applied to suggested list prices for these years, this factor being estimated from the relationship of Sears to suggested list prices in the 1935–40 period.

135

TABLE A8*

Manufacturers' Sales Indexes

Year	Index I	Index II
1931.........	100.0	100.0
1932.........	83.1	69.3
1933.........	112.1	81.5
1934.........	150.7	122.0
1935.........	201.2	161.2
1936.........	276.0	223.2
1937.........	345.2	280.1
1938.........	193.4	258.7
1939.........	270.6	222.0
1940.........	372.5	305.8
1941.........	532.1	403.2
1946.........	513.7	267.3
1947.........	844.1	600.3
1948.........	1,177.0	852.6
1949.........	1,129.3	760.8
1950.........	1,604.5	1,075.7
1951.........	1,196.3	755.3
1952.........	1,206.3	764.0
1953.........	1,464.3	994.2
1954.........	1,339.0	953.4
1955.........	1,573.8	1,120.8

* Sources: This table is based on preceding tables. Thus Index I is derived by adding freezer value to the last column of Table A6 and deflating by Price Index I, Table A4. In Sales Index II, we deflate by Price Index II, Table A4.

TABLE A9*

Inventories at Distributor Level, Refrigerators Only, End of Year

Year	No. of Units in Inventory	First Differences (Nearest 000's)
1935.........	53,948	....
1936.........	103,851	50,000
1937.........	158,537	55,000
1938.........	51,163	−107,000
1939.........	75,707	7,000
1940.........	73,405	15,000
1941.........	71,024	− 2,000
1946.........	47,320	....
1947.........	54,645	7,000
1948.........	223,058	168,000
1949.........	215,015	− 8,000
1950.........	359,570	144,000
1951.........	478,912	119,000
1952.........	334,033	−145,000
1953.........	308,094	− 22,000
1954.........	288,875	− 21,000
1955.........	361,694	73,000

* Source: National Electrical Manufacturers Association.

136

TABLE A10*

EXPORTS OF HOME FREEZERS, UNITED STATES

Year	No. of Freezers Exported	Percentage of Nominal Sales Exported
1946–50	0	0
1951	33,734	3.2
1952	21,776	1.9
1953	40,193	3.7
1954	31,978	3.3
1955	52,189	4.7

* Source: *Electrical Merchandising.*

TABLE A11

UNITED STATES STOCKS OF REFRIGERATION (INCLUDING FREEZERS) WITH ALTERNATIVE DEPRECIATION ASSUMPTIONS*

(*Not* Per Capita)

Year	$K = 0.25$	$K = 0.20$	$K = 0.10$
1931	247	269	322
1932	268	298	373
1933	313	350	447
1934	386	431	553
1935	490	546	699
1936	644	713	906
1937	828	916	1,160
1938	815	926	1,238
1939	882	1,011	1,385
1940	1,034	1,182	1,618
1941	1,307	1,477	1,988
1942	981	1,182	1,790
1943	736	946	1,611
1944	552	756	1,450
1945	415	605	1,305
1946	734	909	1,600
1947	1,239	1,413	2,126
1948	1,928	2,130	2,913
1949	2,420	2,678	3,595
1950	3,134	3,461	4,555
1951	3,177	3,595	4,925
1952	3,170	3,663	5,220
1953	3,356	3,909	5,677
1954	3,438	4,048	6,030
1955	3,658	4,317	6,505

* Based on Price Index I.

Questions might arise as to the extent to which exports and changes in inventories might affect the accuracy of the results. Tables A9 and A10 have been constructed to answer these queries. First, some brief comment. The data shown in Table A7 are for sales (manufacturers'). As a result, the sometimes substantial inventory changes at the manufacturers' level do not distort our data. On the other hand, there are no data for the retail level. The coverage of Table A9 is at least 50 per cent; that for Table A10, almost 100 per cent. Referigerator sales data were net of exports. Table A10 shows freezer exports. It becomes clear that changes in inventory and exports have little significance with respect to distortion of the manufacturers' sales index.

TABLE A12*

MID-YEAR CIVILIAN POPULATION, PER CAPITA STOCKS RE-
FRIGERATION (INCLUDING FREEZERS), WITH ALTERNATIVE
DEPRECIATION ASSUMPTIONS, PRICE INDEX I

YEAR	MID-YEAR POPULATION	STOCK	
		$K = 0.25$	$K = 0.10$
1931	124.1	198.8	259.2
1932	124.9	214.7	297.6
1933	125.7	249.2	356.0
1934	126.5	303.3	437.5
1935	127.4	385.0	548.9
1936	128.2	502.7	706.7
1937	129.0	642.2	899.6
1938	130.0	626.1	952.1
1939	131.0	673.6	1,056.9
1940	132.1	783.0	1,225.2
1941	133.4	980.4	1,490.6
1942	134.9	727.2	1,326.8
1943	136.7	538.4	1,178.4
1944	138.4	398.8	1,047.5
1945	139.9	296.6	932.6
1946	141.4	519.0	1,193.8
1947	144.1	859.8	1,640.0
1948	146.6	1,351.1	2,253.7
1949	149.2	1,899.9	2,749.9
1950	151.7	2,459.1	3,491.8
1951	154.4	2,586.9	3,862.5
1952	157.0	2,676.4	4,187.0
1953	159.7	2,897.5	4,633.1
1954	162.4	2,956.1	4,914.7
1955	165.2	3,132.2	5,300.9

* Sources: As above and *Economic Report of the President, 1957* (civilian population).

c) THE STOCK (CONSUMPTION-OF-SERVICES) SERIES

Since the purpose of Table A11 and Chart I is to show the influence of alternative depreciation rate assumptions on the stock series, these are not on a per capita basis. Table A11 shows United States stocks of refrigeration.

Another issue arises here. How was stock for 1931 computed? This computation had to follow the assumption that suggested list prices were equal to actual prices and that the model mix remained essentially unchanged over the 1922–30 period. Fortunately, since per capita stock has increased enormously over the 1931–55 period, it is obvious that the error involved in this approximation will account for but a tiny part of the variance of the stock series. Using the notation S_{31} for stock in 1931

TABLE A13

PER CAPITA STOCKS, ALTERNATIVE DEPRECIATION
RATES, PRICE INDEX II

YEAR	STOCK		
	$K = 0.20$	$K = 0.25$	$K = 0.10$
1931.......	216.4	198.8	259.2
1932.......	238.5	203.6	287.2
1933.......	278.8	216.6	321.7
1934.......	340.8	257.8	384.1
1935.......	428.6	318.5	469.8
1936.......	556.6	411.5	594.3
1937.......	710.0	523.9	748.7
1938.......	712.4	511.9	790.7
1939.......	772.1	550.5	875.7
1940.......	894.5	640.9	1,013.1
1941.......	1,107.5	778.3	1,205.1
1942.......	876.1	577.5	1,072.6
1943.......	691.7	427.2	952.4
1944.......	546.5	316.5	846.8
1945.......	432.5	235.2	754.1
1946.......	527.9	362.8	868.4
1947.......	830.1	684.0	1,184.7
1948.......	1,234.9	1,085.8	1,629.6
1949.......	1,480.7	1,310.1	1,951.0
1950.......	1,874.0	1,675.5	2,436.1
1951.......	1,962.2	1,723.8	2,643.3
1952.......	2,030.6	1,758.1	2,826.2
1953.......	2,219.2	1,918.8	3,123.1
1954.......	2,332.8	2,002.2	3,351.1
1955.......	2,513.2	2,154.6	3,643.3

and x_t for sales in year t, and k for the depreciation rate, the formula for 1931 stock becomes

$$S_{31} = (1 - k)^9 x_{22} + (1 - k)^8 x_{23} + \ldots + (1 - k) x_{30} + x_{31} .$$

From this point on, the simple $S = (1 - k)S_{t-1} + x_t$ formula becomes operative. The regression variable is S^*, stock per capita, using mid-year population as the deflator. Of course, all data are cast into logs for regression purposes.

TABLE A14

PER CAPITA CONSUMPTION OF SERVICES, AL-
TERNATIVE STRAIGHT-LINE DEPRECIATION
ASSUMPTIONS, PRICE INDEX I

Year	Ten-Year Assumption	Fifteen-Year Assumption
1931.........	31.6	20.8
1932.........	37.9	25.1
1933.........	46.4	31.7
1934.........	57.5	39.4
1935.........	72.3	49.3
1936.........	91.3	63.0
1937.........	114.3	80.5
1938.........	124.3	89.8
1939.........	138.8	102.6
1940.........	159.3	120.2
1941.........	190.2	143.9
1948.........	253.1	220.3
1949.........	306.2	260.1
1950.........	382.3	317.7
1951.........	418.7	352.3
1952.........	488.5	382.8
1953.........	571.9	429.6
1954.........	644.9	466.1
1955.........	729.2	506.7

d) THE INCOME SERIES

Table A15 gives the income series used in the time-series regressions. Disposable income per capita is obtained by deflating the series provided by the United States Department of Commerce by the implicit Gross National Product Deflator. Professor Phillip Cagan provided the weights used in calculating expected income, Professor Milton Friedman's empirical approximation to his permanent-income concept. Current income is weighted by the factor 0.33, and the remaining weights, "moving backward," are 0.211, 0.148, 0.099, 0.067, 0.045, 0.030, 0.020, and 0.013. Chow reports the expected income per capita calculations on page 32 of his book, *The Demand for Automobiles in the United States*. Chow converted the current dollar data supplied him into real dollars in terms of the GNP Deflator, and, since these data extended only to 1953, the present writer extended the series through 1955. Thus column (3), Table A15, is real expected income per capita in the United States.

e) PRICE INDEX NUMBERS FOR 1942-44

Table A16 sets out price indexes calculated on the basis of alternative assumptions described in the text.

II. THE CROSS-SECTION VARIABLES

a) CONVERSION FACTORS

The conversion factor for year t in A17 is constructed by dividing Sears' average realization for t by $P_I(t)$, where $P_I(t)$ is given by Price Index I, Table A4. The use of these factors permits conversion of the crude annual sales data (organized by states) into rates of sales of "stored" refrigeration service (cf. pp. 123–24 above).

TABLE A15*

REAL DISPOSABLE AND EXPECTED INCOME
PER CAPITA, UNITED STATES†

Year (1)	Disposable Income (2)	Expected Income (3)
1931	498.2	546.3
1932	417.4	511.0
1933	394.3	483.8
1934	421.4	511.3
1935	475.2	532.8
1936	525.6	534.1
1937	551.2	532.8
1938	511.0	534.1
1939	547.9	547.8
1940	578.8	567.5
1941	642.7	611.6
1942	719.1	623.9
1943	741.6	636.6
1944	798.0	649.4
1948	721.2	727.1
1949	696.7	730.2
1950	745.8	751.2
1951	743.9	762.8
1952	753.7	773.8
1953	772.3	787.7
1954	775.0	800.0
1955	804.5	815.0

* Sources: *National Income Supplement, Survey of Current Business, 1954; Economic Report of the President, 1957;* and Gregory C. Chow, *Demand for Automobiles in the United States* (Amsterdam, 1957).

† Those who might use these data should take heed of the following further adjustment. Chow, although he does not so indicate, augmented the real expected income per capita variable by a factor of 0.10 in order that the means of the disposable and expected income series be equal, this for technical reasons. I have followed this practice so that this table is equivalent to Chow's Table 1 (*op. cit.*, p. 32).

b) DATA ORGANIZED BY STATES

The following observations might be offered before presentation of Table A18.

1. All cross-sectional variables were ultimately cast into logs except for Regressions XXIX and XXX, as has been noted.
2. The GNP Deflator, as used in deriving the income variable in Table A18, had a 1947 base.
3. In comparing columns (2) and (3) in Table A18 ("refrigeration" vis-à-vis "freezers"), note that these columns have entirely different derivations, as described above. These columns should *not* be compared horizontally.

TABLE A16*

PRICE-INDEX NUMBERS FOR 1942–44, CHAIN LINKED TO
DEFLATED PRICE INDEX NUMBER FOR 1941 (42.8)

YEAR	ASSUMPTION I		ASSUMPTION II	
	$K = 0.10$	$K = 0.20$	$K = 0.10$	$K = 0.20$
1942.........	58.7	85.6	52.2	58.8
1943.........	71.0	114.0	63.3	75.5
1944.........	86.3	157.5	77.0	109.8

* Source: Want-ad sections of *Chicago Tribune, Chicago Sun, Evanston Review,* and *New York Times.*

TABLE A17

CONVERSION FACTORS (r/P), BASED ON
PRICE INDEX I, 1939–54

YEAR	FACTOR	
	Refrigerators	Freezers
1939............	2.72	....
1940............	2.59	....
1941............	2.85	....
1946............	2.76	....
1947............	3.71	....
1948............	4.03	4.67
1949............	4.11	5.80
1950............	3.97	5.00
1951............	4.01	5.24
1952............	4.46	5.79
1953............	4.85	6.40
1954............	4.87	6.34

TABLE A18

PER CAPITA STOCK OF REFRIGERATION INCLUDING FREEZERS; 1954 PER CAPITA
STOCK, FREEZERS ONLY; 1954 "EXPECTED INCOME"; URBANIZATION,
1950; AND MEAN TEMPERATURE, 1954; BY STATES, 1954

State (1)	Refrigeration (2)	Freezers (3)	Real "Expected Income" (4)	Urban (5)	Mean Temperature (° F.) (6)
Maine............	0.5029	0.0329	1186	0.517	44.5
New Hampshire.....	.4852	.0289	1262	.575	44.8
Massachusetts......	.4477	.0180	1538	.844	50.7
Vermont...........	.4088	.0299	1124	.364	44.5
Rhode Island.......	.7588	.0193	1476	.843	51.4
Connecticut........	.5452	.0287	1875	.776	49.7
New York..........	.5833	.0228	1727	.855	50.0
New Jersey.........	.5503	.0245	1743	.866	44.8
Pennsylvania.......	.5289	.0328	1466	.705	54.7
Ohio..............	.5948	.0443	1580	.702	52.7
Indiana...........	.6319	.0512	1468	.599	54.4
Illinois............	.5425	.0364	1720	.776	50.5
Michigan..........	.5706	.0319	1612	.707	48.1
Wisconsin.........	.4990	.0437	1389	.579	47.7
Minnesota.........	.5393	.0505	1303	.545	43.4
Iowa..............	.5619	.0677	1307	.477	50.9
Missouri..........	.7045	.0528	1376	.613	56.5
North Dakota......	.7849	.1064	1017	.266	41.7
South Dakota.......	.7439	.0972	1088	.322	45.8
Nebraska..........	.8011	.0924	1304	.469	51.6
Kansas............	.5305	.0483	1333	.521	57.0
Delaware..........	.6225	.0395	1915	.626	54.2
Maryland.........	.5122	.0295	1537	.690	57.1
Virginia...........	.4630	.0294	1168	.470	59.6
West Virginia......	.5605	.0355	1021	.346	55.8
North Carolina.....	.5347	.0385	945	.337	56.9
South Carolina......	.4609	.0312	981	.367	64.4
Georgia...........	.5758	.0381	985	.453	62.0
Florida............	.7445	.0344	1244	.655	72.3
Kentucky..........	.4925	.0309	964	.368	57.3
Tennessee.........	.6288	.0390	953	.441	62.4
Alabama...........	.4949	.0312	867	.438	68.1
Mississippi........	.5273	.0409	694	.279	65.4
Arkansas..........	.6263	.0472	780	.330	62.4
Louisiana..........	.6341	.0552	1027	.548	70.4
Oklahoma.........	.6301	.0459	1132	.510	61.0
Texas.............	.6274	.0513	1246	.627	66.5
Montana..........	.6546	.0859	1427	.437	38.3
Idaho.............	.5229	.0645	1195	.429	50.8
Wyoming..........	.5812	.0705	1487	.498	44.9
Colorado..........	.6598	.0594	1397	.627	51.4
New Mexico........	.4466	.0400	1100	.502	56.6
Arizona...........	.5375	.0376	1277	.555	70.5
Utah..............	.6096	.0686	1203	.653	51.3
Nevada............	.8399	.0713	1893	.572	49.5
Washington........	.4939	.0397	1561	.632	50.1
Oregon............	.6631	.0602	1456	.539	54.6
California.........	0.5573	0.0346	1741	0.807	60.7

c) DATA ORGANIZED BY FAMILIES

1. *Stocks.*—The Survey Research Center of the University of Michigan data contain five income categories (according to spending units) which are interesting to us. They reveal what percentage of spending units within a given category bought their machines new and what per-

CHART VIII

REFRIGERATOR STOCK HOLDINGS BY INCOME CATEGORY
UNITED STATES AND REGIONS, 1952

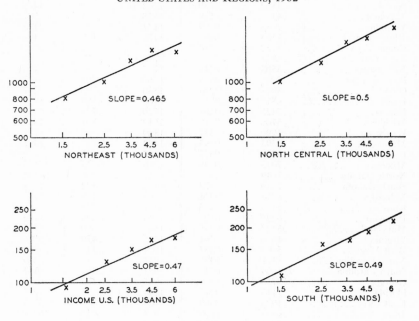

CHART IX

AVERAGE REFRIGERATOR PRICE PAID BY INCOME CATEGORY, 1941

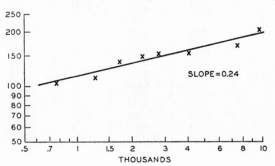

centage bought them used; in what year the machine was purchased if new and, if used, whether the machine was acquired before or after World War II; and what percentage owns no refrigerator at all. Table A19 gives the results of the computations described in the text. The data of Table A19 are shown in double-log form in Charts VIII and IX.

TABLE A19*

INDEX NUMBERS OF REFRIGERATOR STOCK HOLDINGS BY INCOME
CATEGORIES CLASSIFIED REGIONALLY (SPENDING UNITS),
1952, ADJUSTED FOR QUALITY†

	$1,000– $1,999	$2,000– $2,999	$3,000– $3,999	$4,000– $4,999	$5,000– $7,4999
United States......	93.7	131.4	153.7	172.6	177.3
Northeast region...	81.9	100.6	132.0	151.8	149.7
North-central region	100.6	130.2	166.3	183.8	200.1
South............	107.9	159.8	170.8	185.4	216.9
Western..........	62.1	135.2	128.6	168.8	179.6

* Source: Survey Research Center, University of Michigan Adjustments based on Table A18.

† 2,820 cases included in the first ("United States") row, 788 in the second row, 1,051 in the third, 623 in the fourth, and 358 in the fifth.

TABLE A20

AVERAGE EXPENDITURE PER REFRIGERATOR BY BUDGET
CATEGORY, 1941 PURCHASES

Budget Category	Average Expenditure	Budget Category	Average Expenditure
Under $500..........	$102.00	$2,500– $3,000.....	$147.75
$ 500–$1,000........	107.50	$3,000– $5,000.....	159.92
$1,000–$1,500........	114.30	$5,000–$10,000.....	170.71
$1,500–$2,000........	137.67	Over $10,000.......	210.60
$2,000–$2,500........	148.80		

2. *Average prices paid.*—The Bureau of Labor Statistics gives the number of electric refrigerators purchased in 1941 per 100 families at various income levels. It also gives total expenditure on electric refrigerators in 1941 per 100 families similarly classified. Thus, by dividing the total expenditures by the number of machines purchased, we are able to obtain average expenditure per machine by budget category, this with reference to *new* machines purchased. The result is Table A20.

IV

Statistical Demand Functions for Automobiles and Their Use for Forecasting

GREGORY C. CHOW

Statistical Demand Functions for Automobiles and Their Use for Forecasting[1]

In this paper I attempt to assess the principal findings of my *Demand for Automobiles in the United States*[2] in the light of four years' additional data. Section I summarizes the theoretical framework, and Section II gives the main results of this earlier study. Section III tests the consistency of these results with new evidence, while Section IV presents some tentative forecasts of future automobile demand.

I. Theoretical Framework

LONG-RUN DEMAND FOR AUTOMOBILE STOCK

A salient feature of the demand for consumer durables in general, and for automobiles in particular, is that annual purchase is only a part of the total stock available for the satisfaction of wants. Purchase is made primarily to fill the gap between the quantity of total stock desired and the quantity of old stock remaining from the preceding period. In order to explain the demand for purchase, therefore, the demand for desired stock will be first explained. By "desired stock" is meant that level of ownership which actual ownership will approach in the course of time, given that the determining variables remain unchanged.

A difficulty immediately presents itself in obtaining an empirical definition of the stock of automobiles. There are old and new cars and, in any model year, expensive and cheap cars. The wide range of prices for which different makes and ages of cars sell at any one time is itself evidence that the buying public does not consider them all to be equivalent.

In this study the stock of cars was expressed in terms of new-car equivalents, older cars being considered as equivalent to half a new car if their price was half that of new cars, etc. The weights used in converting old cars into new-car equivalents were the relative prices of cars of different ages in 1937. The relative price structure of cars according to age changed remarkably little over the period of the study. The prices of

[1] Support from the Alfred P. Sloan Research Fund of the School of Industrial Management at the Massachusetts Institute of Technology is gratefully acknowledged. The assistance of Thomas C. Thomas has been valuable.

[2] Gregory C. Chow, *Demand for Automobiles in the United States: A Study in Consumer Durables* (Amsterdam: North-Holland Publishing Co., 1957).

149

various ages of cars in any one year were approximated very well by the assumption of a constant percentage rate of depreciation, which is between 22 and 24 per cent for nineteen of the thirty-three years considered, between 21 and 25 per cent for twenty-five of the thirty-three years, and which is in no case less than 19 or more than 30 per cent.[3] The 1937 rate of depreciation was 23 per cent—the median rate for the whole period. Thus we did not have to be concerned with the common index-number problems of changing or unrepresentative weights.

I believe that much misunderstanding of the automobile market has come from the tendency to "count cars." The evidence just cited is strong that the market does not consider all cars to be equivalent and that its preferences as among cars of different ages are remarkably stable over time. This evidence suggests that it is much more meaningful to talk in terms of, say, 25 million new-car equivalents rather than in terms of 55 million cars on the road.

One point should be noted, however. Since our stock data were expressed in terms of new-car equivalents, they do not contain any adjustment for the secular improvement in the quality of automobiles. Had such an adjustment been made, the series on automobile stocks and on new purchases would have shown a greater secular increase, and the series on relative price would have shown a lower secular increase or, more probably, a secular decline. Rather than become involved in the extremely difficult task of making a quality adjustment directly in the data, the alternative course was pursued of including a trend variable as an additional "test variable" in the estimation of the income and price elasticities of demand, net of trendwise movements in the variables, and accordingly "adjusted" for any trendwise change in quality (see eq. [1et] below).

The price data themselves were based on used-car price quotations in newspaper advertisements. "New-car" prices were not used, because of the fact that during the period of the study the relationships between list prices and actual prices paid by purchasers varied greatly. For our purpose the "new-car" price was the price in the used-car market of cars of the current model year. Our series of prices based on used-car quotations is closely similar to the price series of the National Automobile Dealers Association as far back as 1934, but it appears to be more accurate than series derived from other sources for the period prior to 1934.[4]

The stock of automobiles, expressed in terms of the relative prices of cars of different ages, does not necessarily indicate the service yield obtained in any given year. The service yield is measured by the price con-

---

[3] These percentage rates of depreciation can be derived from the average prices of automobiles, classified by age (*ibid.*, pp. 102–3).

[4] *Ibid.*, p. 31.

sumers are paying for the use of their cars for a year, that is, by the amount by which their cars depreciate plus the interest foregone by holding their capital in the form of cars. When automobiles depreciate at a constant rate per annum, the price paid for the use of the stock of cars for a year is proportional to the value of the stock itself. For the years considered in this study, it has hovered in the neighborhood of 30 per cent of the value of the stock.[5] We shall here neglect the relatively small variations which occurred in this fraction and treat "consumption" of automobile services as strictly proportional to the stock, and we shall use the terms "demand for stock" and "consumption demand" interchangeably.

The desired stock of automobiles is taken to depend principally on relative price and real income. Let the desired stock of automobiles $\dot{X}_{jt}$ of the jth consumer in year t be a linear function of the relative price of automobiles to the jth consumer and his real income in year t:

$$\dot{X}_{jt} = a_{jt} + b_{jt}P_{jt} + c_{jt}I_{jt},$$

where the intercept a_{jt} is affected both by the taste of the jth individual and by the variables not taken into account, especially the relative prices of complements and substitutes, at year t. For a given year t, there will be a frequency distribution of each of the five variables, a_{jt}, b_{jt}, P_{jt}, c_{jt}, and I_{jt}, for the group of individuals. Their means are denoted, respectively, by a_t, b_t, P_t, c_t, and I_t. Taking expectations over j on both sides of the above equation, we have $\dot{X}_t = a_t + E(b_{jt}P_{jt}) + E(c_{jt}I_{jt})$. Under the assumptions that b_{jt} and P_{jt} are statistically independent and that c_{jt} and I_{jt} are also statistically independent, the mean demand for desired stock becomes

$$\dot{X}_t = a_t + b_tP_t + c_tI_t.$$

It is further assumed that the mean effects of price and income, namely, b_t and c_t, remain constant through time; thus the t subscripts for these two coefficients can be dropped. We propose to break up a_t into two parts, the average for the period of study a and a random element u_t which summarizes the combined effect of the variables left out. The mean demand for desired stock can now be written as a linear function of mean price and mean income with coefficients independent of time:

$$\dot{X}_t = a + bP_t + cI_t + u_t.$$

[5] The price paid for the use of a car may be defined to include license fees, gasoline, oil, tire, and repair costs, in addition to interest and depreciation, but need not be so defined. Under our more restricted definition, licenses, gasoline, etc., are considered as complementary products, whose prices, relative to the general price level, are assumed in our empirical analysis to have moved in a fashion not highly correlated with the relative price of cars.

Note that we have avoided the problem of changes in the distribution of income by the assumption that c_{jt} is statistically independent of I_{jt}. This assumption implies that the mean of the product of these two variables is the product of their means. A similar aggregation procedure can be applied to demand functions linear in the logarithms of the variables.

We decided to work with a per capita demand function rather than a per family demand function because of the apparent weaknesses of the latter. Assume that both families A and B have the same income and that A has only half as many members as B. Assume also that the other variables affecting demand are identical for the two families. If a per family demand function is employed, A and B should have the same desired automobile ownership. On the other hand, according to a per capita demand function, B's per capita income is only half of A's, and B's per capita demand will be less than one-half of, or B's family demand will be less than, A's, given that income elasticity is higher than unity. The implication of the per capita demand function seems closer to the truth insofar as family B tends to spend more on food and clothing for its members. The same point can be extended to the whole economy. Assuming both national income and the number of families to remain the same, we would predict the same demand for automobile ownership using a per family demand function irrespective of any increase in population. Assuming both national income and population to remain unchanged, we would, using the same demand function with income elasticity higher than unity, predict a *decline* in automobile ownership to follow an *increase* in the number of families—when the number of families increases, income per family declines and demand per family declines proportionally more. These considerations suggest a per capita demand function for desired stock to be the better alternative.

DEMAND FOR ANNUAL PURCHASE UNDER ASSUMPTION OF INSTANTANEOUS ADJUSTMENT

We have proposed to explain the desired stock of automobiles (in equivalent units) per capita by the relative price P of automobiles and real income per capita I. If the desired stock were achieved all the time, purchase per capita during a year would simply be the difference between desired stock per capita at the end of the year and the depreciated old stock per capita from the preceding year. The latter will be assumed to be a fraction k of the per capita stock one year earlier. Not only is k the result mostly of annual depreciation but also it takes into account the effects of scrappage and of the change in population, since it is the ratio of old stock per capita at the end of the year to the entire per capita stock at the beginning of the year. However, numerically, k has been very close to 0.75 because the effect of scrappage has been slight as compared to the effect of depreciation measured by price decline and because the ratio of year-end population to beginning-of-year population has been practically unity.

Purchase of an automobile by a consumer can take the form of trading in a used car for a newer one. Annual purchase of the economy is the sum of individual purchases and, after aggregation, will equal to the number of new cars bought during the year provided that there is no net inflow from or outflow to the stocks in the hands of the dealers. Let new purchase per capita in year t be X_t^1, desired stock per capita at the end of year t be $\dot{X}_t$, and total stock per capita at the end of year $t - 1$ be X_{t-1}. Under the assumption that automobile stock is instantaneously adjusted to its desired level as governed by price and income, annual purchase per capita will be

$$X_t^1 = \dot{X}_t(P_t, I_t, u_t) - kX_{t-1},$$

where u_t, as we have defined it, is a combination of all variables other than price and income that affect the demand for desired stock. This demand function can alternatively be written as

$$X_t^1 = (\dot{X}_t - X_{t-1}) + (1 - k)X_{t-1},$$

breaking up annual purchase into two parts. The first, $\dot{X}_t - X_{t-1}$, is the demand for desired change in stock during the year; the second, $(1 - k)X_{t-1}$, is the demand for replacement of old stock.

When existing stock is adjusted to the desired level instantaneously, the time path of annual purchase generated by a single and permanent shift in the demand for desired stock is illustrated by the following example. This example will be simplified by the assumption of a constant population so that we may refer to either per capita demand or total demand of the economy. Here the rate of depreciation (including scrappage) is taken to be 0.25. Start with Year 1, when total stock is 100 and purchase is 25. Let desired stock in Year 2 be shifted to 110. Such a shift requires the purchase of 35—25 for replacement and 10 to meet the desired change in stock. In the third year, with desired stock still at 110 and depreciated stock from the second year at 0.75 of 110, or 82.5, purchase will be 27.5. An annual purchase of 27.5 will be continued as long as desired stock remains at 110. Two points regarding the effect of a shift in desired ownership on the demand for purchase are illustrated by this example. In the short run, or the second year in our example, a 10 per cent change in desired stock can generate a 40 per cent change in purchase—an increase of 10 units in purchase from the original 25 units. However, in the long run when equilibrium is again reached, the percentage change in purchase (2.5 units of the original 25 units) will be the same as the percentage change in desired stock. Thus the short-run elasticities of demand for purchase will be four times as high as the long-run elasticities of demand for desired ownership under the assumptions that adjustment is instantaneous and that the annual rate of depreciation is 25 per cent. On the other hand, the long-run elasticities of demand for purchase will be the same as the long-run elasticities of demand for desired ownership.

DEMAND FOR ANNUAL PURCHASE WITH TIME LAG

In the above numerical example annual purchases show a time path of 25, 35, 27.5, 27.5, . . . , in successive years as a result of a 10 per cent shift in desired stock. This path showing a sharp jump in the year of the shift and a large drop in the year immediately afterward may appear unreasonable. Why does the adjustment of existing stock to the desired level have to be accomplished in one year? As a matter of fact, there are reasons to the contrary, the most important one being the cost of buying and selling automobiles. If this model of the individual consumer were valid, he would be observed to buy and sell automobiles frequently in response to any changes in price and income. With a positive cost of transaction, the individual may not change his automobile stock at once even if it is somewhat different from his desired ownership. In the aggregate only a fraction c of the desired change in ownership will be assumed to take place in one year, and our theory of demand for purchase will be accordingly modified.

Our previous demand function is

$$X_t^1 = \dot{X}_t(P_t, I_t, u_t) - kX_{t-1},$$

which can also be separated into demand for change in stock and demand for replacement

$$X_t^1 = [\dot{X}_t(P_t, I_t, u_t) - X_{t-1}] + (1 - k)X_{t-1}.$$

If only a fraction c of the desired change in ownership is made during the year, the demand function becomes

$$X_t^1 = c[\dot{X}_t(P_t, I_t, u_t) - X_{t-1}] + (1 - k)X_{t-1}.$$

The adjustment coefficient c is applied to the desired change in stock $\dot{X}_t - X_{t-1}$ rather than the entire purchase $\dot{X}_t - kX_{t-1}$ required to bring existing stock to the desired level, because the latter model would imply an amount purchased in year t, $c[\dot{X}_t - kX_{t-1}]$ insufficient to keep the stock in equilibrium at the end of the year, even if it had been in equilibrium in the beginning of the year. Under our scheme of adjustment purchase will consist of the entire replacement $(1 - k)X_{t-1}$ when there is no desire to change the stock during year t.

By way of a numerical example, we can illustrate the time path of annual purchase resulting from a single shift in desired stock. A rate of depreciation of 0.25 and an adjustment coefficient of .5 due to time lag will be assumed. Again in Year 1, total stock is 100 and purchase is 25. Let desired stock be shifted to 110 in Year 2. The movements of the relevant variables can be summarized:

Year	1	2	3	4	...	∞
Desired stock......	...	110	110	110		110
Change in stock....	...	5	2.5	1.25		0
Actual stock.......	100	105	107.5	108.75		110
Replacement......	...	25	26.25	26.875		27.5
Purchase..........	25	30	28.75	28.125		27.5

Replacement is 25 per cent of actual stock at the end of the preceding year. Purchase can be calculated as the sum of replacement and the change in stock during the year.

Two points concerning the relationship between the elasticities of demand for desired stock and the elasticities of demand for annual purchase are again illustrated by the above example. In the short run (i.e., the year when desired stock is changed), purchase will be changed by 5 units, or 20 per cent, as a result of the 10 per cent change in desired stock. After the incomplete adjustment of existing stock to its desired level is allowed for, the short-run elasticities of demand for purchase are only twice as large as the corresponding elasticities of demand for desired stock. In the long run, purchase will settle down to 27.5 units, or 10 per cent higher than the original amount. The long-run elasticities of demand for purchase are thus identical with the corresponding elasticities of demand for desired stock.

II. Statistical Findings, 1921–53

This section reports on some of the statistical demand functions for automobile stock and for annual purchase in the United States estimated from time-series observations for the period 1921–53 with the theoretical framework set forth above. A more detailed discussion of these functions, as well as demand functions based on alternative hypotheses, can be found elsewhere.[6] The ones chosen here are believed to be more promising for reasons already stated in that reference. They will be confronted with ad-

---

[6] Chow, *op. cit.*

ditional observations not yet available at the time of their estimation and will be used to provide predictions of automobile demand in the long run and in the short run.

We are interested in explaining two variables, automobile stock, X_t (in equivalent units) per capita at the end of the year, and purchase of new automobiles, X_t^1, per capita during the year. The desired level of the former is assumed to be a function of the relative price of automobiles P_t and per capita real income I_t. The latter requires for its explanation another variable, per capita stock at the end of the previous year, X_{t-1}. Table 1 presents observations on these variables. In brief, they are measured as follows.

Variable X_t is a weighted sum of registrations of passenger automobiles in various age groups at the end of year t, divided by population. The weights are proportional to the average prices of automobiles of different ages at the end of 1937, with a one-year-old car (purchased during year t) counting as one unit. Since ownership per capita has been somewhere between 0.04 and 0.13 equivalent units, X_t is recorded in hundredths of a unit, ranging between 4 and 13.

X_t^1 is the number of new automobiles purchased in year t, divided by population, also in hundredths of a unit.

P_t is a price index of automobiles constructed with the stocks at the end of 1937 as weights, divided by the Gross National Product Deflator of the United States Department of Commerce, set equal to 100 for 1937. The prices of automobiles, classified by age, have been obtained from newspaper advertisements at the end of year t.

I_{dt} is per capita disposable personal income of the Department of Commerce, divided by the Gross National Product Deflator, in 1937 dollars.

I_{et} is real "expected income" per capita in 1937 dollars, used by Friedman in *A Theory of the Consumption Function*, defined as a weighted average of past real disposable incomes per capita.[7]

LONG-RUN DEMAND FOR AUTOMOBILE STOCK

Desired stock per capita has been assumed to be a function of the relative price of automobiles as a group, real income per capita, and other variables whose effects are summarized by the variable u_t. It has been pointed out that desired stock may not always be realized because of the time lag in adjustment. However, incomplete adjustment is much more important for the study of annual purchase than for the study of automobile ownership. As first approximations, demand functions for desired

[7] Milton Friedman, *A Theory of the Consumption Function* (Princeton, N.J.: Princeton University Press, 1957).

TABLE 1*

Automobile Stock, Annual Purchase, and Their Determinants, 1921–53

Year	Automobile Stock Per Capita X_t	New Purchase Per Capita X_t^1	Relative Price of Automobiles P_t	Real Disposable Income Per Capita I_{dt}	Real Expected Income Per Capita I_{et}
1920.........	4.677	....	....	....	....
1921.........	4.805	1.354	120.9	407.8	475.2
1922.........	5.426	1.887	111.2	460.4	474.4
1923.........	6.888	2.988	100.6	509.2	493.3
1924.........	7.849	2.776	90.9	509.3	506.6
1925.........	8.418	2.806	81.7	525.6	515.1
1926.........	8.928	2.974	92.6	532.3	528.9
1927.........	8.774	2.273	105.6	543.3	540.3
1928.........	9.130	2.817	91.0	545.1	544.8
1929.........	9.698	3.311	95.1	572.6	563.0
1930.........	9.092	2.153	85.9	525.2	559.3
1931.........	8.106	1.533	102.4	498.2	546.3
1932.........	6.915	.878	107.9	417.4	511.0
1933.........	6.340	1.214	95.6	394.3	483.8
1934.........	6.172	1.524	107.0	421.4	476.0
1935.........	6.530	2.250	105.2	475.2	484.8
1936.........	7.515	2.741	109.3	525.6	511.3
1937.........	8.343	2.719	100.0	551.2	532.8
1938.........	7.786	1.505	109.3	511.0	534.1
1939.........	7.719	2.079	104.9	547.9	547.8
1940.........	8.221	2.622	97.1	578.8	567.5
1941.........	9.178	2.797	120.1	642.7	611.6
1942.........	7.420	....	119.0	719.1	623.9
1943.........	5.790	....	204.7	741.6	636.6
1944.........	4.457	....	356.3	798.0	649.4
1945.........	3.513	....	449.3	787.2	662.5
1946.........	4.057	....	338.6	743.2	707.9
1947.........	5.291	2.198	263.4	696.4	717.4
1948.........	6.101	2.381	236.2	721.2	727.1
1949.........	8.076	3.243	159.7	696.7	730.2
1950.........	10.256	4.170	161.8	745.8	751.2
1951.........	11.463	3.278	161.2	743.9	762.8
1952.........	11.194	2.648	169.6	753.7	773.8
1953.........	12.057	3.594	152.4	772.3	787.7

* Source: Gregory C. Chow, *Demand for Automobiles in the United States* (Amsterdam, 1957), Table 1, p. 32, and Table 2, p. 55. The reader is also referred to the similar sources of Table 2 in Sec. III of the present chapter.

stock are applied to explain actual stock directly. Any differences between the two are supposed to be absorbed by the residual u_t.

We shall first present the statistical demand functions for desired stock
per capita in linear form. They are to serve as the fundamental relationships from which demand functions for annual purchase will be derived.
These functions, both for stock and for purchase, are estimated by the
method of least squares from twenty-eight annual observations in the
period 1921–53, excluding the years 1942–46. For ease of reference they
are numbered in exactly the same way as in my *Demand for Automobiles
in the United States*. Standard errors of the regression coefficients are given
in parentheses. The two measures of income employed are real disposable
personal income per capita of the Department of Commerce and real
expected income per capita used by Friedman to explain total consumption through time. They have been denoted by I_{dt} and I_{et}, respectively.

$$\dot{X}_t = 1.1666 \quad -0.039544P_t \; + \; 0.020827I_{dt} \qquad R^2 = 0.850 \qquad (X1d)$$
$$\phantom{\dot{X}_t = 1.1666 \quad} (0.004522) \qquad (0.001749) \qquad s \;\; = 0.738$$

$$\dot{X}_t = -\,0.7247 \; -0.048802P_t \; + \; 0.025487I_{et} \qquad R^2 = 0.895 \qquad (X1e)$$
$$\phantom{\dot{X}_t = -\,0.7247 \;\;} (0.004201) \qquad (0.001747) \qquad s \;\; = 0.618$$

Price and income have accounted for a very significant portion of the
variance of automobile stock. According to the demand function using
disposable income ($X1d$), price elasticity at mean price 122.8 and mean
per capita stock 8.081 is -0.601; income elasticity at mean income 565.2
and mean stock is 1.46. According to the demand function using expected
income ($X1e$), price elasticity at mean price and mean stock is -0.742;
income elasticity at mean expected income 580.6 and mean stock is 1.83.
Expected income, which has been found by Friedman to be more closely
associated with total consumption than disposable income, has also
turned out to be a better variable for the explanation of automobile stock
from the comparison of the multiple correlation coefficients in the above
demand functions. If disposable income is interpreted as expected income
measured with an error, we can account for the lower income elasticity
estimated from the former. The coefficient of an explanatory variable in a
multiple regression will become smaller when the variable is subject to
error. Error in one explanatory variable will also affect the coefficient of
another variable. This may also account for the difference between the
coefficients of price in the above demand functions.

For the purpose of comparison with these results concerning price and
income elasticities of demand for automobile stock, demand functions
with different functional form, a different dependent variable, and differ-

ent observations were estimated. Linear demand functions in the logarithms of the variables are now assumed. The logarithm of price is
treated as the dependent variable. The years 1942–46 are included, giving
a total of thirty-three annual observations. Using disposable income, we
have

$$\ln P_t = -3.2247 - 0.9014 \ \ln X_t + 1.5564 \ \ln I_{dt} \quad R^2 = 0.898$$
$$\qquad\qquad (0.0875) \qquad\qquad (0.1210) \qquad s \ = 0.146 \qquad (1d)$$

The solution of (1d) for $\ln X_t$ is

$$\ln X_t = -3.5774 - 1.1094 \ \ln P_t + 1.7266 \ \ln I_{dt}$$

Using expected income, we have

$$\ln P_t = -6.6077 - 1.0528 \ \ln X_t + 2.1336 \ \ln I_{et} \quad R^2 = 0.948 \qquad (1e)$$
$$\qquad\qquad (0.0632) \qquad\qquad (0.1133) \qquad s \ = 0.104$$

The solution of (1e) for $\ln X_t$ is

$$\ln X_t = -6.2763 - 0.9498 \ \ln P_t + 2.0266 \ \ln I_{et}$$

Elasticities with respect to disposable income and expected income are
now, respectively, 1.73 and 2.03, as compared with 1.46 and 1.83 obtained
from the linear demand functions. The new estimates of price elasticity,
−1.11 and −0.950, are somewhat higher than the previous estimates
−0.601 and −0.742. The two sets of estimates are different partly because there are two regressions between stock and price, after the effect
of income is netted out. A partial regression of stock on price will give a
lower price elasticity than the corresponding partial regression of price
on stock. It should be pointed out that the war years are included in
estimating the demand functions of constant elasticities. Only when the
ratios between the variables observed do not change violently will the
linear demand functions give similar elasticities to the ones given by the
demand functions linear in logarithms. In 1945, to take the extreme case,
the ratio of price to stock was 449.3 to 3.513, or 127.9, much higher
than the ratio 15.20 between mean price and mean stock for the twenty-
eight years included in the linear regressions. Therefore, in 1945, the price
elasticity according to ($X1e$) would be −6.24. Insofar as the observations
in the war period are consistent with the demand functions of constant
elasticities, they are not consistent with the linear demand functions.

A more rigorous test can be performed in order to choose between disposable income and expected income for inclusion in a demand function
for automobile stock. Hotelling has shown that the partial correlation coefficients between the same dependent variable and two alternative ex-

planatory variables can be compared by "Student's" t distribution.[8] The t ratio for comparing the partial correlation between $\ln P_t$ and $\ln I_{dt}$, given $\ln X_t$, and the partial correlation between $\ln P_t$ and $\ln I_{et}$ is 2.079 with 29 degrees of freedom. The null hypothesis that these two partial correlations are the same would be rejected at the 2.5 per cent level, against the alternative hypothesis that the latter is higher. A trend variable t, which begins at one for 1921 and increases by one in each successive year, is added to the demand function (1e) but fails to yield any significant improvement.

$$\ln P_t = -5.8538 - 1.0480 \ \ln X_t + 2.0074 \ \ln I_{et} + 0.002383 \ t \quad (1et)$$
$$ (0.0645) (0.2563) \phantom{\ln I_{et} +} (0.004325)$$

Our findings so far seem to justify the conclusion that price and income alone have traced a large part of the variations in automobile stock. Expected income has turned out to be a better variable for explaining automobile consumption than disposable income. Income elasticity is probably somewhere between 1.4 and 2.0. Price elasticity probably ranges between -0.6 and -1.0.

DEMAND FOR ANNUAL PURCHASE WITH TIME LAG

Using the linear demand functions for automobile stock $(X1d)$ and $(X1e)$ as the basic relationships, we will attempt to explain annual purchase of automobiles. As pointed out in the theoretical section, demand for purchase per capita is related to the demand for desired stock per capita in the following way.

$$X_t^1 = c[\dot{X}_t(P_t, I_t, u_t) - X_{t-1}] + (1-k)X_{t-1},$$
$$= c\dot{X}_t(P_t, I_t, u_t) + (1-k-c)X_{t-1}.$$

Besides price and income, which determine the demand for desired stock, ownership at the beginning of the year will influence purchase during the year.

The statistical results, first estimated in conjunction with disposable income and then with expected income, from the same twenty-eight observations as were included in the linear demand functions for desired stock are:

[8] Harold Hotelling, "The Selection of Variates for Use in Prediction with Some Comments on the General Problem of Nuissance Parameters," *Annals of Mathematical Statistics*, XI (1940), 271–83.

$$X_t^1 = 0.07791 \quad - \quad 0.020127 \ P_t + 0.011699 \ I_{dt} - 0.23104 \ X_{t-1}$$
$$(0.002648) \qquad (0.001070) \qquad (0.04719)$$

$$R^2 = 0.858$$
$$s = 0.308$$

$$(4s)$$

$$X_t^1 = -0.39966 - 0.025936 \ P_t + 0.014307 \ I_{et} - 0.29709 \ X_{t-1}$$
$$(0.005939) \qquad (0.002583) \qquad (0.09549)$$

$$R^2 = 0.628$$
$$s = 0.499$$

$$(1xf)$$

Price and income elasticities of demand for stocks of automobiles can be derived from the results presented above. The coefficient of purchase with respect to price (-0.02 in [$4s$]) is equal to the partial derivative of desired stock with respect to price, multiplied by the adjustment coefficient c. To obtain the elasticity of desired stock with respect to price, divide (-0.02) by the estimated adjustment coefficient times mean stock and multiply the result by mean price. The estimated adjustment coefficient, c, is obtained from the coefficient of X_{t-1}, which is an estimate of $(1 - k - c)$. Recall that k is known to be very close to 0.75.

According to ($4s$), then, the price elasticity of demand for stock is -0.63, the income elasticity 1.70, and the adjustment coefficient .48. These elasticity estimates compare with -0.60 and 1.46, obtained from equation ($X1d$), which also used disposable income but assumed full rather than partial adjustment.

According to ($1xf$), the price elasticity of demand for stock is -0.72, the income elasticity 1.88, and the adjustment coefficient .55. The elasticity estimates here are very close to the figures -0.74 and 1.83 obtained in the comparable full adjustment equation, ($X1e$).[9]

It is interesting to compare the relative performances of the disposable- and expected-income variables in the partial-adjustment model just presented with their relative performances in the full-adjustment model presented earlier. The disposable-income variable accounts for considerably more of the variation in purchases than the expected-income vari-

---

[9] We can obtain separate estimates of the adjustment coefficient, c, from the ratios of the price and income parameters in the partial-adjustment equations ($4s$) and ($1xf$) to those in the comparable full-adjustment equations ($X1d$) and ($X1e$), respectively. For the disposable-income equations ($4s$) and ($X1d$), these estimates are 0.51 (obtained from the ratio of the price parameters) and 0.57 (obtained from the ratio of the income parameters). In the expected-income equations ($1xf$) and ($X1e$), the estimates are 0.53 (price) and 0.57 (income). These estimates are remarkably close to those obtained directly from equations ($4s$) and ($1xf$).

able. Yet expected income performs better than disposable income in explaining variations in the stock of automobiles on the road.

These results can be interpreted in at least two ways. First, we may view the expected-income variable as playing part of the role of the adjustment coefficient. When complete adjustment of stock is assumed, the disposable-income formulation has no way of taking into account a slow approach of stocks to a new equilibrium level, while the expected-income formulation does, because the income variable itself only changes in each year by a fraction of the distance between its recent level and the new level of disposable-income. Once partial adjustment is permitted, the adjustment coefficient itself accounts for the slow approach of stocks to their new level. On this interpretation the disposable-income formulation is the correct one, and the expected-income variable performs better in explaining variations in stocks only because the averaging procedure built into it acts as a partial surrogate for the adjustment mechanism.

On the second interpretation expected and "unexpected" income are allowed to play separate roles. Unexpected income is defined as $I_{dt} - I_{et}$. Equation (4se) represents an attempt to explore this interpretation. The model on which it is based is

$$X_t^1 = a' + b'P_t + c'I_{et} + d'X_{t-1} + e'(I_{dt} - I_{et})$$

or

$$X_t^1 = a' + b'P_t + (c' - e')I_{et} + d'X_{t-1} + e'I_{dt}$$

$$X_t^1 = 0.14400 - 0.018857\,P_t - 0.001357\,I_{et} - 0.21378\,X_{t-1}$$
$$(0.003903) \quad\quad (0.003018) \quad\quad (0.061547)$$
$$+\, 0.012467\,I_{dt} \quad\quad R^2 = 0.859$$
$$(0.002026) \quad\quad\quad s = 0.314$$

(4se)

According to this regression, the coefficient c' of expected income is .0111 (.0125 − .0014), while the coefficient e' of unexpected income is .0125. Since the responsiveness of purchases to unexpected income is virtually the same as to expected income, this interpretation is not operationally distinguishable from the disposable-income formulation presented earlier.

TESTS OF SERIAL CORRELATION OF REGRESSION RESIDUALS

The statistical analysis up to this point has revealed that automobile ownership is closely associated with price and expected income and that automobile purchase can be explained by price, disposable income, and existing stock. In the case of demand for ownership, we have estimated the linear regression ($X1e$) using per capita stock as the dependent variable and the regression (1e) using the logarithm of price as the dependent variable. In the case of demand for annual purchase we have estimated the linear regression (4s). In each case the number of explanatory variables is extremely small. There is no doubt that many factors have been left out. Their combined effect, as shown by the regression residuals, may vary systematically through time. It is desirable to examine the behavior of the residuals of each of the regressions, (X1e), (1e), and (4s), and find out the extent to which they are serially correlated.

Two statistics are available for testing the serial correlation of the residuals in a regression. The Durbin-Watson statistic is defined as the ratio of the sum of squares of the first differences of the residuals to the sum of squares of the residuals themselves.[10] Applied to regression residuals, the von Neumann ratio is computed as the ratio of the mean of the squares of the first differences of the residuals to the mean of the squares of the residuals.[11] In either case a smaller ratio indicates positive serial correlation, while a large ratio indicates negative serial correlation. We will test the null hypothesis of no serial correlation against the one-sided alternative hypothesis that there is positive serial correlation at 5 per cent level of significance. Durbin and Watson have divided the values of their statistic into three regions: values smaller than d_L leading to the rejection of the null hypothesis; values larger than d_U leading to the acceptance of the null hypothesis; and values between d_L and d_U leading to an inconclusive test. On the other hand, if the von Neumann ratio falls below a certain value k, the null hypothesis is rejected; otherwise, the null hypothesis is accepted. The results of both tests are summarized below.

	Durbin-Watson Statistic	d_L	d_U	Von Neumann Ratio	k
(X1e)........	1.31	1.26	1.56	1.36	1.45
(1e)........	1.53	1.32	1.58	1.58	1.49
(4s)........	1.43	1.18	1.65	1.49	1.45

The Durbin-Watson test is inconclusive for all three regressions. The von Neumann test leads to barely rejecting the null hypothesis for (X1e) and to barely accepting the null hypothesis for (1e) and (4s). To claim that the residuals are positively correlated, one might need somewhat stronger evidence than this. But the evidence is strong enough to make the absence of serial correlation doubtful.

[10] J. Durbin and G. S. Watson, "Testing for Serial Correlation in Least Squares Regression. II," *Biometrika*, XXXVIII (1951), 159–78.

[11] B. I. Hart and John von Neumann, "Tabulation of the Probabilities for the Ratio of the Mean Square Successive Difference to the Variance," *Annals of Mathematical Statistics*, XIII (1942), 207–14.

III. Consistency of Statistical Findings with New Observations

NEW OBSERVATIONS (1954–57)

Four years have elapsed since the statistical study summarized in Section II was made. This is an opportune moment to examine the validity of our previous findings in the light of the new observations now available. The statistical demand functions previously found most promising will be confronted with the new data. To do so, our first step is to bring the time-series observations in Table 1 up to date. The new series, from 1954

TABLE 2*

AUTOMOBILE STOCK, ANNUAL PURCHASE, AND THEIR
DETERMINANTS, 1954–57

Year	Automobile Stock Per Capita X_t	New Purchase Per Capita X_t^1	Relative Price of Automobiles P_t	Real Disposable Income Per Capita I_{dt}	Real Expected Income Per Capita I_{et}
1953.........	12.057	....	....	....	....
1954.........	12.052	3.408	141.3	769.6	795.9
1955.........	13.072	4.338	141.3	793.3	808.8
1956.........	13.430	3.543	141.5	805.2	822.3
1957.........	13.462	3.496	151.1	798.0	828.8

* Source: Table 3. I_{et} is a weighted mean of I_{dt}, $I_{d(t-1)}$, . . . , and $I_{d(t-8)}$, with weights 0.34403, 0.23526, 0.16089, 0.11003, 0.07524, 0.05146, 0.03518, 0.02406, and 0.01646.

to 1957, are presented in Table 2. The basic data from which Table 2 is derived will be given in Table 3. Tables 4, 5, and 6 will further supplement the basic data in Table 3.

CONSISTENCY OF DEMAND FUNCTIONS FOR AUTOMOBILE STOCK

From the statistical findings up to 1953, it has been concluded that desired stock of automobiles per capita can best be explained by the relative price index P_t and real expected income per capita I_{et}. We have estimated two statistical demand functions using these variables. The first is a linear regression of X_t on P_t and I_{et}, denoted by $(X1e)$. The second is a linear regression of $\ln P_t$ on $\ln X_t$ and $\ln I_{et}$, denoted by $(1e)$. The values of the dependent variables calculated from these regressions for the four years 1954–57 are now compared with the observed values shown in Table 2.

	1954	1955	1956	1957
X_t estimated from $(X1e)$.......	12.665	12.993	13.328	13.025
X_t observed minus estimated...	− 0.613	0.079	0.102	0.437
$\ln P_t$ estimated from $(1e)$......	5.023	4.972	4.978	4.993
$\ln P_t$ observed minus estimated.	− 0.072	− 0.021	− 0.026	0.025

The residuals of the observed values from the estimated values are very small. They do not indicate any shifts in the pattern of demand for automobile stock during the four years 1954–57. As a matter of fact, they are amazingly small in view of the standard errors of the two regressions, 0.618 for $(X1e)$ and 0.104 for $(1e)$. For those who like to see the statistical results presented in the form of a test of significance, we have performed the standard test by the analysis of covariance to decide whether the last four observations have come from the same regression as the previous observations.

TABLE 3

Basic Data for the Derivation of Table 2

Year	Total Automobile Stock (Thousands)*	New Purchase (Thousands)†	Absolute Price of Automobile Stock‡	Disposable Income (Billions of Current Dollars)§	GNP Deflator (1937 = 100)‖	Total Population (Millions)#
1954....	19,575	5,535	286.12	253.1	202.5	162.42
1955....	21,604	7.170	289.44	268.7	204.9	165.27
1956....	22,574	5,955	298.50	285.6	211.0	168.09
1957....	23,036	5,982	330.81	298.9	218.9	171.12

* Weighted sum of registrations of passenger automobiles of different model years by the relative prices in 1937. Registration figures are shown separately in Table 4. Prices of automobiles in different age groups at the end of 1937 are given in Table 6. At the end of each year, a one-year-old (or current-year) model is one unit, a two-year-old model is 540/644 unit, a three-year-old model is 403/644 unit, and so forth.

† "New Passenger Car Registration," published annually in *Automotive Industries: Annual Statistical Issue* (Philadelphia: Chilton Co.).

‡ Absolute price index of automobile stock (unadjusted) derived from data of National Automobile Dealers Association, Table 5, multiplied by 0.921. Except for the war years, this price index has been practically proportional to the price index based on newspaper advertisements, Table 6. The parallel movements between these two sets of prices can be seen from Tables 5 and 6. The ratios of the latter to the former index are 0.917, 0.918, 0.899, and 0.913, respectively, for the years 1950–53, with a mean of 0.912.

§ "Disposable Personal Income of the United States Department of Commerce," *Business Statistics: A Supplement to the Survey of Current Business, 1957* (biennial edition), p. 4, and *Survey of Current Business,* February, 1958, p. 8. This series is new as compared with the one originally used. It has been multiplied by a factor of 0.9944 for the purpose of extending the old series.

‖ Gross National Product Deflator with 1947 as 100, *Survey of Current Business,* July, 1957, p. 25, and February, 1958, p. 7, divided by 0.592 for conversion into 100 for 1937.

Total population of continental United States including armed forces overseas, *Statistical Abstract, 1957,* p. 5, and *Survey of Current Business,* February, 1958, p. S-11.

Briefly, the method of analysis of covariance employed here can be described as follows.[12] Suppose that n observations are used to estimate a regression on p parameters ($p - 1$ explanatory variables plus one intercept). Suppose also that their are m additional observations, and we are interested in deciding whether they are generated by the same regression model as the first n observations. To perform the analysis of covariance, we need the following sums of squares:

[12] See, e.g., Maurice G. Kendall, *The Advanced Theory of Statistics* (London: Charles Griffin & Co., 1946), II, 242 ff.

A sum of squares of $n + m$ deviations of the dependent variable from the regression estimated by $n + m$ observations, with $n + m - p$ degrees of freedom.

B sum of squares of n deviations of the dependent variable from the regression estimated by the first n observations, with $n - p$ degrees of freedom.

C sum of squares of m deviations of the dependent variable from the regression estimated by the second m observations, with $m - p$ degrees of freedom.

Then the ratio of $(A - B - C)/p$ to $(B + C)/(n + m - 2p)$ will be distributed as $F(p, n + m - 2p)$ under the null hypothesis that both groups of observations belong to the same regression model.

To perform the analysis of covariance for $(X1e)$, we first compute the regression with both the first twenty-eight and the additional four observations.

TABLE 4*

STOCKS OF PASSENGER AUTOMOBILES CLASSIFIED BY AGE

(In Thousands)

Age (In Years)	1937	1954	1955	1956	1957
1	3,550	4,589	6,701	5,916	5,800
2	3,280	5,723	4,583	6,700	5,900
3	2,280	3,675	5,700	4,577	6,700
4	1,780	5,387	3,638	5,652	4,550
5	1,370	6,102	5,290	3,575	5,600
6	1,000	4,773	5,914	5,072	3,350
7	1,720	2,766	4,434	5,539	4,800
8	1,950	2,608	2,466	3,871	4,750
9	2,540	1,624	2,162	2,021	3,250
10	1,330	....	1,277	1,637	1,500
11	750	....	....	891	1,350
12	440	....	....	....	600
13	300	464	....	....	....
14	70	1,782	294	....	....
15	10	1,205	1,127	185	....
16	....	693	755	699	100
17	....	344	420	476	440
18	....	481	206	261	200
19	....	420	234	109	100
20	....	130	225	205	50
21	....	130	100	205	135
22	....	130	100	65	135
23	....	45	100	65	30
24	....	130	30	65	30
25	....	42	60	10	30
26	....	....	25	30	....

* Source: Registrations of passenger automobiles, by model year, at the end of each calendar year, from the Econometric Institute, Inc. They are similar to the numbers of passenger cars in use by model year as of the following July 1, based on data from the Reuben H. Donnelley Corporation and published annually in *Automotive Industries: Annual Statistical Issue* (Philadelphia: Chilton Co.).

$$\dot{X}_t = -0.7482 - 0.048800 \; P_t + 0.025526 \; I_{et} \qquad R^2 = 0.943$$
$$\qquad\qquad (0.003553) \qquad (0.001171) \qquad\qquad s = 0.591 \tag{X1e'}$$

The sum of squares, A, of the deviations around this regression is 10.1155. $B + C$ is 9.6130. The ratio $F(3, 26)$ is therefore 0.45. In order to interpret the new observations as coming from a different structure at the 5 per cent level of significance, F would have to be at least 2.98—much larger than the one obtained. As it is to be expected, function $(X1e')$ turns out to be almost identical with $(X1e)$.

Similarly, we have computed $(1e)$ by combining the first thirty-three with the additional four observations.

$$\ln P_t = -6.4998 - 1.0600 \; \ln X_t + 2.1187 \; \ln I_{et} \qquad R^2 = 0.947$$
$$\qquad\qquad (0.0544) \qquad\qquad (0.0965) \qquad\qquad s = 0.0988 \tag{1e'}$$

In this case, the ratio $F(3, 31)$ is found to be 0.15—also much smaller than the 5 per cent critical value of 2.91.

TABLE 5*

RETAIL PRICES OF AUTOMOBILES CLASSIFIED BY AGE
ESTIMATED BY THE NATIONAL AUTOMOBILE
DEALERS ASSOCIATION

(In Current Dollars)

Age (In Years)	1950	1951	1952	1953	1954	1955	1956	1957
1	$1,881	$2,120	$2,445	$2,298	$2,244	$2,423	$2,477	$2,651
2	1,512	1,676	1,825	1,685	1,628	1,690	1,787	1,943
3	1,261	1,397	1,484	1,302	1,243	1,245	1,309	1,494
4	1,054	1,144	1,218	1,026	931	894	957	1,087
5	927	954	968	826	728	651	674	765
6	......	833	799	621	541	500	479	538
7	......	......	691	501	375	342	352	484
8	......	......	......	423	304	250	255	290
9	529	......	......	......	256	198	*192*	226
10	*475*	421	......	......	......	*180*	136	*204*
11	360	*384*	329	......	......	......	100	135
12	305	265	*298*	221	......	......	......	100
13	260	220	190	*202*	174	......	......	......
14	220	181	154	101	*161*	39	......	......
15	190	160	124	82	46	29	27	......
Absolute price index of automobile stock (unadjusted)	320.86	343.74	374.51	335.53	313.73	317.37	327.30	362.73

* Source and notes: Prices are national averages of used-car prices in December of each year estimated by the National Automobile Dealers Association. In each column the figures below the one italicized are obtained by free-hand extrapolation from the figures above the line plotted on a semilog paper. Absolute price index of automobile stock (unadjusted) is the ratio of the value of the 1937 stocks (Table 4) by these prices to the value of the same stocks by the 1937 prices given in Table 6.

CONSISTENCY OF THE DEMAND FUNCTION FOR ANNUAL PURCHASE

The demand function that has been selected as best explaining per capita purchase of automobiles is (4s). We will present the values of per capita purchase estimated by this function for the four years 1954–57.

	1954	1955	1956	1957
X_t^1 estimated from (4s).........	3.452	3.730	3.630	3.270
X_t^1 observed minus estimated...	−0.044	0.608	−0.087	0.226

Inspection of the residuals reveals that they are not unduly large relative to 0.308, the standard error of estimate for (4s). The year 1955 is an

TABLE 6*

RETAIL PRICES OF AUTOMOBILES CLASSIFIED BY AGE
FROM NEWSPAPER ADVERTISEMENTS
(In Current Dollars)

Age (In Years)	1937	1950	1951	1952	1953
1..........	$644	$1,783	$2,016	$2,167	$2,221
2..........	540	1,458	1,567	1,735	1,538
3..........	403	1,117	1,224	1,346	1,180
4..........	327	893	979	1,087	907
5..........	247	851	851	882	702
6..........	180	....	730	651	504
7..........	150	....	....	576	391
8..........	*112*	....	....	....	320
9..........	87	434	....	....	....
10..........	67	426	370	....	....
11..........	52	320	376	209	....
12..........	40	192	257	248	224
13..........	31	*165*	*195*	178	173
14..........	24	125	148	*135*	179
15..........	19	95	113	103	*117*
16..........	15	72	86	78	92
17..........	11	55	65	60	71
18..........	9	42	50	46	56
19..........	7	32	38	35	43
20..........	5	24	29	27	34
21..........	4	18	22	20	26
22..........	3	14	17	15	20
23..........	2	....	13	12	16
24..........	2	....	....	....	12
25..........	1	....	....	....	....
26..........	1	....	....	....	....
Absolute price index of automobile stock......	100.00	294.31	315.75	336.86	306.30

Source and notes: Prices are averages of newspaper advertisements at the end of each year (Chow, *op. cit.*, pp. 102–3). Absolute price index of automobile stock is the ratio of the value of the 1937 stocks (Table 4) by the above prices to the value of the same stocks by the prices at the end of 1937 (*ibid.*, p. 106).

exception, where we find the residual to be twice as large as the standard error.

Again the analysis of covariance is performed by first computing the regression including the last four observations.

$$X_t^1 = -0.07391 - 0.020218\ P_t + 0.011875\ I_{dt} - 0.22130\ X_{t-1}$$
$$\ (0.002603)\qquad (0.001050)\qquad (0.04216)$$

$$R^2 = 0.880 \qquad (4s')$$
$$s = 0.307$$

The sum of squares, A, of the thirty-two deviations from this regression is 2.6444, with 28 degrees of freedom. The sum of squares, B, of the twenty-eight deviations from ($4s$) is 2.2818, with 24 degrees of freedom. The sum of squares, C, of the deviations of the last four values of X_t^1 from the regression based on the last four observations is zero, since the regression has four parameters to be estimated. C being zero, the F ratio becomes the ratio of $(A - B)/4$ to $B/24$. Numerically, this $F(4, 24)$ equals 0.95, leading to the acceptance of the hypothesis that automobile purchases in the last four years have been governed by the same relationship as before.

To see how far the sales estimates by ($4s$) are from the actual sales in millions of new cars, we have multiplied the per capita estimates by the population figures in Table 4.

	1954	1955	1956	1957
Sales estimated................	5.607	6.165	6.102	5.597
Actual minus estimated sales...	−0.072	1.005	−0.147	0.385

Actual sales in 1955 were a million units above the estimated value. Note that the standard error of regression ($4s$) in terms of total sales for the size of population as of 1955 would be about a half-million. The standard error for a prediction using ($4s$) would of course be greater.

IV. The Use of Statistical Demand Functions for Forecasting

LONG-RUN FORECASTING

Although the main purpose of the statistical analysis presented above has been to ascertain the extent to which the prevalent theoretical framework of consumer demand, modified to take account of the problem of existing stock, can explain past variations in automobile ownership and automobile sales, a possible by-product of such an analysis is its usefulness for predicting sales in the future. In this section we shall reflect on the implications of our findings on automobile demand in the long run and in the short run. Looking ahead ten years from now, we may wish to foresee the magnitudes of the forces governing automobile purchase. Is the market now saturated in the sense that annual purchases in the future will not be any higher than the present level? If not, at what level will the demand in 1968 be? On the other hand, looking one year ahead, we may wish to form an idea of the total purchase of automobiles. These questions are by no means easy to answer. It is our hope to bring a few of the important factors to bear and to suggest some partial answers to them.

At the outset it is well to point out the limiting assumptions on which our partial answers will be based. First of all, the demand relationships that we have estimated will be assumed to hold in the future, at least until 1968. Second, as it has been pointed out, the primary interest in our statistical analysis has been the estimation of the effects of a few variables that are considered important in the economic theory of demand. Only their effects on automobile sales will be considered. Whatever predictions we make are predictions of the partial effects of these variables, while the combined effect of all other variables is held constant. Third, all we have estimated are statistical demand functions. Accordingly, only the shifts in the demand curves will be examined. The quantity demanded, be it stock or purchase, cannot be specified without an additional assumption concerning the supply of automobiles.

Our first task is to make a forecast of automobile demand in 1968. Long-run demand for automobile purchase will be derived from long-run demand for automobile stock. The short-run factors such as time lag do not concern us here, since our present purpose is to get a rough order of magnitude of the demand ten years from now rather than to predict the fluctuations in demand from year to year. With this in mind, we can regard the desired stock as being actually fulfilled and make no distinction between actual stock and desired stock. A forecast will first be worked out on a per capita basis and then translated to the total number of automobiles.

Given the per capita demands for desired stock at the ends of two consecutive years in the future, $\dot{X}_t$ and $\dot{X}_{t-1}$, a long-run forecast of per capita demand for purchase in year t can be regarded as $\dot{X}_t$ minus $k\dot{X}_{t-1}$. Alternatively, this relationship can be written as

$$X_t^1 = (\dot{X}_t - \dot{X}_{t-1}) + (1 - k)\dot{X}_{t-1}.$$

A long-run forecast of demand for purchase is thus broken into two parts, the change in desired stock during the year $(\dot{X}_t - \dot{X}_{t-1})$ and the demand for replacing the stock at the beginning of the year $(1 - k)\dot{X}_{t-1}$. For predicting the sales of automobiles in 1968, therefore, calculations of the change in desired stock during 1968 and of the replacement of the stock at the end of 1967 have to be made.

A few comments on replacement sales are in order at this point to make clear our position on the question of possible saturation in automobile sales. Saturation is understood to be the state of affairs in which existing ownership is sufficient to satisfy demand in the near future, so that annual purchase will be declining or, in any case, will not be increasing. There has been some conjecture that the automobile market is already saturated now in 1958. However, our analysis seems to point to the contrary. Since one used car is not a perfect substitute for a new car and since the annual rate of depreciation is close to 25 per cent, roughly a quarter of the existing automobile stock needs to be replaced just to keep the ownership level from falling. In other words, the replacement demand is around a quarter of the number of automobiles (in new-car equivalent units) being used currently. At the end of 1957 there were 23.0 million units of automobiles registered, as shown in Table 3. A quarter of this stock, or 5.75 million units, would be needed annually for replacement alone even if per capita income and population were to remain unchanged. Expected increases in per capita income and in population will raise annual demand above 5.75 million in a manner to be described presently.

To estimate replacement demand in 1968, we first need an estimate of the demand for desired stock at the end of 1967. The latter in turn requires estimates of per capita income and population in 1967. As we have concluded previously, the measure of income appropriate for determination of desired stock is expected income. It is beyond our scope to dwell on elaborate forecasts of income and population. We will simply project past trends of these two variables into the future and investigate into the effects of these variables, so projected, on the demand for automobiles. From 1921 to 1957, real expected income per capita was growing at an average rate of 1.5 per cent per year; from 1946 to 1957 it was growing at an average rate of 1.4 per cent. For projecting expected income from 1957 on, 1.4 per cent will be used. Compounded continuously for ten years, this rate amounts to a 15 per cent growth from the expected income per capita in 1957. The result of this projection is 953 for the expected income in 1967. Since the end of World War II, population in the United States has been rising at an average rate of 1.7 per cent per year. Using this rate for projecting population from 1957, we obtain 203 million as the estimated population in 1967.

Let us see how the projected growth of expected income affects our demand curves for desired stock per capita. The relationships between desired stock and price, given an expected income of 828.8 as it was in 1957, are derived from functions $(X1e')$ and $(1e')$:

$$\dot{X}_t = 20.408 - 0.048800\, P_t, \tag{$X1e'$}$$

$$\ln \dot{X}_t = 7.300 - 0.9434 \ln P_t. \tag{$1e'$}$$

Given an expected income of 953 as projected for 1967, these demand curves become

$$\dot{X}_t = 23.578 - 0.048800\, P_t, \tag{$X1e'$}$$

$$\ln \dot{X}_t = 7.579 - 0.9434 \ln P_t. \tag{$1e'$}$$

By comparing the two pairs of intercepts, we find that the growth of income alone will increase the per capita demand for desired stock by an absolute amount of $(23.578-20.408)$ or 3.170 (hundredths of an equivalent unit) according to $(X1e')$ and by a factor of $e^{(7.579-7.300)}$ or 1.322 according to $(1e')$.

What do the above indicated shifts in the per capita demand curves mean in terms of per capita demand for desired stock in 1967, total demand for desired stock in 1967, and total demand for replacement in 1968? It would be more revealing to deal with the quantities demanded rather than the demand curves in all cases. Merely for the sake of expressing our results in terms of the quantities demanded, the price in 1957 will be used in the following calculations. Assuming the price index to be 151.1 as it was in 1957, we proceed first to calculate the desired stocks per capita in 1957 from $(X1e')$ and $(1e')$. These figures are then raised by the effects of the projected growth in expected income to form estimates of desired stock per capita at the end of 1967. The corresponding estimates of total desired stock can be obtained, given our projected population of 203 million. One-quarter of total desired stock at the end of 1967 will constitute our forecast of replacement remand in 1968. These calculations are shown below.

	Desired Stock Per Capita, End of 1957 (Hundredths)	Desired Stock Per Capita, End of 1967 (Hundredths)	Total Desired Stock, End of 1967 (Millions)	Replacement Demand, 1968 (Millions)
$(X1e')$....	13.03	16.20	32.9	8.2
$(1e')$......	13.01	17.20	34.9	8.7

Predictions based on both $(X1e')$ and $(1e')$ are exhibited here for comparison. Equation $(X1e')$ is a regression with per capita stock as the dependent variable, whereas $(1e')$ is a regression of the logarithm of relative price. But both calculations show that the projected increases in per capital income and in population would be enough to raise replacement sales to over 8 million in 1968 if the relative price of automobiles were to remain unchanged.

To arrive at the demand for purchase in 1968, the demand due to the change in desired stock should be added to replacement demand. Under the same assumption of constant price, desired stock per capita will be changed from 16.20 to 16.54 during the year 1968 according to $(X1e')$ as per capita income is expected to rise by 1.4 per cent. This increase of 0.34 in desired stock per capita, when multiplied by the projected population in 1968, is converted to 0.7 million automobiles as the increase in total desired stock. The sum of .7 million and the 8.2 million for replacement is the complete estimate of demand for purchase in 1968 according to $(X1e')$. Similar calculations based upon function $(1e')$ are shown here also.

	Desired Stock Per Capita, End of 1968 (Hundredths)	Change in Desired Stock Per Capita during 1968 (Hundredths)	Change in Total Stock during 1968 (Millions)	Demand for Purchase during 1968 (Millions)
$(X1e')$....	16.54	0.34	0.7	8.9
$(1e')$......	17.68	0.48	1.0	9.7

It should be emphasized that the estimates of 8.9 million and 9.7 million are not forecasts of actual automobile sales in 1968; rather they are intended to indicate effects of the projected increases in per capita income and population on the demand for automobiles under the arbitrary assumption that relative price of automobiles is to remain constant.

Another way to indicate the shift of total demand for purchase resulting from the projected increases in per capita income and population is by the rise in price which would be necessary to keep total purchase in 1968 at the same level as in 1957. Here we are concerned with automobile purchases as governed by the long-run factors in these two years. Therefore, we can rephrase our question. How much need the price rise be in order to keep total *desired* stock at the end of 1968 the same as total *desired* stock at the end of 1957? If total stock is prevented from growing, purchase will consist entirely of replacement. Purchases in these two years are considered equal if the desired stocks are equal. According to $(X1e')$, per capita desired stock is 13.03 in 1957. In order to keep total desired stock in 1968 the same as in 1957, when population increases from 171.1 to 206.4 million, per capita desired stock in 1968 has to be reduced to 10.80. The price index required to achieve this level of per capita stock, under the assumption that expected income increases to 966.4 in 1968, is 269, which can easily be verified by substitutions into $(X1e')$. Similar substitutions into (1e′) give a price index of 255. Thus the growths in per capita income and population would be sufficient to raise the relative price of automobiles by some 70 per cent in the next ten years if total automobile stock were not adjusted upward. Such a price would be close to one prevailing at the end of 1947, as given in Table 1.

Our views on the long-run prospects of automobile sales can be summed up briefly. Expected income and population, if they are to grow at the same rate as in the last decade, will increase the total demand for automobiles significantly. In 1968 the number of automobiles demanded would be in the neighborhood of 9 million if the relative price of automobiles were not to move up at all; price would have to move up to the level which prevailed at the end of 1947 in order to keep total demand from exceeding the present demand. In reaching these conclusions, I have not been oblivious of the hazards of long-run forecasting in economics. But no better alternative has occurred to me than the application of the measures of price and income effects from past observations.

SHORT-RUN FORECASTING

We have seen that a long-run forecast of automobile purchase consists of two parts, demand for replacement and demand due to the change in desired stock. Replacement demand is the more important component, and it is simply one-fourth of the demand for desired stock. In essence, therefore, forecasting purchase in the long run amounts to forecasting the desired stock. However, the process of short-run forecasting, by which is meant forecasting for the next year, is different. Its emphasis is on the *adjustment* of existing stock to the desired level and not on the desired stock as such. This difference has two manifestations. First, since adjustment has to start from a given existing stock, short-run forecasting requires the stock at the beginning of the year as an additional variable. Second, a given percentage change in desired stock, by widening its discrepancy from the existing stock, will bring about a higher percentage change in current purchase even if only half of the discrepancy is filled within one year. In other words, the income and price elasticities of demand for purchase in the short run will be higher than the corresponding elasticities of demand for desired stock (or for long-run purchase).

As before, the variables affecting per capita purchase will first be considered. The effect of population on total purchase will become clear afterward. In discussing these variables, we will refer to the statistical demand function (4s′) which relates per capita purchase to per capita income, relative price of automobiles, and existing stock per capita. Disposable income has been found successful in explaining the purchase of automobiles.

From ($4s'$) the short-run income elasticity of demand for purchase is estimated to be 2.71 in 1957. Income elasticity being so high, there is little
doubt that the violent fluctuations of automobile sales in the United
States have been largely due to the fluctuations in disposable income. It
would be impossible to evaluate the short-run prospect of automobile purchase without having evaluated the short-run prospect of disposable income. Granted that forecasting income one year ahead is difficult, it is
essential for the prediction of automobile purchase one year ahead.

While income is the only variable selected for the specification of the
demand curve for desired stock, both income and existing stock affect
the demand curve for purchase in the short run. Existing stock exercises
a negative influence on the current demand for purchasing autombles.
The higher the existing stock, the less is the purchase needed to fill the
gap between desired stock and existing stock. A familiar historical illus-
tration is the period immediately after World War II, when the accumu-
lation of automobile stock continuously shifted the demand curve for
purchase downward and led to the decline in the price of automobiles.
According to ($4s'$), an increase of per capita stock at the beginning of the
year by one unit has the partial effect of reducing per capita purchase
during the year by 0.22 unit. As far as its role in forecasting is concerned,
existing stock is a variable that can already be observed and does not require a separate forecast itself.

After the demand curve for purchase is specified by income and existing stock, the quantity demanded remains to be determined simultaneously with the relative price of automobiles. Because our study has been confined to the demand side, it can be used to indicate only the shift in the
demand curve. It will be remembered that we have expressed the shift in
the long-run demand for desired stock by the shift in the quantity demanded provided that price were to remain the same. We will also express the demand curve for purchase in the year 1958 by the quantity demanded under the arbitrary assumption that price in 1958 remains
unchanged.

A forecast of the total demand for automobile purchase is simply the
product of per capita demand and population. It is obvious that, given the
per capita demand, total demand will be an increasing function of, and in
fact proportional to, the size of population. However, an increase in
population, given the same total disposable income in real terms, will
exert a depressing influence on the total demand for automobiles. Assume
that population increases by y per cent without being matched by any
increase in total income. Per capita income will be reduced by y per cent.
Since short-run income elasticity is nearly 3, per capita demand for pur-

chase will drop by 3y per cent. Total demand for purchase, now from a larger population, will be 2y per cent less than before. Whenever the per capita demand for a commodity is elastic with respect to income, a *ceteris paribus* increase in population, by reducing per capita demand more than proportionally, tends to lower total demand at the same time.

What does the examination of the above factors reveal in regard to the prospect of automobile demand in 1958? Regression (4s') summarizes the effects of these factors. We will consider the demand curve for total purchase as governed by per capita income, existing stock, and population and will provide an estimate of what the quantity demanded would be if there should be no change in price. Although this study does not enable us to make a forecast of actual sales of automobiles in 1958, it does help indicate the partial effects of income, existing stock, and population on automobile demand. The main purpose of studying these partial effects is to understand the impact of the current recession in 1958 on automobile sales within our analytical framework. The change in existing stock per capita, from the beginning of 1957 to the beginning of 1958, is negligible, as shown in Table 2. Therefore, any shift in the demand curve for sales in 1958 would have to come mainly from population and income. It appears reasonable to assume an increase of 1.7 per cent in population in 1958. As far as income is concerned, statistics available now (May, 1958) seem to show very little decline in total disposable income in money terms but a continued rise in the general price level. Even if total disposable income in money terms remains stable, a 3.3 per cent rise in the price level (somewhere in between the 3.7 per cent in 1957 and the 3.0 per cent in 1956 as derived from the data on the GNP Deflator in Table 3) coupled with a 1.7 per cent increase in population will reduce disposable income per capita in real terms by 5 per cent. The shift in automobile demand between 1957 and 1958 under these assumptions about population and income can be calculated from (4s'). The shift in the quantity demanded, given the relative price of automobiles as of 1957, is shown below.

	Purchase Per Capita Estimated from (4s') (Hundredths)	Population (Millions)	Total Purchase (Millions)
1957.....	3.375	171.1	5.775
1958.....	2.894	174.0	5.036

Population and real income, by themselves, would reduce estimated automobile sales from 5.8 million in 1957 to 5.0 million in 1958. Let us remember that we have analyzed the partial effects of only two variables and are thus far from having obtained a forecast of automobile sales in 1958. This shows how limited our model (4s') is for the purpose of forecasting. Even under the ideal condition that all explanatory variables in (4s′) are known for certain, the standard error of the regression is considerable. It is 0.307 hundredths of an automobile unit per capita, or, translated into total purchase by the population in 1957, it is approximately 0.525 million new automobiles. It therefore appears that, in its application to short-run forecasting of automobile purchase, our model can be used merely to trace the partial effects of a very few variables while leaving a sizable margin of error. But this is as far as the model can go.

FURTHER COMMENTS ON THE DEMAND FOR AUTOMOBILES IN 1958

Just before this manuscript went to press, the editor gave me the opportunity to add a few words on the demand for automobiles in 1958. With more information available now (May, 1959), I would like first to examine the consistency of demand function (4s′) with automobile purchase in 1958 and then to comment further on the usefulness of (4s′) as a forecasting device in the short run.

The basic data in Table 3 can readily be extended to 1958:

1. "Total Automobile Stock" at the end of 1957 is 23,083 thousand new-car equivalent units, estimated from automobile registrations by age groups in *Automotive Industry Statistical Issues* (Philadelphia: Chilton Co., 1959), page 87.

2. "New Purchase" is 4,651 thousand (*ibid.*, p. 82).

3. "Absolute Price of Automobile Stock" (unadjusted) is 370.65, based on the following average prices in December, 1958, estimated by the National Automobile Dealers Association:

1958	1957	1956	1955	1954	1953	1952	1951	1950
$2,595	$2,027	$1,563	$1,212	$864	$603	$417	$296	$233

The absolute price index, adjusted, to obtain comparability with the index used in estimating (4s′), is 370.65 multiplied by 0.912, or 338.03.

4. "Disposable Income" is 305.3 billions of current dollars, obtained by raising disposable income figure in Table 3 for 1957 by 2.13 per cent. This percentage results from comparing the revised estimates of disposable income for 1957 and 1958 (*Survey of Current Business*, February 1959, p. 3).

5. "GNP Deflator" equals 224.2, which is 2.4 per cent higher than the 1957 figure. This percentage increase is also found in the preceding reference.

6. "Total Population" is 174.06 millions (*ibid.*, p. S-11).

For the year 1958 the data in Table 2 become:

X_{t-1}	X_t^1	P_t	I_{dt}
13.489	2.672	150.8	782.3

These figures, when substituted into equation (4s′), give 3.182 per cent of a new-car equivalent per capita, as compared with the observed 2.672

In absolute terms this means an estimate of 5.539 million automobiles as compared with the observed 4.651 million. Thus our model performed poorly in 1958, although not so poorly as in 1955. Nevertheless, the model is far from being rejected statistically by the observation in 1958. The deviation of the observed purchase per capita in 1958 from the estimated figure according to (4s') is .510. In order to test whether this deviation is large enough to reject the hypothesis that (4s') remains stable, we can construct a prediction interval[13] based on regression (4s'). The standard error in prediction is obviously larger than the standard error of the regression, since the regression coefficients themselves are estimates and are therefore subject to sampling variations. The standard error of regression (4s') being 0.307, the observed deviation of 0.510 would not lead to rejecting the null hypothesis that (4s') remains stable in 1958. It should be pointed out again that, while our short-run model for purchase fails to be rejected on statistical grounds, it is not a very useful model for prediction mainly because of the large standard error.[14]

In the last subsection on "Short-Run Forecasting," I made some assumptions on the changes in disposable income, the general price level, and population in 1958. It was pointed out that an increase in population per se would have a negative effect on automobile purchase and that an increase in the general price level per se, insofar as it deflates income and the absolute price of automobiles by the same percentage, would also have a depressing effect on the demand for new automobiles. Mainly because disposable income turned out to be higher, and the general price level turned out to be lower, than my previous speculations, the new estimate of automobile sales from (4s') is higher than the previous estimate. The section on "Short-Run Forecasting" has been included for publication with the hope that it may convey some of the difficulties in forecasting in addition to my own mistakes.

[13] In a paper "Tests of Equality between Sets of Coefficients in Two Linear Regressions," *Econometrica*, July, 1960, I have shown that the prediction interval test is a special case of the analysis of covariance. I am unable to give a prediction interval based on (4s') numerically because the computations, including the inverse of the matrix of the covariances of the explanatory variables, have unfortunately been lost.

[14] Recently, the U.S. Bureau of Labor Statistics has been collecting data on prices of new and used cars. It has found that the price of new automobiles increased by 9.3 per cent, and the price of used automobiles increased by 9.0 per cent, from July, 1957, to November, 1958, as recorded in *Economic Report of the President* (Washington, D.C.: Government Printing Office, 1959), p. 96. Using these percentage increases would improve our estimate somewhat but would not conceal the fact that factors excluded in (4s') exercised considerable influence on automobile demand in 1958.

V

The Demand for a Durable Input: Farm Tractors in the United States, 1921–57

ZVI GRILICHES

The Demand for a Durable Input: Farm Tractors in the United States, 1921–57[1]

I. INTRODUCTION

THE starting point of this study was a strong doubt that economics had no more to offer in explanation of the great mechanization of agriculture in the United States following World War I than the assertion that this phenomenon was an "adaptation by the agricultural sector to technological innovation." The first farm tractors were developed early in this century, and by 1920 the tractor had a form quite similar to that of today. Between 1920 and 1957 the number of tractors on United States farms increased almost twenty-fold (see Chart I). Except for a slowing-down of the growth in the depressed years in the early 1930's, the time series of the number of United States farm tractors has the smooth ogive shape of "growth" curves. It is tempting, therefore, to "explain" this time series as a single smooth, though gradual, "response" to the initial "stimulus" of an innovation.

The slackening of the growth of number of tractors on farms in the early 1930's, of course, suggests that there may be more to "mechanization" than smooth response to stimulus. This suggestion is strongly supported by the time series, also shown in Chart I, on gross annual farmers' capital expenditures (in 1935–39 dollars) on tractors. The gross investment series shows the same marked cycles and year-to-year fluctuations that we have come to expect in series of annual purchases of durable goods.

Farm machines, of which farm tractors are an important example, are durable productive agents whose services are inputs in the production of agricultural outputs. The theory of the firm suggests that the demand for these services—that is, for the stock of farm machines (tractors)—depends upon the price of the machines, the prices of inputs that are close substitutes or complements, the rate of interest, and similar "economic" variables. The test of the alternative explanation of "mechanization" suggested by the theory of the firm is in the goodness of the fit to the data

[1] I am indebted to Yehuda Grunfeld, Trygve Haavelmo, A. C. Harberger, Lester S. Kellogg, H. Gregg Lewis, and T. W. Schultz for valuable comments and to the Farm Income Branch, AMS, USDA, for making available to me their unpublished data. This study is part of a larger investigation of changes in agricultural inputs supported by a National Science Foundation grant.

181

182   *The Demand for Durable Goods*

of a demand function for farm machines containing these economic variables.

Thus what began as an investigation of "adaptation to technological innovation" became an econometric study of the demand for farm tractors. The parameters of a demand function, however, are not single-purpose tools. In particular, knowledge of the demand function for farm tractors may also provide useful knowledge on the responsiveness of farm investment to cyclical fluctuations in the demand for agricultural products and on the elasticity of farm output with respect to the prices of farm products and inputs.

CHART I

UNITED STATES TRACTORS ON FARMS: NUMBERS AND GROSS
INVESTMENT, 1920–57

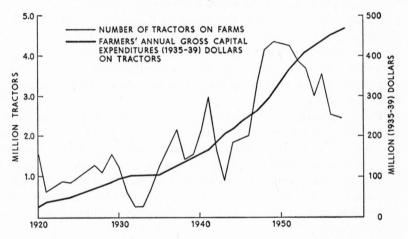

Farm tractors are producer durable goods. In the literature on the demand for durable goods most attention has been given to consumer durables, particularly automobiles. For a list of automobile studies see Chow and the literature cited there.[2] The recent work of Nerlove on automobiles uses an approach very similar to that used in this paper.[3] For other studies

[2] G. C. Chow, *Demand for Automobiles in the United States* ("Contributions to Economic Analysis," Vol. XIII [Amsterdam: North-Holland Publishing Co., 1957]).

[3] Marc Nerlove, "A Note on Long-Run Automobile Demand," *Journal of Marketing*, July, 1957; his *Distributed Lags and Demand Analysis of Agricultural and Other Commodities* (USDA Agriculture Handbook No. 141 [Washington, D.C., 1958]); and his "On the Nerlove Estimate of Supply Elasticity: A Reply," *Journal of Farm Economics*, Vol. XL, No. 3 (August, 1958).

of the demand for durable goods see Stone and Rowe[4] and the papers by Burstein and Muth in this volume. The list of studies of the demand for pruducer durable goods is even shorter. I know only of the steel demand studies by Lewis.[5] There is only one published study of aggregate farm investment, by Kendrick and Jones,[6] and it does not go beyond relating gross farm capital expenditures to lagged farm income. Hathaway has studied the cyclical fluctuations of farm investment but made no attempt to estimate the parameters of the investment function.[7] The only other studies of the demand for farm machinery and tractors known to me are the yet unpublished studies by Fettig[8] and by Cromarty.[9] None of the farm investment studies, however, takes adequate account either of the stock and flow problem or of the problem of lags in the adjustment of demand to changes in the underlying conditions.

The plan of this study is as follows: Section II develops the underlying theoretical model and discusses some of the statistical difficulties involved in estimating its parameters. Section III describes briefly the sources of data and the construction of the major variables from these data. Section IV presents the results of fitting alternative stock demand equations and derived investment functions to the data. Section V contains a discussion of the problems involved in measuring the stock of tractors, presents several alternative measures, and explores the empirical implications of the differences among these measures. Section VI summarizes the study and draws some of its implications for the analysis of cyclical fluctuations in farm investment and the responsiveness of farm output to changes in product and factor prices.

[4] J. R. N. Stone, and D. A. Rowe, "The Market Demand for Durable Goods," *Econometrica*, Vol. XXV, No. 3 (July, 1957); and their "Dynamic Demand Functions: Some Econometric Results," *Economic Journal*, Vol. LXVIII (June, 1958).

[5] H. G. Lewis, "Studies in the Elasticity of Demand for Steel" (unpublished Ph.D. thesis, University of Chicago, 1947).

[6] J. W. Kendrick and C. E. Jones, "Farm Capital Outlays and Stock," *Survey of Current Business*, Vol. XXXIX, No. 8 (August, 1953).

[7] D. E. Hathaway, "Agriculture and the Business Cycle," in U.S. Congress, Joint Economic Committee, *Policy for Commercial Agriculture* (Washington, D.C., November 22, 1957), pp. 51–76.

[8] L. P. Fettig, "Purchases of New Farm Tractors and Machinery in Relation to the Non-Farm Business Cycle" (unpublished M.S. thesis, Michigan State University, 1958).

[9] W. A. Cromarty, *The Demand for Farm Machinery and Tractors* (Michigan State University Technical Bulletin [Lansing, 1960]).

II. THE MODEL

THEORETICAL CONSIDERATIONS

The demand for any input is derived from the demand for the product, the production function, and the supply conditions of other factors. Furthermore, the demand for a *durable* input is a demand for a stock, not a flow. It is the *stock* of machines (tractors) that enters the production function as an input, not the annual purchases of new machines. Hence the "investment function," the demand function for new purchases, must be derived from the demand for the stock. Given a production function, the assumption of competitive product and factor markets, and profit maximization, the stock demand for an input depends on the price of the product, the price of the input, the prices of other inputs, and, if it is a durable input, the rate of interest.[10]

In deriving a demand function, it is important to specify what is and what is not being held constant. For the purposes of this study the definition that seemed most useful was one that makes the demand for the stock of tractors a function of all the relevant prices, including the rate of interest, but allows output and other inputs to vary. This study, thus, differs from most consumer demand studies in the absence of a "scale" variable like income. But this is quite consistent with theory. In the conventional theory of the firm, the firm has no "budget restraint," and the production function is its only constraint.

I assume that this demand function is homogeneous of degree zero in all the prices. That is, a doubling of the price of the product and of all input prices, but holding the rate of interest constant, will not change the "desired" stock of tractors or the desired level of any of the other inputs. Using this property, we can express all prices as ratios, reduce the number of variables by one, and take care of the price "deflation" problem by using one of the relevant prices as a deflator.[11] Equation (1) summarizes schematically the general form of the stock demand function:

[10] The form of this demand function depends upon the form of the assumed production function. For example, the Cobb-Douglas production function will lead to demand functions for inputs that are linear in the logarithms of their variables.

[11] Strictly speaking, this theoretical discussion is valid only for a particular firm or farm. However, I shall proceed to apply it, without further qualification, to the whole industry. Throughout this study I follow the tradition of empirical demand analysis and beg the aggregation question. For a discussion of some of the problems involved in aggregation see H. Theil, *Linear Aggregation of Economic Relations* ("Contributions to Economic Analysis," Vol. VII [Amsterdam: North-Holland Publishing Co., 1954]), and Y. Grunfeld and Z. Griliches, "Is Aggregation Necessarily Bad?" *Review of Economics and Statistics*, Vol. XLII (February, 1960).

$$T_t^* = f\left(\frac{P_T}{P_p}, \frac{P_T}{P_0}, \ldots, r, X\right),\tag{1}$$

where T^* = desired stock of tractors, P_T = price of tractors, P_p = price of products, P_0 = price of other factors, r = rate of interest, and X = other variables. Notice that all prices appear as ratios to the price of tractors.[12]

The distinction between the "desired" and "actual" stock of tractors is a crucial feature of my model. The above demand function determines the "desired" stock of tractors; it says nothing about the "actual" stock of tractors. In most empirical demand studies it has been typically assumed that the "desired" stock always equals the "actual" stock or, what is almost the same thing, that all the adjustment is completed in one year. Neither assumption is a good one for durable goods. Adjustment takes time, and it may easily take more than one year to adjust to a disequilibrium, especially if we are not very sure where the equilibrium is and how long it is going to remain there. If prices and other variables fluctuate widely, we may not take the trouble to adjust unless we are convinced that the change is "permanent" or until we accumulate convincing evidence.[13] It is reasonable to suppose that the rate at which adjustment takes place will depend on the difference between the "desired" level of stock and its actual level. The simplest model of the adjustment process assumes that the change in actual stock is proportional to the difference between the "desired" and actual stock:

$$T_t - T_{t-1} = b(T_t^* - T_{t-1}),\tag{2}$$

where T_t is actual stock and b is a constant "adjustment" coefficient.

This is a very simple adjustment model which may not do justice to the complexity of the problem. It simply assumes that "response" is proportional to "stimulus." Actually, the adjustment process itself is affected by a whole set of economic considerations, and the relationship may not remain linear when large changes in stock are called for. There may be also asymmetries or "irreversibilities" in this process. For example, in a closed system it may be impossible to dispose of the existing stock of

[12] This somewhat strange repeated usage of the price of tractors divided by other prices is consistent with the homogeneity assumption. It arose out of looking at different "real" tractor prices: prices of tractors relative to price of labor, and so on.

[13] Considerations like these lie behind Friedman's "permanent versus transitory income" hypothesis (Milton Friedman, *A Theory of Consumption Function* [Princeton, N.J.: Princeton University Press, 1957]) and the distributed lag models of Nerlove, *Distributed Lags and Demand Analysis of Agricultural and Other Commodities.*

capital except as it wears out or is scrapped. This provides a floor, in the short run, for the possible magnitude of downward adjustments. On the upside, adjustments calling for a very large increase in actual stock may run into various production bottlenecks, and this may also impose a ceiling on the magnitude of short-run adjustments. I shall ignore these complications. The most important reason for overlooking them is that it would require a much more complicated model to take them into account.[14] And while equation (2) may present an oversimplified picture of the adjustment process, it is still much better than the assumption that all the adjustments are instantaneous.

It is convenient to assume that both the "desired" or "long-run" demand function (1) and the adjustment equation (2) are linear in the logarithms of the variables. This is equivalent to assuming that the production function is of a Cobb-Douglas form and that the adjustment equation is

$$\frac{T_t}{T_{t-1}} = \left\{ \frac{T_t^*}{T_{t-1}} \right\}^b . \tag{3}$$

Equations (1) and (3) imply the "short-run" stock demand equation

$$\log T_t = ba_0 + ba_1 \log X_{1t} + \ldots + (1-b) \log T_{t-1} + bu_t , \tag{4}$$

where the X's stand for the various independent variables, the a's are the elasticities of the "long-run" demand function (1), the ba's are the "short-run" elasticities, b is the "adjustment coefficient," and u_t is a disturbance attached to equation (1). This, then, is essentially the usual type of demand equation except that the lagged value of the dependent variable has been introduced as an additional independent variable.[15]

[14] Given the low estimates of the adjustment coefficients, to be presented below, it is unlikely that the "floor" or "ceiling" would be actually hit and present a real obstacle to this simple model. For example, a fall as large as 20 per cent in the "real" price of tractors is quite infrequent. Given a long-run elasticity of demand of -1.5, a 20 per cent fall in the "real" price of tractors would imply a 30 per cent fall reduction in the "desired" stock of tractors. But with an adjustment coefficient of .2 this would only imply a 6 per cent reduction in the first year, a drop that is substantially smaller than the depreciation of the existing stock.

[15] Because of the high intercorrelation of $\log T_t$ and $\log T_{t-1}$, the multiple correlation coefficients for (4) should be taken with a grain of salt. The relevant measure of success is, then, the partial correlation or "significance" of the coefficients of the other independent variables. That our results will not be spurious can be shown by considering the following form of (4):

$$\log T_t - \log T_{t-1} = ba_0 + ba_1 \log X_t + \ldots - b \log T_{t-1} + bu_t . \tag{5}$$

In (5) the first differences of the logarithms of T are related to all prices and $\log T_{t-1}$. There is now no strong intercorrelation. Nevertheless, it is a fact that, if we estimate

The coefficient of the lagged dependent variable subtracted from unity is an estimate of the "adjustment coefficient," b. The ratios of the other coefficients to this estimate of b are estimates of the "long-run" elasticities, the a's.

Alternatively, we can derive a flow-demand equation in which the dependent variable is the annual purchase of tractors (G_t = gross farm capital expenditures on tractors in 1935–39 dollars). Gross investment is the sum of net investment and replacement demand or depreciation. Net investment, of course, is the change in actual stock and is determined by the model outlined above. For simplicity, let us assume that replacement demand is proportional to the existing stock. This is equivalent to assuming a declining balance depreciation formula. To preserve some of the advantages of a logarithmic model, I assume, in addition, that the "desired" demand function (1) is semilogarithmic. That is,

$$e^{T_t^*} = a_0 X_1^{a_1} X_2^{a_2} \ldots e^{u_t} \tag{6}$$

$$T_t - T_{t-1} = b(T_t^* - T_{t-1}), \tag{7}$$

$$G_t = T_{t+1} - T_t + dT_t, \tag{8}$$

where d is the depreciation coefficient and where the stock T_t is dated at the beginning of the year or period. Taking the logarithm of (6), substituting it into (7), substituting (7) into (8), and simplifying, we get the gross investment equation

$$G_t = b \log a_0 + ba_1 \log X_{1t} + \ldots + (d - b)T_t + bu_t, \tag{9}$$

where the coefficient of stock equals now the difference between the depreciation and the adjustment coefficients.[16]

Apart from the difference in form assumed for equations (1) and (2),

---

(4) and (5) independently, we shall get exactly the same coefficients (except for the coefficient of $\log T_{t-1}$, which will equal $-b$) and exactly the same significance levels for the other variables. The only thing that will differ will be the multiple correlation coefficient, and it will usually be lower in (5) than in (4). But even this is only an apparent difference. The residual variance will be the same, and the multiple correlation coefficients will differ only because they are measured relative to a different base, relative to the variance of different dependent variables. All this happens because (5) is just a linear recombination of (4). Thus our results are independent of the high correlation between $\log T_t$ and $\log T_{t-1}$. Different versions of the same model, where there is no such intercorrelation, would produce exactly the same estimates of the relevant parameters, and these estimates would have the same standard errors.

[16] Since (9) is not linear in the logarithms of all the variables, the a's and ba's are not elasticities any more. They are slope coefficients. To derive elasticities, they have to be divided by the appropriate levels of stock or gross investment.

there is no theoretical difference between (4), the stock-demand equation, and (9), the investment function. But there is a practical difference. The data on the stock of tractors are poor, and the conceptual problems of the "right" measure of stock are very large. It may, therefore, be desirable to experiment with a variety of alternative measures of stock. Computationally, the flow formulation, equation (9), is much more convenient for these purposes.

STATISTICAL CONSIDERATIONS

I have used the least-squares method to estimate the coefficients of the stock demand and the gross investment functions. In both equations one of the independent variables, lagged stock, is the lagged value of a dependent variable. If the disturbances—the u's in equations (4) and (9)—are serially correlated, the least-squares estimates may be seriously biased. For the problem at hand the danger of bias is greatest for the estimate of the adjustment coefficient. The bias is likely to come about in the following way. It is unreasonable to suppose that the demand equations (4) and (9) include all the relevant variables. If both these omitted variables, and the dependent variable are serially correlated, it is likely that the omitted variables will be also correlated with the lagged value of the dependent variable. This will lead to an upward bias in the estimate of the coefficient of the lagged dependent variable and, therefore, to a downward bias in the estimate of the adjustment coefficient.[17] For this reason the adjustment coefficients estimated in the next section must be taken with a grain of salt. Their low values may be the consequence of omitting variables that change slowly over time rather than the result of a slow rate of adjustment by farmers to a difference between their actual stock of tractors and the stock they may desire.

There is a second, but I believe much less important, source of bias, "the simultaneous equations problem." Prices and quantities are simultaneously determined by a system of supply and demand equations; thus an equation fitted to price and quantity data may estimate a supply function rather than a demand function or neither one of these.

In the case at hand, however, both the price of agricultural output and the prices of agricultural inputs can be assumed to be predetermined. Tractor purchases are unlikely to influence agricultural product prices in the short run, both because the output effect of these purchases is likely

---

[17] For further discussion of this problem of bias see G. E. Barndow, "A Note on the Nerlove Estimate of Supply Elasticity," *Journal of Farm Economics*, Vol. XL (August, 1958); Nerlove, "On the Nerlove Estimate of Supply Elasticity: A Reply," *op. cit.*; and Z. Griliches, "Distributed Lags, Disaggregation, and Regional Demand Functions for Fertilizer," *Journal of Farm Economics*, February, 1959.

to be small and because agricultural output is subject to relatively large random (weather) fluctuations. The price paid for tractors is not affected much by the level of tractor purchases in the short run (within the season). Tractors are produced and sold by a few major firms that announce the price early in the model year and rarely vary it within the season. In the short run the price paid for tractors, therefore, may be assumed to be predetermined. This assumption gains support from the probable high elasticity of both the short- and the long-run supply function of tractors.

III. The Data and the Major Variables

G_t = farm gross capital expenditures on tractors in 1935–39 dollars. The undeflated data are from the USDA, *Farm Income Situation*. They are deflated by an unpublished index of prices paid by farmers for tractors (1935–39 = 100) made available by the Farm Income Branch of the Agricultural Marketing Service, USDA.

T_t = value of the stock of tractors on farms, January 1, in 1935–39 prices. These are unpublished USDA figures used in calculating depreciation for the net farm income estimates. The formulas used by the USDA in estimating the stock figures is:

$$T_t = (1 - d) T_{t-1} + (1 - \tfrac{1}{2} d) G_{t-1} ,$$

where d is the assumed rate of depreciation. This is equivalent to applying a declining balance depreciation formula to past accumulated gross investment. In recent years the USDA has been using 0.185 (18.5 per cent) as its rate of depreciation for tractors. The USDA, however, used much higher depreciation rates in the past and reduced them slowly in response to what it believed to be increases in the expected length of life of tractors. The actual USDA estimates are based on a slowly falling rate of depreciation, $d_{1910} = 0.40$, $d_{1920} = 0.30$, $d_{1930} = 0.25$, $d_{1940} = 0.20$, with the median d being around 0.23. I shall defer the discussion of the conceptual problem of measuring "the stock of tractors" to a later section.

X_{1t} = the index of prices paid for tractors divided by the index of prices received for crops. The index of tractor prices is the unpublished USDA index mentioned above. The index of prices received by farmers for all crops, 1910–14 = 100, is from USDA, *Major Statistical Series of the U.S. Department of Agriculture* (Agriculture Handbook No. 118 [Washington, D.C., 1957]), I, 15.

X_{2t} = the rate of interest: the farm mortgage interest rate, average rate for loans held by principal lenders from USDA, *Major Statistical Series of the U.S. Department of Agriculture*, VI, 22.

The preceding variables account for a high proportion of the variability in our dependent variables (see Tables 1 and 2). Several other variables, however, were introduced experimentally into these demand functions: the stock of horses on farms; the price of tractors relative to the wage paid to hired farm workers; the price of tractors relative to the price of motor supplies (gasoline, oil, tires, etc.); "real equity," deflated owners' net equity in agriculture (as a measure of "liquidity" or "capital rationing"); and trend. The variables will be described in the next section.

In addition to the problem of measuring stock, dealt with in a later section, two other measurements problems deserve comment. First, do the tractor stock and gross investment series take into account changes in the "quality of tractors"? The deflated series of *expenditures* on tractors does take into account quality changes for which a price is paid. For example, the series probably takes adequate account of the increase in horsepower, since there appears to be a relatively simple relationship between horsepower and the price of a tractor.[18] Furthermore, it is probably true that no revolutionary changes in tractor design have taken place since 1920.

From the standpoint of development, the 1920 tractor, taken collectively, embodied fundamental engineering and designing found perhaps in more refined form in tractors of the present day. The one-piece cast-iron frame, replaceable wearing parts, force-feed and pressure-gun lubrication, enclosed transmission, carburetor manifolding, air cleaner, electric lighting and starting, the high-tension magneto ignition with impulse starter, enclosed cooling system, anti-friction bearings, alloy and heat treated steels, and the power take-off had all been introduced and some experiments had been made with rubber tires. The lightweight low-price tractor had been designed and widely accepted, and several fairly successful motor cultivator-type units were on the market.

By this time, the advantage of the tractor as a farm power unit had been well established, and the number of companies manufacturing tractors had passed the 160 mark and tractor production 200,000 units, compared with 15 and 4,000, respectively, in 1910. The number of tractor manufacturers reached a peak of 186 in 1921.[19]

There was, on the other hand, a continuing stream of small improvements making for a much superior product today. Neither the quantity nor the price measures can reflect all these "quality" aspects. To the extent that the omitted "quality" changes are correlated with other independent variables, their omission may lead to bias in our estimates of the co-

---

[18] This is one of the major reasons for preferring deflated expenditures to numbers purchased as the dependent variable.

[19] R. B. Gray and E. M. Dieffenbach, "Fifty Years of Tractor Development in the U.S.A.," *Agricultural Engineering*, XXXVII (June, 1957), 393.

efficients of these variables and, in particular, to an upward bias in the estimate of the price elasticity.[20]

The second measurement problem is that of measuring the relevant rate of interest. Only for the farm mortgage rate are data available for a substantial period of time. But mortgage rates are notoriously inflexible, and their fluctuations probably underestimate substantially the fluctuations in the real marginal rate of interest paid by farmers. Similarly, published tractor prices may underestimate the fluctuation in the real price of tractors because they may fail to take into account changing discounts, loan terms, and the like.[21] To the extent that the price and interest figures have too little variability, the estimates of their coefficients will be biased upward.

IV. Results

Table 1 presents estimates of the coefficients of the stock-demand model fitted to the data. Equation (1.1) corresponds to the naïve stock-demand model in which it is assumed that the adjustment coefficient is unity—that is, that adjustment of actual to desired stock is instantaneous. In equation (1.2), fitted to data for the same time period as equation (1.1), the adjustment coefficient is estimated from the data rather than imposed upon them. The effect is to increase the multiple correlation coefficient to a very high level and, more importantly, greatly to increase the statistical significance of the estimated coefficient of the price variable, X_1. Notice that all the estimated coefficients of 1.2 are highly significant.

The estimated adjustment coefficient is approximately .17, suggesting that farmers adjust the actual stock of tractors slowly to short-run changes in prices and the rate of interest. The estimate of the short-run real price elasticity is approximately 0.25 and that for the long-run elasticity about −1.5. The estimates of the elasticities with respect to the rate of interest are even higher: approximately −1.0 in the short run and −6.0 in the long run.

In fitting equations (1.1) and (1.2), the war years were omitted. Equation (1.3), otherwise comparable to (1.2), was fitted to data that included the war years. The inclusion of the data for the war years lowers

[20] To the extent that the error in the price measure results also in an error in the opposite direction in the quantity measure, the bias will be toward a price elasticity of −1.

[21] E.g., the reported dealers' gross margins in the farm equipment retailing industry dropped from 20.2 per cent in 1952 to 17.9 per cent in 1953 and rose again to 19.0 per cent in 1956. From the *1957 Cost of Doing Business in the Farm Equipment Retailing Industry* (St. Louis: National Retail Farm Equipment Association).

The Demand for Durable Goods

the multiple correlation coefficient and the statistical significance of the estimates of all three coefficients.

Table 2 presents the results of fitting the gross investment equation to the data. The multiple correlation coefficient is high, and the estimated coefficients are highly significant. Table 3 shows the estimates of stock-demand elasticities derived from the gross investment equation. If the

TABLE 1

ESTIMATES OF THE UNITED STATES FARM DEMAND FOR TRACTORS
STOCK MODEL

(Dependent Variable $= \log T_t$)*

EQUATION No.	TIME PERIOD COVERED	COEFFICIENTS OF THE LOGARITHMS OF			R^2§	b‖	a_1#	a_2#
		X_{1t-1}†	X_{2t-1}‡	T_{t-1}				
(1.1).......	1921–41, 1948–57	−0.519 (0.231)††	−4.933 (0.477)	....	0.793	1.00**	−0.5	−4.9
(1.2).......	1921–41, 1948–57	− .254 (.042)	−1.188 (0.154)	0.827 (0.028)	.994	.173	−1.5	−6.9
(1.3).......	1921–57	−0.218 (0.051)	−0.855 (0.170)	0.864 (0.035)	0.987	0.136	−1.6	−6.3

    * T_t = value of the stock of tractors on farms, January 1, in 1935–39 dollars.

    † X_{1t-1} = index of prices paid for tractors divided by an index of prices received for all crops.

    ‡ X_{2t-1} = the rate of interest.

    § R^2 is the square of the multiple correlation coefficient.

    ‖ b is the adjustment coefficient calculated by subtracting the coefficient of $\log T_{t-1}$ from 1.

    # a_1 is the "long-run" price elasticity, and a_2 is the "long-run" elasticity of the demand for tractors with respect to the farm mortgage rate of interest, calculated by dividing the estimated coefficients by b.

    ** Assumed.

    †† Figures in the parentheses are the calculated standard errors.

TABLE 2

ESTIMATES OF COEFFICIENTS OF THE UNITED STATES FARM
TRACTOR INVESTMENT FUNCTION

EQUATION No.	TIME PERIOD COVERED	COEFFICIENTS OF			R^2
		$\log X_{1t}$	$\log X_{2t}$	T_t	
(2.1)*.........	1920–40, 1947–56	−353.5 (57.9)	−1,333 (178)	0.0995 (0.0195)	0.929
(2.2′).........	1920–40, 1947–56	−359.7 (64.0)	−1,385 (202)	.0849 (.0225)	.913
(2.3′).........	1920–41, 1947–57	−375.7 (64.9)	−1,470 (193)	.0704 (.0212)	.905
(3.0′).........	1920–41, 1948–57	−417.1 (68.0)	−1,594 (203)	.0609 (0.0214)	0.910

    * Equations denoted by a prime use slightly revised data that became available in the summer of 1958. $N_{2.1, 2.2'} = 31$, $N_{2.3'} = 33$, $N_{3.0'} = 32$.

depreciation coefficient is .23 (the median rate used in computing T_t), the estimated adjustment coefficient is .17.[22] Since the stock-demand function underlying the gross investment relation is semilogarithmic, the elasticities are not constant but depend on the existing level of stock. Thus the estimated elasticities at the 1957 levels of stock are substantially lower than those estimated for the mean level of stocks. Note, however, that the elasticities estimated in the stock demand model (Table 1) fall between the mean level and the 1957 level elasticities estimated from the investment function. In summary, both models indicate an adjustment coefficient of about .17, a "real" price elasticity of about −.25 in

TABLE 3

ESTIMATES OF STOCK-DEMAND ELASTICITIES DERIVED FROM EQUATION (2.3′), ASSUMING THAT $d=0.23$ AND, THEREFORE, $b=0.17$*

	ELASTICITIES WITH RESPECT TO THE			
	"Real" Price of Tractors X_1		Rate of Interest X_2	
	Short Run	Long Run	Short Run	Long Run
At the mean......	−0.45	−2.63	−1.76	−10.3
At 1957 stock levels	−0.20	−1.16	−0.78	− 4.5

* To estimate the adjustment coefficient and the stock elasticities from the investment function it is necessary to make an assumption about the average rate of depreciation d and to adjust for the fact that some of the gross investment depreciates during the year it is bought. Assuming that $d = 0.23$, we multiply all the coefficients of (2.3′) by $(1 - \frac{1}{2}d) = 0.885$ and get −332, −1,301, and 0.0623, respectively. Subtracting 0.0623 from 0.23 leads to an estimate of $b = 0.1677$. Dividing through by b gives us the coefficients of the "long-run" stock demand function, and dividing through by the appropriate stock levels, its elasticities.

the short run and −1.5 in the long run, and an elasticity of the stock demand for tractors with respect to the farm mortgage rate of about −1.0 in the short run and −5.0 in the long run.[23]

Tables 4 and 5 report on efforts to improve these results by introducing additional variables. One of the first additional variables to be tried, the

[22] A lower assumption about d would have led to lower short-run and higher long-run elasticities.

[23] The estimated interest elasticities are probably substantially too high. There may be two reasons for this overestimate: (1) The interest-rate series used is very sluggish, underestimating the real variability in the marginal rates of interest. This would bias both the short-run and the long-run estimates upward. (2) Given the general sluggishness of interest rates, there may be no or very little lag in the response to changing rates. If this is true, then the distributed lag model may not be applicable to this variable, and it may be incorrect to divide its coefficient by the estimated adjustment coefficient. If this latter consideration holds, it would lead to an upward bias only in the estimate of the "long-run" interest elasticity.

The Demand for Durable Goods

price of tractors relative to the "price" of labor (X_3), had the "wrong" sign in the stock model (Table 4, eq. [1.4]) but was not significantly different from zero.[24] X_3 has the "right" sign (for a substitute factor) in the investment function (Table 5, [eq. 2.5]) but is not significant statistically.

The possible impact of the existing stock of horses and mules on the demand for tractors prompted the introduction of H_t, the value of the stock of horses and mules on farms in 1935–39 dollars.[25] The coefficient of H_t has the right sign in both the stock and the investment functions but is not significantly different from zero in either (Table 4, eq. [1.5], and

TABLE 4

ADDITIONAL STOCK REGRESSIONS

EQUATION No.	TIME PERIOD COVERED	COEFFICIENTS OF					R^2
		$\log X_{1t-1}$	$\log X_{2t-1}$	$\log X_{3t-1}$*	$\log T_{t-1}$	$\log H_{t-1}$†	
(1.4)......	1921–57	−0.259 (0.127)	−0.814 (0.208)	0.052 (0.146)	0.886 (0.071)	....	0.987
(1.5)......	1921–41, 1948–57	−0.261 (0.043)	−1.192 (0.154)	....	0.768 (0.061)	−0.079 (0.072)	0.994

* X_3 = the index of prices paid for tractors divided by the index of wages paid for hired farm labor.
† H = the value of the stock of horses and mules on farms, January 1, in 1935–39 dollars.

Table 5, eq. [2.4]). In both cases the coefficient of H_t is about one-tenth of the coefficient of T_t, though both are measured in the same units. The data indicate that changes in the stock of horses and mules had very little impact on the demand for tractors.

Johnson has emphasized repeatedly the importance of capital gains and capital rationing in explaining farmer's demand for durable assets.[26]

[24] X_3 = index of prices paid for tractors divided by the USDA index, 1910–14 = 100, of wages paid for hired farm labor. The tractor-price index is the previously mentioned unpublished USDA index. The wage index is from USDA, *Major Statistical Series of the U.S. Department of Agriculture*, I, 63.

[25] H_t = number of horses and mules on farms, January 1, multiplied by the average 1935–39 value per head. The numbers of horses and mules are from USDA, *Power and Machinery on Farms and Related Data* (ARS 43–26, [Washington, D.C., February 14, 1958]). Average value per head in 1935–39 was computed from data given in USDA, *Livestock on Farms and Ranches on January 1* (Statistical Bull. 88 [Washington, D.C., 1950]). Attempts to weight horses and mules separately, or to use animal units fed instead of numbers, made very little difference.

[26] Glenn L. Johnson, "Supply Function—Some Facts and Notions," in Heady *et al.* (eds.), *Agricultural Adjustment Problems in a Growing Economy* (Ames: Iowa State College Press, 1958).

TABLE 5

ADDITIONAL INVESTMENT REGRESSIONS

Equation No.	Time Period Covered	$\log X_{1t}$	$\log X_{2t}$	$\log X_{3t}$*	$\log X_{4t}$†	$\log X_{5t}$‡	$\log X_{6t}$§	T_t	H_t‖	R^2
(2.4)	1920–40, 1947–56	−361 (66)	−1,291 (257)	......	......	......	......	0.091 (0.041)	−0.010 (0.044)	0.929
(2.5)	1920–40, 1947–56	−267 (115)	−1,338 (188)	−192 (156)	−298 (364)	......	......	.111 (.056)	......	.933
(2.6')	1920–41, 1947–57	−433 (83)	−1,261 (266)	......	......	227 (220)	......	.050 (.027)	......	.909
(2.7')	1920–41, 1947–57	−378 (75)	−1,453 (306)	......	......	......	147 (199)	0.069 (0.032)	......	0.905

* X_3 = index of prices paid for tractors divided by an index of wages paid to hired farm labor.

† X_4 = "real" equity. Proprietors' equity in agriculture deflated by an index of prices paid by farmers for commodities used in production.

‡ X_5 = index of prices paid for tractors divided by the index of prices paid for motor supplies.

§ X_6 = time; t = 20, . . . , 41, 47, . . . , 57.

‖ H_t = value of the stock of horses and mules on farms, January 1, in 1935–39 prices.

A measure of "real" proprietors' equity in agriculture, X_4, therefore was computed and introduced experimentally into the investment model.[27] How should such a variable be introduced into the gross investment function? Does it belong in the demand equation itself, or should it, rather, enter via the adjustment equation? A simple way of introducing it is to assume that the demand for tractors depends on the effective or marginal rate of interest. For a given "market" rate of interest, the higher the equity, the lower is the effective rate of interest. If the relationship among the "effective" rate, the "market" rate, and "equity" is linear in the logarithms, the logarithm of equity should appear linearly in the final estimation equation. Although there is a substantial positive correlation between gross investment in tractors and real equity ($r^2 = 0.678$), the coefficient of X_4 (Table 5, eq. [2.5]) is statistically insignificant and has the wrong sign. This may be due either to the unimportance of equity to the investment process, to my inability to capture the relevant aspects of "equity" in this measure, or, though less likely, to the use of an incorrect functional form.

An effort to improve results by adding a complementary factor, X_5 the price of tractors relative to the prices paid for motor supplies, was also unsuccessful (Table 5, eq. [2.6']).[28] Though its coefficient has the "right" sign for the price of a complementary factor, its contribution was not significantly different from zero at the conventional significance levels.[29]

The final variable tested, log X_{6t}, is a simple logarithmic time trend introduced to represent all slowly changing forces not accounted for by the other variables. The coefficient of log X_6 is also not statistically significant (see Table 5, eq. [2.7']). This is an important result. It implies the rejection of many alternative hypotheses giving "trend" a prominent role.

[27] Sources: 1940 to date, from *Balance Sheet of Agriculture*. Before 1940, computed by adding to the published USDA value of real farm estate the unpublished USDA estimates of the inventory value of machinery and equipment on farms, the Goldsmith figures on the inventory value of feed and livestock on farms, the Goldsmith figures on the financial assets of farmers, and subtracting the Goldsmith estimates of the financial liabilities of farmers. The two series were linked at 1940 and divided by the index of prices paid by farmers for commodities used in production to arrive at a series on farmers' equity in constant dollars. For the Goldsmith figures see R. W. Goldsmith, *A Study of Saving in the United States* (Princeton, N.J.: Princeton University Press, 1956), Vol. I.

[28] X_5 = index of prices paid for tractors divided by the USDA index, 1910–14 = 100, of prices paid by farmers for motor supplies (gasoline, motor oil, tires, etc.). The motor supplies price index is taken from USDA, *Agricultural Prices*, October, 1957, Supplement 1 and subsequent issues.

[29] The contribution of log X_5 becomes statistically significant when it is introduced in conjunction with another measure of stock (see Table 7).

V. ALTERNATIVE MEASURES OF STOCK

Econometric studies often raise more questions than they answer. For me, an important question to emerge from this study is: What is the "right" way of measuring stock? The theoretical literature is full of the difficulties involved in the concept of "stock of capital," while the empirical literature abounds in makeshift measures and expedient compromises. I know of almost no attempt to investigate the empirical implications of alternative stock measures. It would take us too far afield to explore all that this implies here, in particular, as I intend to pursue it in detail elsewhere. It will suffice to indicate that a first step toward answering the question of the "right" way of measuring stock is the realization that it does not have a unique answer. Different measures of stock will be useful in answering different questions.

The USDA estimates of the stock of tractors on farms are a by-product of the "net farm income" calculations. They were developed to provide depreciation estimates to be subtracted from the gross income figures. My first doubts about the adequacy of the USDA stock series were aroused when I realized that the "official" estimates were based on a declining rather than constant rate of depreciation. The rate of depreciation is 0.4 in 1910, declines to 0.3 in the 1920's, to 0.25 in the 1930's, and to 0.2 in the 1940's. This can, however, be explained on the basis of the lengthening average life of tractors. The USDA chooses as its depreciation rate that rate which will depreciate the purchases to a small percentage (scrap value, say, 5 per cent) of their original value at the end of their *expected* service life. An 18.5 per cent rate would depreciate a new purchase to about 5 per cent of its original value in fifteen years, the expected useful life-span of a tractor now assumed by the USDA.[30] Over the years, as the expected life of tractors has increased, the USDA revised its depreciation rate downward.

Nowhere does the USDA explicitly defend its choice of the depreciation rate. At 18.5 per cent depreciation, a four-year-old tractor has only 44 per cent of its original value left. Almost half of the "value" of a tractor disappears in the first three years (46 per cent). In view of the

[30] The difficulties that beset this approach can be brought out by considering the following: The USDA depreciates *all* tractors over their *average* expected life. Consider the purchase in Year 0 of 100 tractors, each with an expected service life of ten years. This can be viewed as the purchase of 1,000 tractor-service-years. Using the USDA method of depreciation, the stock measure in Year 10 would indicate that only 50 tractor-years have remained from the original purchase of 1,000. But actually, if the distribution of service life is reasonably symmetric about its average, 500 tractor-years will be still there. At the age of the *average* life-expectancy only one-half of the original population are dead.

fact that tractors, by and large, lack the fashion elements that make for a high rate of depreciation of motorcars, the depreciation rate used by the USDA seems rather high.

We can get independent evidence on the rate of depreciation from the used-tractor market data. Two firms publish annual tractor trade-in guides ("blue books"), and auction prices of used tractors are currently being published in *Implement and Tractor*. Table 6 summarizes some of the available data in the "blue books."[31] Except for the first year, the calculated depreciation rates are substantially below the USDA rate. The data point to a declining-balance depreciation model, with a rate somewhat higher in the 1930's than in the 1950's. Over the whole period the depreciation rate computed from the relative prices of different age tractors (leaving the first year out) is around 11 per cent.[32] If we add another percentage point for the "pure accident rate," the depreciation rate is still only 12 per cent, which is substantially lower than the 18.5 (and higher) rate used by the USDA.[33]

Even this estimate may be too high. The value of a used tractor may decrease with age because it is deteriorating in its physical performance, because its expected life is decreasing, or because it is expected that better tractors will be available in the future ("obsolescence"). For some purposes, only the first reason, physical deterioration in a tractor's ability to perform its services, may be relevant.[34] It is not at all obvious that for

[31] Auction-price data are difficult to summarize because of the very large variance in the reported prices. On the whole, however, the implied depreciation rates in auction prices are very close to the "blue book" data with the possible exception of somewhat lower depreciation of old (ten years and older) tractors.

[32] The estimates of the first year's depreciation are unreliable and may not be relevant. The denominator is the "list price" which very few people pay, and last year's model is usually more than one year old (probable median age is around fifteen to sixteen months). Also, part of the first year's large drop in price is due simply to the "loss of virginity," the simple fact of passage from "new" to "used" which may be irrelevant for our calculations.

[33] For a very interesting discussion of one depreciation model see J. S. Cramer, "The Depreciation and Mortality of Motor Cars," *Journal of the Royal Statistical Society*, Ser. A, Vol. CXXI, No. 1 (1958).

[34] This may be especially true if we want to use our measure of capital for productivity comparisons. Neither expected obsolescence nor a reduction in the expected lifespan of a particular machine is then a valid reason for reducing its weight (writing it down) in our measure of the physical stock of capital. On this see my paper on "Output over Input Indexes and the Measurement of Technological Change" (unpublished). As far as physical deterioration is concerned, all the available evidence points to much lower rates of "depreciation." For example, in 1956 about 35 per cent of all wheel tractors on farms were between six and ten years old, and about 30 per cent were ten years

TABLE 6*

DEPRECIATION OF FARM TRACTORS AS MEASURED BY RELATIVE PRICES OF USED TRACTORS OF DIFFERENT AGES (BUT SAME MAKE AND MODEL) IN A GIVEN YEAR

(P_t/P_{t+1}: Average of Price Ratios of "Adjacent-Year" Tractors of Same Make and Model)

YEAR	1	2	3	4	5	6	7	8	9	10	11	12	13	AVERAGE FOR TRACTORS OLDER THAN ONE YEAR
1958 (fall)†	0.81	0.91	0.91	0.91	0.91	0.91	0.91	0.91	0.91	0.91	0.91	0.90	....	0.91
1958 (spring)‡	.78	.92	.91	.89	.90	.90	.90	.90	.88	.87	.85	....	....	.89
1956§	.76	.90	.89	.90	.91	.91	.91	.91	.91	.91	.91	.91	....	.91
1952‖	.79	.91	.91	.92	.92	.93	.93	.94	.94	.94	.93	....	....	.93
1950#	.81	.91	.92	.89	.89	.87	.87	.87	.87	.86	.83	....	....	.86
1948 (fall)**	.73	.90	.90	.91	.91	.91	.90	.89	.90	.89	.88	.90	....	.90
1948 (spring)††	.81	.90	.95	.92	.92	.91	.89	.89	.90	.87	....	....	....	.89
1946‡‡	0.73	.90	.91	.91	.90	.89	.89	.91	.89	.90	.89	.88	0.87	.90
1941§§	....	.87	.87	.86	.87	.87	.87	.86	.84	.84	....	....	....	.86
1937‖‖	....	0.87	0.86	0.86	0.89	0.89	0.88	0.88	0.84	0.82	....	....	....	0.87

* 1950–58 figures are based on "Average Resale Prices" given in various trade manuals. 1948 and earlier figures are based on "Average As-Is Values" or "Trade-In Values." From 1950 on, when data are available for both concepts, except for the first year, both concepts give practically identical results. At most, the "As-Is Values" depreciate by about one percentage point faster, each year, than the "Resale Values." These averages are based on a "representative" rather than a random sample of 30–75 per cent of all the available observations.

† *Official Tractor and Farm Equipment Guide* (St. Louis: National Retail Farm Equipment Association, Fall, 1958). Average N, number of paired observations for each two adjacent years, is 23.

‡ *National Farm Tractor and Implement Blue Book* (Chicago: National Market Reports, 1958), Ave. N = 29.

§ *Official . . . Guide* (Fall, 1956), Ave. N = 22.
‖ *Official . . . Manual* (Spring, 1952), Ave. N = 22.
Blue Book (1950), Ave. N = 22.
** *Official . . . Manual* (Fall, 1948), Ave. N = 15.
†† *Blue Book* (1948), Ave. N = 10.
‡‡ *Official . . . Manual* (1946), Ave N = 15.
§§ *Official . . . Manual* (1941), Ave. N = 23.
‖‖ *United Tractor and Combine Trade-In Manual* (National Federation of Implement Dealers' Associations, 1937), Ave. N = 19.

our purposes a stock measure based on "value" depreciation is superior to one based on "physical-service" depreciation. An alternative extreme assumption is that of "one-horse shay": a tractor does not deteriorate in service until it is scrapped or falls apart. This assumption leads to the use of the total number of tractors on farms, irrespective of age, as the stock variable.

TABLE 7

INVESTMENT REGRESSIONS: ALTERNATIVE MEASURES OF STOCK

EQUATION No.	TIME PERIOD COVERED	COEFFICIENTS OF						R^2
		log X_1	log X_2	log X_5	T^*	$T_2\dagger$	$T_3\ddagger$	
(2.1)...	1920–40, 1947–56	−354 (58)	−1,333 (178)	....	0.100 (0.020)	....	....	0.929
(2.8)...	1920–40, 1947–56	−384 (58)	−1,345 (185)	....	....	0.070 (0.015)	....	.925
(2.3')...	1920–41, 1947–57	−376 (65)	−1,470 (193)	....	.070 (.021)	....	....	.905
(2.9')...	1920–41, 1947–57	−395 (67)	−1,479 (218)	....	....	....	24.9 (9.0)	.896
(2.91')..	1920–41, 1947–57	−353 (66)	−1,605 (213)	....	.191 (.088)	....	− 50.5 (35.6)	.911
(2.93')..	1920–41, 1947–57	−504 (73)	−1,156 (228)	755 (229)	.343 (.088)	....	−141.9 (41.5)	.936
(3.1')...	1920–41, 1948–57	−558 (77)	−1,204 (222)	787 (222)	0.295 (0.090)	....	−126.8 (41.2)	0.941

* T = USDA estimate of the value of the stock of tractors on farms in 1935–39 prices. Average $d = 0.23$.
† T_2 = cumulated gross investment assuming that $d = 0.12$ and that T_2 (1920) = T (1920).
‡ T_3 = number of tractors on farms.

Table 7 presents the results of using three alternative measures of stock in the tractor investment function: (1) T = USDA estimate based on an average $d = 0.23$; (2) T_2 = cumulated past gross investment, $d = 0.12$; and (3) T_3 = the total number of tractors on farms.[35] The most striking

---

and older. It is rather doubtful that they did only 24 and 9 per cent of the work done by a new tractor, respectively. But this is what is implied by an 18.5 per cent depreciation rate for seven- and twelve-year-old tractors. Actually, the six- to ten-year-old-tractors worked only 11 per cent less hours than the one- to five-year-olds, and the over-ten-year-old tractors still worked as many as 63 per cent of the hours worked by a typical one- to five-year-old tractor in 1956. This does not indicate a very high rate of "physical deterioration." The source of these figures is USDA, ARS, *The National Survey of Farm Machinery, 1956: Selected Tables from Forthcoming Publications* (Washington, D.C., June 18, 1958).

[35] T_3 is taken from USDA, *Changes in Farm Production and Efficiency* (Statistical Bull. 233 [Washington, D.C., August, 1958]).

feature of this table is how little difference it makes which measure we use. While the USDA measure yields the highest R^2, the differences in fit between the various regressions are not statistically significant. Moreover, the coefficient of X_1 and X_2 are practically unaffected by the substitution of different stock measures.[76] It seems that we are unable to differentiate between alternative stock measures on the basis of goodness-of-fit criteria.

A very interesting result, however, emerges from a comparison of (2.9') with (2.91'). In (2.9') the stock measure is the number of tractors instead of the USDA depreciated value of stock estimate used in (2.3'). The coefficient of the number of tractors has the same sign as the coefficient of the USDA stock estimate in (2.3'), and the R^2 is only a few points lower. But when *both* measures are introduced in (2.91'), the sign of T_3, the coefficient of the number of tractors on farms, becomes negative and is almost twice as large as its standard error. When log X_5 is introduced ([2.93'] and [3.1']), the coefficient of T_3 is significantly different from zero, while T, the USDA estimate, also retains its significance and opposite sign. This indicates not only that T and T_3 measure somewhat different things in the sense that each of them has an independent contribution to make to the explanation of G_t but also that the different things measured by T and T_3 have actually opposite effects on G_t.

Beside having increased the multiple correlation coefficient and the significance levels of T_3, equations (2.93') and (3.1') represent a substantial improvement over (2.9') and (3.0') for two additional reasons: (*a*) the serial correlation of the residuals is greatly reduced when log X_5 and T_3 are added to the other explanatory variables[37] and (*b*) equations (2.93') and (3.1') perform much better in the recent post–World War II period than equations (2.9') and (3.0). The predictive performance of (2.9') and (2.93') is charted in Chart II.

It is not too difficult to see how two different stock measures could both contribute significantly to the explanation of gross investment. The first measure of stock, T, assumes a declining-balance depreciation world in which the marginal productivity of a four-year-old tractor is one-half of the marginal productivity of a new tractor and, furthermore, that the age distribution of the stock of tractors does not matter as long as its value is the same. The second measure, T_3, goes to the opposite extreme

[36] Nor are they affected much by the introduction of other variables. The surprising stability in the estimates of these coefficients is also recorded in Table 5.

[37] We cannot reject the hypothesis of positive serial correlation of the residuals for equation (2.9'), but we can reject it for (2.93'). The Durbin-Watson coefficients are 1.11 and 1.79, respectively.

and assumes that a twenty-year-old tractor is as good as a new one. Only the number of tractors matters, not their value. But the truth may lie somewhere in between these two extremes. If this is so, then the use of both measures together could provide a better approximation of the "true" measure of stock than is accomplished by the use of either one of the "extreme assumption" stock measures separately.

It is less obvious, however, why the coefficients of these two measures should have opposite signs—the coefficient of "value," T, being positive,

CHART II

FARMERS' GROSS CAPITAL EXPENDITURES ON TRACTORS, 1935–39 DOLLARS

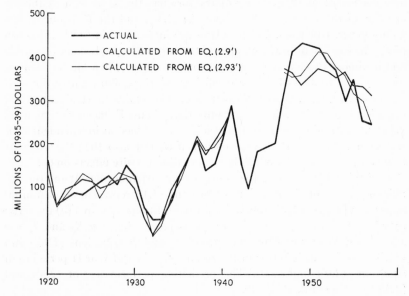

and the coefficient of "numbers," T_3, negative. To understand this, we have to recall how lagged stock affects gross investment in our model. Gross investment consists of replacement plus net investment. The impact of lagged stock on replacement demand is positive. The impact of lagged stock on net investment is negative. The actual sign of the coefficient of the stock of tractors in the investment function is then indeterminate, a priori. It depends on whether d, the rate of depreciation is higher or lower than b, the adjustment coefficient. A possible interpretation of the results of (2.91′), (2.93′), and (3.1′) is that, in some way, T, the depreciated value of the stock of tractors on farms, measures better the forces affecting replacement demand, whereas T_3, the number of tractors on farms, measures better the depressing effects of the existing quantity of capital on net investment.

This interpretation may not appear so surprising if we reconsider the problem of the "ideal" measures of investment and capital.[38] If machines do not deteriorate much with age (i.e., we are close to a "one-horse-shay" world), then the demand for capital as a productive asset is a demand for a *number* of machines; whether these are old or new is irrelevant as long as they will do the job. The choice of the optimal durability of capital will usually be made on different grounds, the most important being the "cost of durability," speculative considerations, and transactions costs. Whatever are the determinants of the *value* of capital, there will be, at any one point, a particular "desired" level. Once it is achieved, and unless other variables change, the desire to maintain this level may determine replacement demand. That is, the *value* concept of capital may be the relevant measure for determining replacement demand. On the other hand, if some of the variables change and there is now a desire for a different scale of production or a different ratio of factors, this demand will be for an additional *number* of machines. How many more machines this implies and how fast the adjustment will be may depend more on the existing number of machines than on their *value*. That is, the number of existing machines may be a better measure than their depreciated value of the depressing effect of an existing stock of capital on net investment.

If we introduce the possibility of maintenance and repairs (i.e., the possibility of producing a "four"-year-old tractor from a five-year-old), this can provide another explanation of our results. Maintenance and repairs are to some extent a substitute for purchases. The larger the number of old machines on farms, the more scope there is for the production of "additional," or "newer" tractors from old ones. Hence, given a particular desired level of stock, we might expect smaller purchases of new tractors the larger is the number of old tractors on farms (keeping the value of the stock constant). Given an increase in the desired stock, the existence of larger numbers would imply less purchases and more repairs.[39]

There are, thus, several ways in which we can interpret the coefficients

---

[38] In this paragraph I draw heavily on conversations with Trygve Haavelmo. I have also had access to his unpublished manuscript, "A Study in the Theory of Investment."

[39] Our results may have, however, a purely statistical interpretation. It is possible that there is serial correlation in investment above and beyond the serial correlation that is explained by the model and the independent variables that it contains. One way of taking this into account would have been to introduce lagged investment explicitly into our model. We did not do this, but the combination of value and numbers may perform the same role as lagged investment. Numbers will be high relative to value when purchases in the last year or last couple of years have been lower than usual. If there is serial correlation in investment, this will imply that purchases this year will also be lower. Conversely, a high value of the stock relative to numbers would occur in periods of above-average gross investment and would imply more of the same in the future.

of T and T_3 in these equations. One of them would be to identify the coefficient of T with d, the replacement or depreciation coefficient, and the coefficient of T_3 with b, the adjustment coefficient. It is simpler, however, to assume that, whatever is the division of roles between these variables, the sum of their coefficients should still add up to $(d-b)$. Before we can do this, we have to convert T_3 into the same units (dollars) as T. If we assume that T is a reasonably good measure of the *value* of all tractors on farms, we can use its average value per tractor for the years 1920–41, 1947–57, to adjust the coefficient of $T_3(\Sigma_t T_t/\Sigma_t T_{3t} = \$376)$. If, as I believe, the USDA measure underestimates the value of tractors on farms,

TABLE 8

ESTIMATES OF $(d-b)$ AND b FROM DIFFERENT
INVESTMENT EQUATIONS*

EQUATION No.	d	ASSUMED AVERAGE VALUE OF A TRACTOR ON FARMS IN 1935–39 DOLLARS	ESTIMATED	
			$(d-b)$	b
(2.3').........	0.23	$376	0.06	0.17
(2.91')........	.23	$376	.05	.16
	.12	$595	.02	.10
(2.93')........	.23	$376	− .03	.26
	.12	$595	− .03	.15
(3.1').........	.23	$376	− .04	.27
	0.12	$595	−0.03	0.15

* All the coefficients are multiplied first by $(1 - \frac{1}{2}d)$. For example, in (3.1'), assuming $d = 0.12$ and that a unit of T_3 is worth $595, we derive: $(d - b) = 0.94 \ (0.295/1.64 - 126.8/595) = -0.03$. Multpilying by -1 and adding 0.12 gives us the estimate $b = 0.15$.

we can use the average value per tractor derived from the T_2 series using a lower (.12) rate of depreciation $(\Sigma T_2/\Sigma T_3 = \$595)$. In this case, however, we should adjust the coefficient of T downward by dividing it through by 1.64, the ratio of average T_2 to T, and use a $d = 0.12$ in estimating the adjustment coefficient.

Table 8 summarizes the different estimates of $(d-b)$ and b derivable from equations (2.9'), (2.91'), (2.93'), and (3.1'). There is little difference between the estimates of (2.9') and (2.91'). However, the introduction of log X_5, the price of tractors relative to the price of motor supplies, does make a difference. If we accept a d of 0.23, then equations (2.93') and (3.1') indicate an adjustment coefficient substantially higher than .17. This is not too surprising, since we had good reason to expect a downward bias in the estimate of the adjustment coefficients. If we accept, however, the hypothesis that the USDA depreciation rates are too high and use a value estimate based on $d = 0.12$, the estimated adjustment coefficients are again very close to .17.

As was indicated before, this section was largely intended to raise questions rather than to answer them. Some of the lines of attack that we could take in answering them have been indicated above, and I do intend to pursue them further elsewhere. More work is needed, however, both on the theoretical side and on the empirical side. We need to know what the "right" measure is from the theoretical point of view, how to measure capital in practice, and how much difference it actually makes.

VI. Conclusions and Implications

Both the stock-demand model and the gross investment model indicate a stock-price elasticity of demand of about -0.25 in the short run and about -1.5 in the long run and an interest elasticity of about -1.0 in the short run and -5.8 in the long run. The estimated adjustment period is rather long, the adjustment coefficient being about .17, but this result could be due to the downward bias in the estimates of this coefficient.

Low short-run *stock*-demand elasticities do not imply that *gross investment* is very stable with respect to changes in the relative price of tractors. In fact, the *short-run* price elasticity of *investment* is much higher. It is -1.9 at the mean level of investment and -1.4 at the 1957 level of investment.[40] Thus a 10 per cent rise in the relative price of tractors (or a 10 per cent drop in crop prices) in 1957 would have resulted in the same year in a 14 per cent drop in the demand for the output flow of the tractor industry. Even though the *stock*-demand elasticities are small, they still imply very large fluctuations in *investment*.

While small recessions may not result in large changes in the demand for durable agricultural inputs produced in the non-farm sector, this is not a consequence of the "stability" of the demand for durables but rather the result of the relative stability of the consumer demand for agricultural products, particularly food. On the other hand, agricultural *prices* do fluctuate substantially as a result of changes in government policy, export demand, weather, and other factors. For example, between 1947 and 1957 the "real" price of tractors changed on the average by 8 per cent from year to year, and in two of these ten years it changed by more than 17 per cent. Such changes in prices reflect themselves immediately in large changes in the demand for capital items.

Low short-run stock elasticities do imply, however, that the effect on agricultural output of a change in the relative price of inputs is small in the short run. This is consistent with the generally accepted notion that

[40] Based on equation (2.3′).

the aggregate agricultural supply function is very inelastic. The *long-run* stock elasticities, however, are quite high, implying that there may be a large supply response if the change in relative prices persists for more than one or two years. Given time, a favorable price relationship leads to substantial investment in capital items and eventually, also, to expansion in agricultural output.

APPENDIX

TABLE A1

STOCK-DEMAND FUNCTION: FIRST-ORDER CORRELATION
COEFFICIENTS SQUARED, 1921–41, 1948–57

Log	r^2			
	$\log X_{1t-1}$	$\log X_{2t-1}$	$\log H_{t-1}$	$\log T_{t-1}$
$T_t{}^*$......	(−)0.001	(−)0.755	(−)0.900	0.976
$X_{1t-1}\dagger$....	....	(−)0.033	(−) .006	.001
$X_{2t-1}\ddagger$....			0.632	(−) .680
$H_{t-1}\S$.....				(−)0.920

　　* T_t = value of the stock of tractors on farms, in 1935–39 prices.
　　† X_1 = price of tractors relative to price received for all crops.
　　‡ X_2 = rate of interest.
　　§ H_t = value of the stock of horses and mules in 1935–39 prices.

TABLE A2

TRACTOR INVESTMENT FUNCTION: FIRST-ORDER CORRELATION COEFFICIENTS
SQUARED, UNREVISED DATA, 1920–40, 1947–56

	r^2						
	$\log X_1$	$\log X_2$	$\log X_3$	$\log X_4$	$H_t{}^*$	T_t	$T_{2t}\dagger$
$G_t\ddagger$......	(−)0.054	(−)0.706	(−)0.491	0.678	(−)0.713	0.740	0.708
$\log X_1$...	....	(−)0.033	.444	(−) .081	(−) .030	(−) .001	.001
$\log X_2$....			0.101	(−) .352	0.765	(−) .550	(−) .575
$\log X_3$....				(−)0.703	N.c.‖	(−) .456	N.c.‖
$\log X_4\S$...						.870	N.c.‖
$H_t{}^*$......						(−)0.850	(−)0.908
T_t......							N.c.‖

　　* H_t = the value of horses and mules on farms in 1935–39 prices.
　　† T_{2t} = the value of the stock of tractors on farms in 1935–39 prices computed by cumulating past gross investment using a 12 per cent rate of depreciation.
　　‡ G_t = gross farm capital expenditures on tractors in 1935–39 prices.
　　§ X_4 = net proprietors' equity in agriculture in 1910–14 prices.
　　‖ Not computed.

TABLE A3

TRACTOR INVESTMENT FUNCTION: FIRST-ORDER CORRELATION COEFFICIENTS
SQUARED, REVISED DATA, 1920–41, 1947–57

	r^2						
	$\log X_1$	$\log X_2$	$\log X_3$	$\log X_5$	$\log X_6$	T	$T_3{}^*$
G_t†	(−)0.045	(−)0.694	(−)0.453	0.549	0.637	0.672	0.664
$\log X_1$‡		(−)0.036	.426	.137	.045	(−)0.000	.003
$\log X_2$§			0.111	(−) .714	(−) .891	(−) .542	(−) .606
$\log X_3$‖				(−)0.076	(−) .130	(−) .465	(−) .392
$\log X_5$#					0.957	.652	.760
$\log X_6$**						0.738	.857
T††							0.972

* T_3 = number of tractors on farms, January 1.

† G_t = gross capital expenditures by farmers on tractors in 1935–39 prices.

‡ X_1 = index of tractors prices divided by the index of prices received for all drops.

§ X_2 = farm mortgage rate of interest.

‖ X_3 = tractor prices divided by the index of wages paid to farm labor.

X_5 = tractor prices divided by an index of prices paid for motor supplies.

** X_6 = time; $t = 20, \ldots, 57$.

†† T = depreciated value of the stock of tractors on farms, in 1935–39 prices, USDA estimate, January 1.

VI

The Determinants of Corporate Investment

YEHUDA GRUNFELD

The Determinants of Corporate Investment

THIS study attempts to explain the year-to-year variations in investment expenditures by individual corporations in the period 1935–54. Its principal findings are:

1. Profits, which in most previous studies performed extremely well as an "explanatory" variable of investment, appears on first sight to perform well here too. But a close examination indicates that the role of profits is probably that of a surrogate variable. It tends to be correlated with some of the main forces causing changes in investment and therefore with investment as well. But there are other variables which reflect these forces better and more directly, and hence it seems more appropriate to explain investment by means of the variations of these variables rather than profits.[1]

2. The principal variable of this type is the "market value of the firm," that is, the value placed upon the firm by the securities markets. When taken in conjunction with an estimate of the replacement value of the physical assets of the firm, this variable appears to be a sensitive indicator of the expectations upon which investment decisions are based. Furthermore, and in part because of lags in the process of physical investment, this variable signals changes in investment before they actually occur.

3. By allowing for variations in expectations of future returns, it was possible to identify the influence of changes in the rate of interest on investment decisions. For the corporations analyzed, the rate of interest seemed to exert a stronger influence on investment decisions than what would be expected from the results of previous studies.

In the course of the study of eight corporations an explanatory model

[1] A partial list of studies that deal with the effect of profits on investment includes: J. Tinbergen, *A Method and Its Application to Investment Activity* (Geneva: League of Nations Economic Intelligence Service, 1939); C. F. Roos, "The Demand for Investment Goods," *American Economic Review*, XXXVIII (1948), 311–20; L. R. Klein, "Studies in Investment Behavior," *Conference on Business Cycles* (Universities–National Bureau Committee for Economic Research) (New York, 1951); P. W. Andrews and E. Brunner, *Capital Development in Steel: A Study of the United Steel Companies Ltd.* (Oxford, 1951); R. Eisner, "Expectations, Plans, and Capital Expenditures: A Synthesis of Ex-post and Ex-ante Data" (unpublished manuscript); J. Bronfenbrenner, "Factors Controlling Investment Programs and Their Realization" (unpublished manuscript); and J. R. Meyer and E. Kuh, *The Investment Decision: An Empirical Study* (Cambridge, Mass.: Harvard University Press, 1957).

is developed which is tested by applications to additional firms and by examination of the predictive value of the model for two additional years for the same eight firms.

I. The Dependent Variable: Investment

The definition of gross investment used in this study is gross additions to plant and equipment plus maintenance and repairs. This differs from the official Department of Commerce definition of gross investment in that it excludes investment in inventories and includes maintenance and repairs expenditures. Inventory investment was excluded because it was felt that it responds to different stimuli from those affecting investment in plant and equipment. Its inclusion would accordingly only blur our focus on fixed investment. Maintenance and repairs expenditures were included because of the large degree to which these expenditures can (and apparently do) substitute for purchases of new plant and machines. Our focus is on gross rather then net investment because of the sensitivity of the latter variable to arbitrary accounting procedures (such as depreciation) and because for the analysis of cyclical changes in investment it is gross rather than net investment which is of interest.

Since the general price level changed radically over the period of the study, it was necessary to deflate dollar expenditures on investment by some relevant price index. The index used was the "Implicit Price Deflator of Producers Durable Equipment." The construction of this index is described as follows:

Bureau of Labor Statistics wholesale price indexes and Interstate Commerce Commission price indexes were the major data used for deflating producer's purchases of durable equipment, in a product detail which went somewhat beyond that in which the current dollar estimates are published for the years 1929–52. Further breakdowns were estimated, for deflation purposes, in instances in which there were indications that the alternative procedure of dividing broader current dollar components by fixed weight composite price indexes might yield significantly erroneous results.[2]

While it would, of course, have been desirable to have a separate deflating index for each corporation studied, with the weights adjusted to its typical "mix" of capital equipment, we had to content ourselves with a more general index.

The study itself can best be described as a series of experiments with the data of eight large companies, testing plausible hypotheses against one another and searching for the hypothesis or set of hypotheses that

---

[2] U.S. Department of Commerce, Office of Business Economics, *A Supplement to the Survey of Current Business, National Income* (1954 ed.), p. 156.

seemed to explain the data. Some hypotheses gave negative results immediately and could be dropped after testing on a few corporations, while others were examined for all eight companies. Special attention was of course paid to those hypotheses which had appeared to stand up well in earlier studies.

The eight companies were examined in the following order: (1) Atlantic Refining Company, (2) United States Steel Corporation, (3) Union Oil Company of California, (4) Goodyear Tire and Rubber Company, (5) Diamond Match Company, (6) American Steel Foundries, (7) General Motors Corporation, and (8) General Electric Company.

The study was restricted to large corporations mainly because it is for them that the best data are available. We must accordingly be cautious about extrapolating the results of the present study to really small companies, whose investment behavior may be governed by additional forces and constraints. Two of the companies in the present study, Diamond Match and American Steel Foundries, would probably be classified as medium sized rather than giant.

The period studied for each corporation was 1935–54. The year 1935 was chosen as the starting point because from that year data on expenditures on gross investment and on maintenance and repairs were collected by the Securities and Exchange Commission for all corporations. The last year merely signifies the fact that the present study was started in 1955. One of the gains of having the study under way so long is that it was possible later to test with data from 1955 and 1956 the hypothesis developed from the data of earlier years.

The main source of data for investment and maintenance and repairs was *Moody's Industrial Manual,* which records these data as submitted by the corporations to the Securities and Exchange Commission. These records were checked with the annual reports of the corporation, and discrepancies were reconciled by studying the breakdown of investment outlays that is contained in the annual reports of a number of corporations for most years studied.

In Table 1 we present a survey of the sort of variations in investment we are trying to explain.

It is clear that there were substantial variations in investment over the period considered, even apart from trend, and a substantial number of turning points. Further, the statistics of the individual corporations and the aggregate seem reasonably similar to those for the economy as a whole, suggesting that our sample is not grossly unrepresentative of aggregate investment in terms of its broad movements.

It is striking that the measures of variability that apply to investment including maintenance and repairs are almost uniformly lower than the corresponding measures excluding maintenance and repairs. However, readers should be warned against making ready inferences, for this result would normally emerge, so long as expenditures on maintenance and repair were less volatile than expenditures on new plant and equipment. The inclusion of maintenance and repair expenditures does, however, have significant effects. On the average for our eight corporations, investment measured in the two ways moves in the same direction in no more than

TABLE 1

INDICATIONS OF VARIABILITY OF INVESTMENT

Corporation	Coefficient of Variation		Percentage Variation around Trend*		No. of Turning Points	
General Motors................	.50	(.68)†	33	(.52)†	6	(6)†
General Electric..............	.46	(.57)	29	(.43)	6	(6)
United States Steel............	.30	(.46)	54	(.76)	7	(9)
Atlantic Refining.............	.24	(.23)	44	(.87)	12	(13)
Union Oil....................	.38	(.41)	26	(.36)	12	(12)
Diamond Match...............	.54	(1.11)	42	(.37)	10	(9)
Goodyear Tire and Rubber......	.34	(.36)	40	(.63)	11	(13)
American Steel Foundries.......	.46	(.50)	99	(1.00)	9	(9)
Aggregate of eight corporations..	.37	(.47)	24	(.42)	8	(8)
Economy as a whole‡..........	...	(.47)	..	.....	..	(8)

* "Percentage Variation around Trend" was computed from the variance of investment around a straight trend line divided by the variance of investment (it is equal to $\sqrt{1 - r^2}$, where r^2 is the coefficient of determination of the trend line).

† Figures in parentheses refer to gross investment excluding maintenance and repairs.

‡ Computed from expenditures of producers durable equipment in constant dollars 1935–53. Source: *Supplement to the Survey of Current Business, National Income* (1954 ed.).

eighteen out of the twenty years considered. Also, of the roughly seventy-five individual company peaks or troughs reached by investment measured in one of the two ways, only some three-quarters are synchronous with peaks or troughs in investment measured in the other way. In three cases we have actually a peak measuring investment in one way and a trough measuring investment in the other way.

Regardless of which way we measure investment, however, one salient characteristic of its movements appears: about two-thirds of the individual company peaks occur when the aggregate of the eight corporations showed a peak, while the fraction of individual troughs coinciding with troughs in the aggregate is much lower (one-third when investment includes maintenance and repairs and one-sixth when it does not). A particular advantage we obtained by using the measure including maintenance and repairs was the fact that we were able to include the war years in our analysis. We did not find evidence that during the war years investment behavior as measured by investment including maintenance and repairs was fundamentally different from investment behavior in other years. The restrictions on the purchase of capital goods apparently induced firms to increase their maintenance and repairs expenditures so as to carry out the "net investment" that they would have otherwise carried out by purchasing new equipment.[3] (The trough in aggregate investment for the economy as a whole of 1943 appears also in the aggregate investment of the eight corporations when investment is measured excluding maintenance and repairs. This trough disappears if we include maintenance and repairs in our measure of investment.)

II. Profits, Expected Profits, and Liquidity

At first glance it appears that the good performance of profits in "explaining" investment in past studies is repeated here. Table 2 indicates that both lagged and current profits have substantial correlations with investment in practically all cases. (Note that the entries in Table 2 are for r^2, not r. This convention will be followed throughout this paper.) Profits here are defined as net income to surplus (after taxes), deflated by the implicit price deflator of gross national product (GNP).[4]

The role of profits in explaining investment is a puzzling one. Tinbergen's classic justification asserted that realized profits measured expected profits and that "it is almost a tautology to say that investment is governed by profits expectations."[5] Actually, it is not obvious at all that realized profits measure expected profits, and even the assertion that expected profits govern investment is far from being a tautology. Realized profits clearly can result from unexpected changes, and, if the new circumstances are thought to be transitory, no incentive to invest need result. Likewise, realized profits may rise, and may have been anticipated to rise, as the normal payoff on a past investment; such a rise in profits would be "expected" but would not lead to new investment. It is thus

---

[3] The inclusion of maintenance and repairs in the measure of investment is equivalent to assuming that new replacement equipment and maintenance and repairs expenditures are perfect substitutes. But the exclusion of maintenance and repairs from the measurement of investment is equivalent to assuming that new replacement investment and maintenance and repairs expenditures cannot be substituted for each other at all.

[4] The GNP deflator was chosen because we considered it desirable that the price deflator should reflect the movement of prices of all the commodities in the economy rather than a single one.

[5] *Op. cit.*, p. 34.

clear that not all rises in profits signify increases in the incentive to invest; and, correspondingly, not all increases in the incentive to invest are reflected in rises in profits. Shifts in investment incentives usually reflect changes in the evaluation of future conditions, and, while such changes are sometimes connected with current happenings which bring greater profits, this is by no means always the case.

One fairly general formulation of the relationship between profits and investment states that the net addition to capital stock will be proportional to the excess of the observed profit rate over the "normal" rate. Three alternative interpretations of this relationship are given below.

1. Profits (P_t) rise above normal (aM_t), where M_t is the replacement value of existing capital stock and a is a constant. The new situation

TABLE 2*

COEFFICIENTS OF DETERMINATION (r^2) AMONG INVESTMENT (I), LAGGED PROFITS (P_{-1}), AND CURRENT PROFITS (P)

	CORPORATION								AGGREGATE OF EIGHT CORPORATIONS
	G.M. (1)	G.E. (2)	U.S.S. (3)	A.R. (4)	U.O. (5)	D.M. (6)	G.T.R. (7)	A.S.F. (8)	(9)
(1) $r^2_{IP_{-1}}$	.235	.376	.414	.480	.270	.196	.524	.049	.420
(2) r^2_{IP}	.284	.418	.474	.570	.441	.100	.562	.173	.434

* Sources: Profits obtained from net income to surplus as reported in *Moody's Industrial Manual* deflated by the implicit price deflator of GNP as measured in the *Survey of Current Business*.

giving rise to the change is expected to continue. The firm immediately adjusts its capital equipment by the full amount corresponding to these altered expectations, say, $i_{t+1} = K(P_t - aM_t)$, where i_{t+1} is net investment in $t + 1$.

2. A similar situation as in 1 emerges, but the firm, being cautious, adds to its capital stock only a fraction of the amount in 1, anticipating to continue investing if the changed situation continues to prevail. This leads to $i_{t+1} = \beta K(P_t - aM_t)$.

3. A similar situation as in 1 emerges, but the technical difficulties of adding to plant and equipment prevent the firm from making more than a fraction γ of the desired adjustment. This leads to $i_{t+1} = \gamma K(P_t - aM_t)$.[6]

In all these formulations net investment is a positive function of profits and a negative function of the existing capital stock. Simply put, high profits in dollar terms may provide an incentive to invest to the extent

[6] See L. M. Koyck, *Distributed Lags and Investment Analysis* (Amsterdam: North-Holland Publishing Co., 1954).

that they are over and above the normal return on existing capital, but they do not provide such an incentive when they are simply the payoff on existing capital.

While net investment i_{t+1} is a negative function of the existing capital stock, gross investment need not be, because gross investment includes replacement and maintenance and repairs, which will tend to be larger, the larger is the capital stock. In estimating the general relationship

$$I_{t+1} = a + bP_t + cM_t, \tag{1}$$

we accordingly anticipate a positive estimate of b, if profits play a significant role in influencing investment decisions, but the estimate of c can be either positive or negative, depending on whether the "replacement effect" of the existing capital stock outweighs the "net investment" effect or vice versa.[7]

It is clear that, in testing the effect of profits in explaining investment, we should make allowance for the possible influence of the existing capital stock. To approximate this variable, we accumulated net investment in plant and equipment expressed in real terms. Since the capital stock enters linearly in equation (1), and since the constant term is of no special significance for the hypothesis we are testing, we were free to set the initial (i.e., 1935) capital stock at an arbitrary value. Starting from this year, we accumulated gross investment in plant and equipment, deflated by the Implicit Deflator of Producers Capital Equipment, less depreciation allowances, adjusted as indicated below, and deflated by a ten-year moving average of the wholesale prices of metals and metal products. This procedure was necessitated by the fact that neither data on gross investment nor data on the implicit price deflator are available prior to 1929. We could accordingly neither estimate real depreciation in any year by taking an appropriate fraction of real gross investment in previous years nor deflate current dollar investment by an appropriate average of preceding years' implicit price deflators.

Our first "compromise" was to use the wholesale price index of metals and metal products (converted to base year 1947 for comparability) rather than the implicit price deflator for the purpose of translating

---

[7] This fact has been recognized by Klein, who used a stock of capital measure in his investment equations. Any formulation in which net investment is a positive function of the excess of desired over actual capital stock has this property. To a linear approximation net investment, $i_{t+1} = j + k(M_t^* - M_t)$, where $M_t^* =$ desired capital stock, while replacement demand is equal to $f + gM_t$. Gross investment, I_{t+1}, is therefore equal to $j + f + kM_t^* + (g - k)M_t$. It depends positively or negatively on M_t, depending on whether the replacement effect, here measured by g, does or does not outweigh the net investment effect, here measured by $-k$.

adjusted current dollar depreciation allowances into real terms. Our second compromise was the use of a ten-year moving average of prices rather than an average of varying durations and with varying weights depending on the company in question and the time pattern of its investment.[8]

Nominal depreciation data as they appeared in the books of a corporation were adjusted in two ways. First, accelerated depreciation, where identified, was deducted from the depreciation figure in the year in which it appeared and added back in that year and subsequent years at the "normal" rate (see n. 8). Second, deflated depreciation allowances, when plotted against the real stock of plant and equipment, generally yielded a quite good fit. In the few cases in which depreciation seemed grossly excessive for the stock of plant and equipment from which it derived, the excess of depreciation over "normal" was treated as accelerated depreciation in the manner described above.

[8] Assuming that nominal depreciation is on a straight-line basis and that the time duration of each year's investment is "average," we could anticipate nominal depreciation in year $n + 1$ to be

$$D_{n+1} = (1/n) \sum_{t=1}^{n} I_t.$$

The real depreciation in year $n + 1$ will be a corresponding sum of the $1/n$ fractions of real investment:

$$D^*_{n+1} = (1/n) \sum_{t=1}^{n} I_t/P_t.$$

The deflator Π_{n+1} will accordingly be

$$\frac{D_{n+1}}{D^*_{n+1}} = \Pi_{n+1} = \frac{\displaystyle\sum_{t=1}^{n} I_t}{\displaystyle\sum_{t=1}^{n} I_t/P_t}.$$

We could not compute this "ideal" deflator for the whole period because of the unavailability of data on investment before 1935, but we did compute it for the last five years of the period, choosing it in such a way as to make

$$(1/n) \sum_{t=1}^{n} I_t$$

correspond most closely to actual depreciation allowances. A simple ten-year moving average of metals and metal products prices corresponded quite closely with the index thus obtained: in no case was there a difference of more than 3 per cent in the total magnitude of the deflator.

The results of multiple regressions of investment on the stock of plant and equipment and lagged profits are shown in Table 3. It is apparent from this table that the introduction of the stock of plant and equipment into the equation has a devastating effect on the correlation between investment and profits. The partial coefficients of determination of investment and lagged profits are in most cases close to zero.

Two cases form exceptions to the above findings. For American Steel Foundries neither lagged profits nor the stock of plant and equipment seem to show any substantial correlation with investment. Both variables

TABLE 3

PARTIAL COEFFICIENTS OF DETERMINATION OF INVESTMENT, PROFITS, AND STOCK OF PLANT AND EQUIPMENT

	CORPORATION								AGGREGATE OF EIGHT CORPORATIONS
	G.M. (1)	G.E. (2)	U.S.S. (3)	A.R. (4)	U.O. (5)	D.M. (6)	G.T.R. (7)	A.S.F. (8)	(9)
(1) $r^2_{IP_{-1} \cdot M_{-1}}$.	$(-).074$	$(-).009$	.211	.086	$(-).011$	.048	.094	.035	$(-).010$
(2) $r^2_{IM_{-1} \cdot P_{-1}}$.	.790	.459	.067	.340	.637	.573	.160	.000	.834
(3) $R^2_{I \cdot M_{-1}P_{-1}}$.	.839	.658	.457	.569	.742	.656	.599	.050	.841
(4) $r^2_{IM_{-1}}$	.827	.655	.298	.528	.739	.643	.569	.016	.841

NOTATION

I = Real gross investment plus maintenance and repairs.
P = Real net income in current year.
P_{-1} = Real net income in previous year.
M_{-1} = Real stock of plant and equipment at end of previous year.
r^2 = Coefficient of determination.
R^2 = Multiple coefficient of determination.
A negative r is shown in parentheses.

"explain" only 5 per cent of the variance in investment. The other and more important exception to the above statements is United States Steel, for which profits seem to perform fairly well in spite of the introduction of the stock of plant and equipment.

Our results do not confirm the hypothesis that profits are a good measure of those expected profits that will tend to induce investment expenditures. The observed simple correlation between investment and profits seems to be due to the fact that profits are just another measure of the capital stock of the firm and one that is in most cases inferior to the measure that we have constructed.

The observed correlation of investment with profits has intrigued many writers and induced them to offer other explanations for it besides the expected profits hypothesis. A very popular interpretation of this relationship is the "liquidity hypothesis." Most writers who employ the liquidity hypothesis do not go into any detail as to the mechanism by which profits produce liquid assets and liquid assets induce investment. Presumably it is believed that, when a firm obtains a large amount of profits, they will usually be in the form of liquid assets and that these liquid assets will be spent on new capital goods. [9] It is clear that this is not necessarily the case. Profits may increase while liquid assets are decreasing, and vice versa. There is no direct and obvious connection between profits and liquidity. A part of the profits may be represented by increases in accounts receivable and inventories and not retained by the firm as liquid assets. Thus a better measure of the inflow of liquid assets than net profits may be represented by net profits plus depreciation allowances minus dividends, minus increases in inventories plus net decrease in accounts receivable. But even such a "corrected" variable will not be a true measure of the net inflow of liquid assets into the firm, and many other "corrections" of that kind could be devised. If this process of deriving the net inflow of liquid assets into the firm is followed through to its logical conclusion, it turns out that the best way of measuring the flow of liquid assets is to compare the *stocks* of liquid assets owned by the firm at adjacent periods. Furthermore, it is much more reasonable to believe that investment will be affected by the *stock* of liquid assets at the disposal of the firm will rather than the flow of these assets. The stock of liquid assets can be measured by combining cash and marketable securities at the disposal of the firm at a certain point of time. It is also possible to deduct from this stock of liquid assets the outstanding short-run or long-run obligations.

Table 4 shows the partial coefficients of determination between investment and deflated current profits and between investment and the deflated value of the stock of current assets. In each case the stock of plant and equipment is taken as given. [10] In neither case is there evidence of a substantial positive relation.

Several other variables which might be thought to have some positive correlation to the liquidity position of the firm were examined graphically and found to have no consistent positive partial correlation with invest-

[9] See, e.g., Meyer and Kuh, *op. cit.*, p. 204.

[10] The stock of plant and equipment is taken as given because the normal liquidity requirements of a firm will vary with its size. The amount of liquid assets which would induce substantial investment (under the liquidity hypothesis) in a firm of size S might just meet the normal liquidity requirements and therefore induce no investment if the firm were of size $2S$.

ment. (In these cases the partial relation was obtained by plotting the residuals from a graphical regression of investment on the stock of plant and equipment against the residuals from a graphical regression of the "liquidity variable" in question on the stock of plant and equipment.) The additional "liquidity" variables so treated were (1) sales, (2) net income plus depreciation and obsolescence minus dividends, and (3) for one firm (United States Steel), cash plus marketable securities minus current liabilities. In each of the above cases the variable in question was deflated by the GNP deflator.

TABLE 4

COEFFICIENTS OF DETERMINATION OF INVESTMENT OF STOCK OF LIQUID ASSETS AND CURRENT PROFITS

	CORPORATION								AGGREGATE OF EIGHT CORPORATIONS
	G.M. (1)	G.E. (2)	U.S.S. (3)	A.R. (4)	U.O. (5)	D.M. (6)	G.T.R. (7)	A.S.F. (8)	(9)
(1) $r^2_{IL_{-1}\cdot M_{-1}}$....	(−).030	.016	.041	(−).000	*	*	*	*	(−).000
(2) $r^2_{IP\cdot M_{-1}}$....	(−).228	(−).029	.343	.190	.065	(−).042	.130	.174	(−).012

* Not computed.

NOTATION

I = Real gross investment plus maintenance and repairs.
M_{-1} = "Real" stock of plant and equipment at December 31 of previous year.
P = Current real net income.
r^2 = Coefficient of determination.

The only substantial positive partial correlation which we found in the entire examination of "liquidity" variables was that for United States Steel between investment and current profits. Recalling that United States Steel also showed the highest partial correlation between investment and lagged profits, we are warned against interpreting the investment-current profits correlation as representing a "liquidity" effect. This warning is reinforced by the poor relationships between investment by United States Steel and either the stock of liquid assets (partial r^2 = .04) or the stock of liquid assets minus current liabilities (partial $r < 0$).

Although the evidence presented thus far argues forcefully that neither current nor lagged profits have a significant influence on investment, once the existing capital stock of the firm is taken into account, we shall present yet another series of tests of these relationships: an analysis of co-movements. In this analysis we are concerned only with the direction of year-to-year movements in our variables. The criterion of co-movement[11] is different from that of a correlation coefficient, or even from the evidence obtained from the scatter diagrams. For the correlation co-efficient and for the scatter diagrams, the magnitudes of the movements of the variables are of utmost importance. Even if two variables move over time always in the same direction but the relative magnitudes of these movements change, we may obtain no relation if we plot the two variables on a scatter diagram. Conversely, two variables that show a strong positive association when plotted each against the other on a scatter diagram may move for many years in opposite directions, pro-vided that, when they move together, the variables change by much larger magnitudes than when they move in opposite directions.

Co-movement analysis is particularly useful in testing against the null hypothesis. In the present case, we have on the basis of correlation analysis concluded that there is probably no relation between profits, either lagged or current, and investment. If there is indeed no relation, this should be revealed also by the non-parametric test of co-movement analysis. If the lack of relation should fail to be confirmed by the co-movement test, we shall have to treat our prior conclusions with consider-able caution.

Table 5 summarizes the co-movements of investment, profits, and the stock of plant and equipment. Next to the actual number of co-move-ments in any case we present the "expected" number. This "expected" number is derived on the assumption that the variables in question are in fact independent. Thus, for example, if, as in the case of General Motors, investment went up in sixteen out of the twenty years, while profits went up in thirteen out of the twenty, we would anticipate on the assumption of independence $(16/20) \times (13/20) \times 20$ co-movements of the variables, in which both were going up, and $(4/20) \times (7/20) \times 20$ co-movements of the variables in which both were going down. The expected total of co-move-ments is therefore 11.8, which compares with 13 co-movements actually observed.

It appears that, in particular, current profits tend to move with invest-ment more often than we would anticipate on the basis of independence. The question arises as to whether this relationship may not be analogous to the relatively high simple correlations observed between profits and investment, which we found to disappear when the stock of plant and equipment was taken into account. We cannot, unfortunately, obtain in

---

[11] The term "co-movement" has been adopted from Milton Friedman, "An Em-pirical Study of the Relationship between Railroad Stock Prices and Railroad Earnings for the Period 1921–31" (unpublished Master's thesis, Department of Economics, University of Chicago).

co-movement analysis an analogue to partial correlation. However, by concentrating attention on turning points in investment, we can learn a good deal about the separate influences of our variables.

Table 6 presents a summary of the co-movements of several variables with investment one year after peaks and after troughs in investment expenditure. It is notable that the stock of plant and equipment performs well in troughs but not in peaks. The reason for this is that the stock of plant and equipment has for most companies an almost uninterrupted upward trend. It therefore "predicts" that investment will go up practically all the time and is, of course, "right" one year after troughs and typically "wrong" one year after peaks. Current profits succeed about equally well in "predicting" the direction of movement of investment after peaks and after troughs. It is therefore quite clear that the co-movement observed earlier between current profits and investment is not

TABLE 5

CO-MOVEMENTS OF INVESTMENT, PROFITS, AND STOCK OF
PLANT AND EQUIPMENT

CORPORATION	CO-MOVEMENT OF					
	I and P_{-1}		I and P		I and M_{-1}	
	No. of Comparisons					
	19		20		19	
	Observed	Expected	Observed	Expected	Observed	Expected
General Motors.....	14	11.2	13	11.8	13	13.9
General Electric....	14	9.9	12	10.6	10	11.0
United States Steel..	14	9.4	14	10	10	10.1
Atlantic Refining...	10	9.3	13	9.7	10	9.1
Union Oil..........	7	9.4	13	10.0	11	12.0
Diamond Match....	8	9.4	13	9.8	9	9.4
Goodyear Tire and Rubber..........	11	9.4	14	10	11	10.8
American Steel Foundries........	9	9.6	13	10	10	12.0
Aggregate of eight corporations......	13	10.4	15	10.8	12	11.7

NOTATION

I = Real gross investment plus maintenance and repairs.
P = Real net income in current year.
P_{-1} = Real net income lagged one year.
M_{-1} = Stock of plant and equipment at end of previous year.

solely due to the tendency for current profits and the stock of plant and equipment to move together. Some independent influence of current profits, though not of lagged profits, on investment is suggested by these data. Thus, so far as profits are concerned, both the expectation and the liquidity hypotheses can at best be validated by using as their measure current profits. But then we would imply that the important investment decisions are made simultaneously with the act of spending funds on investment goods. Apart from the fact that such an explanation is devoid of any predictive value, it does not seem to be a reasonable explanation of

TABLE 6*

CO-MOVEMENTS OF INVESTMENT, PROFITS, AND STOCK OF PLANT AND EQUIPMENT ONE YEAR AFTER TURNING POINTS IN INVESTMENT

CORPORATION	I AND P				I AND M				I AND P_{-1}				I AND M_{-1}			
	Pe†		Tr‡		Pe		Tr		Pe		Tr		Pe		Tr	
	Co	Con-tra	Co	Con-tra	Co	Con-tra	Co	Con-tra	Co	Con-tra	Co	Con-tra	Co	Con-tra	Co	Con-tra
General Motors.....	2	1	2	1	2	1	2	1	3	0	1	2	0	3	1	2
General Electric.....	2	1	2	1	0	3	3	0	2	1	1	2	0	3	1	2
United States Steel..	2	2	3	0	0	4	2	1	2	2	2	1	0	4	1	2
Atlantic Refining....	4	2	5	1	0	6	6	0	1	5	4	2	0	6	6	0
Union Oil..........	4	2	4	2	0	6	6	0	2	4	2	4	0	6	6	0
Diamond Match....	4	1	2	3	3	2	1	4	2	3	1	4	3	2	1	4
Goodyear Tire and Rubber..........	4	2	4	1	0	6	5	0	2	4	2	3	0	6	5	0
American Steel Foundries........	5	0	4	0	0	5	4	0	1	4	2	2	0	5	4	0
Total............	27	11	26	9	5	33	29	6	15	23	15	20	3	35	25	10

* For notation see Table 5.
† Pe = Peak.
‡ Tr = Trough.

a firm's behavior. Clearly, some longer-range decisions than these "instantaneous" ones are made by the firm, the causes of which are not measured by current profits. Thus, instead of trying to transform current profits into a measure that will yield "parametric" results, it seems more profitable to look for a measure of those expectations that are not measured by real profits. We will now turn our attention to this problem.

III. THE MARKET VALUE OF THE FIRM AND INVESTMENT

The failure of profits to explain investment may be due to the fact that realized profits are a bad measure of expected profits. The discrepancy between "measured profits" and the relevant expected profits is due to two main factors. (1) "Net income" is not always a reliable measure of profits that have been realized by the firm. Recall, for example, the problem of depreciation allowances and in particular the so-called accelerated depreciation allowance. (2) Even if changes in net income were a perfect measure of changes in realized profits, they may not yield us any indication as to what changes in expected profits have occurred.

It is very unreasonable to believe that the management of a corporation will base its expectations of future demand conditions for the product and of future supply conditions of factors only on the information that is contained in realized profits, assuming that these conditions will prevail for the infinite future. Many changes in supply conditions are anticipated to take place in the future, though these changes are not yet recorded in current profits. Such changes are, for example, technological developments in methods of production that are already known but have not yet been applied. Forecasts of demand conditions for the product in the future are also made by management on the basis of information that is not contained in current or lagged realized profits of the firm. General factors affecting the industry in which the firm operates, the condition of other industries that produce substitute or complementary products, and the "outlook" of the economy as a whole are factors that have an important influence on expected future demand conditions of the firm and are not necessarily recorded by realized profits.

We now ask ourselves whether it is possible to construct a variable that can be objectively measured and that will represent all the relevant information on beliefs and expectations about the future and hence offer a good explanation of investment behavior. A variable that seems to meet these requirements is the "market value of the firm." All the corporations that are included in the present study are publicly traded and have, therefore, at any point of time, a total value that the market is placing on them. This total market value of the firm may be thought of as the present value of all future earnings of the firm net of the costs of possible future additions to capital, but including future interest on existing debt. The future earnings that the market is expecting and on which it is basing its valuation of the firm are not necessarily identical with those expected by the managers of the firm. But it is reasonable to expect that these two sets of expectations will not differ very substantially for long periods of time.

An advantage of the "value of the firm" as an explanatory variable of investment behavior lies in the fact that it measures the result of a complex market mechanism that tries to achieve essentially the same goal as ourselves, namely, to summarize and evaluate all the information that is relevant to the future demand conditions of the firm's product and the supply conditions of its factors so as to obtain a reliable forecast of its future profits. The participants in the stock market have of course strong economic incentives to base their decisions on a careful examination of all the relevant existing information. Not everybody in the stock market has to obtain all the information available or know how to evaluate such information in order for the value of the firm to be a useful variable for our purposes. It suffices that a relatively small group of informed, well-trained and well-financed traders will act on the basis of all the information available for the market value of the firm as a whole to summarize that information.[12]

Finally, an important advantage of the variable "the value of the firm" is that its measurement is not directly dependent on accounting practices. In this respect it has clearly a great advantage over current or past profits or any combination thereof.

THE MEASUREMENT OF THE VALUE OF THE FIRM

Our measurement of the value of the firm for any given year is obtained by summing up the market value of all the outstanding shares and the book value of all debt outstanding on December 31 of the preceding year.[13] This figure is then deflated by the implicit price deflator of GNP.

In principle, we would like to obtain the *market* value of the outstanding debt of the corporation, since this market value will be equal to the present value of payments to debtors as computed with the existing relevant rate of interest. However, a large part of a corporation's debt is not publicly traded and hence does not have a market value. The only way left open for us was to take the book value of all these untraded types of debt from the balance sheets of the corporations. For those corporations which had bonds outstanding with quoted prices we were able to compare the book value of this kind of debt with its market value. For all cases that were compared we found that, if we take total value of

---

[12] The view expressed in the text is in contrast to common notions about the stock market held by many economists. The following citation is a forceful presentation of the opposite view to that expressed in the text: "For most of these persons [professional investors] are, in fact, largely concerned, not with making superior long-term forecasts of the probable yield of an investment over its whole life, but with foreseeing changes in the conventional basis of valuation a short time ahead of the general public. They are concerned not with what an investment is really worth to a man who buys it 'for keeps,' but with what the market will value it, under the influence of mass psychology, three months or a year hence. . . . We have reached the third degree, where we devote our intelligence to anticipating what average opinion expects the average opinion to be. And there are some, I believe, who practice the fourth, fifth and higher degrees" (John Maynard Keynes, *The General Theory of Employment, Interest and Money* [London: Macmillan & Co., 1936], pp. 154–56).

[13] In some cases we used the average of the share prices of December 31 and January 31. This procedure will be discussed later.

debt with bonds at market value and compare it to total value of debt with bonds at book value, the difference never exceeded 4 per cent of the value of the total debt as measured by the second method. Since total debt comprises, for all corporations considered, only a small fraction of their total market value and since prices of stocks fluctuate much more violently than prices of bonds, we decided that it was not worthwhile to compute the market value of the outstanding bonds of the corporations in order to obtain total debt. Thus the book value of debt was chosen to represent the total value of debt.[14]

THE CO-MOVEMENTS OF INVESTMENT AND
THE VALUE OF THE FIRM

Is there any evidence that the value of the firm shows a substantial co-movement with investment? The first two columns of Table 7 answer this question for the eight corporations studied and for the aggregate of the eight corporations. The first and second columns of Table 7 compare the observed co-movements with the expected co-movements of investment with the value of the firm in the previous year. The comparison shows that there exists a substantial difference among the corporations. For three corporations—Atlantic Refining, Union Oil, and Diamond Match—the observed co-movements are essentially equal to the expected ones. But for the other five corporations and for the aggregate the number of observed co-movements exceeds substantially the number of expected co-movements. This is especially true for General Motors and General Electric.

In Table 8 we compare the observed and expected ratio of co-movements to the total number of movements of investment with the value of the firm, lagged profits, current profits, and the stock of plant and equipment, respectively. The difference between observed and expected ratio of co-movements is largest for investment with the value of the firm. Although current profits has a slightly larger number of observed comovements with investment than the value of the firm, the expected

---

[14] This decision saved us a very sizable amount of work because several of the corporations had a number of types of bonds outstanding at any point of time. A slightly less utilitarian reason for being satisfied with the book value of bonds rather than with their market value is that we are primarily interested in measuring variation in expectations about future earnings of the corporations which are not directly reflected in the bond prices. The payments for the bonds are clearly much less dependent on the variations in future earnings of the firm than stock prices. Anyway, if the error involved in our method of measuring debt has any effect, it will be in the direction of reducing the "performance" of the value of the firm as an explanatory variable of investment. We have not found any reason for it to introduce any "spurious" correlation with investment.

ratio is much larger. The co-movement between investment and current profits seems therefore to be due more to an influence of a common trend than to the co-movement between investment and the value of the firm. Thus the first examination of the co-movements of investment with the value of the firm is encouraging enough to justify an examination of this relation in further detail.[15]

[15] Some supporting evidence to the fact that the movements in stock prices "predict" turning points in business activity is presented in Geoffrey H. Moore, *Statistical Indica-*

TABLE 7

CO-MOVEMENTS OF INVESTMENT AND VALUE OF FIRM ONE YEAR AFTER
TURNING POINTS FOR EIGHT CORPORATIONS, 1935–54

			I AND V_{-1}			
	I AND V_{-1}		Peaks		Troughs	
CORPORATION	Observed Co.	Expected Co.	Success	Failure	Success	Failure
General Motors.............	17	11.9	3	0	3	0
General Electric............	15	9.7	3	0	3	0
United States Steel.........	12	9.7	3	1	3	0
Atlantic Refining...........	9	9.4	2	4	3	3
Union Oil..................	11	10.7	3	3	5	1
Diamond Match............	10	9.4	3	2	3	2
Goodyear Tire and Rubber..	12	9.6	4	2	2	3
American Steel Foundries....	11	8.8	3	2	1	3
Aggregate of eight corporations..................	12	10.7	4	1	3	1

TABLE 8*

RATIO OF CO-MOVEMENTS TO TOTAL NUMBER OF COM-
PARISONS FOR ALL EIGHT CORPORATIONS, 1935–54

	Observed	Expected
1. Investment and the value of firm at the end of previous year.........................	.638	.522
2. Investment and profits of previous year.....	.579	.526
3. Investment and profits of current year......	.656	.639
4. Investment and the stock of plant and equipment at end of previous year..............	.552	.681

* Note that the co-movement of investment and current profits is based on 160 comparisons, while the other three co-movements are based on 152 comparisons.

Columns (3)–(6) of Table 7 show the number of successes and failures in predicting turning points of investment by observing the movement of the value of the firm at the end of the previous year. Whenever the value of the firm decreased one year before a peak in investment or increased one year before a trough in investment, we recorded a success in predicting the turning point. In the opposite case we recorded a failure in predicting a turning point.[16] Of the 38 peaks observed, 24 were successfully predicted, and of the 35 troughs, 23 were successfully predicted. It is interesting to note that around 3 peaks and 3 troughs seems to be the number of successful predictions for all corporations. In particular, for the two corporations, General Motors and General Electric, which really experienced only three peaks and three troughs, the predictions are perfect. If we aggregate investment and the value of the firm over the eight corporations, we observe that, of 5 peaks observed, 4 are successfully predicted by the value of the firm and, of 4 troughs, 3 are successfully predicted.

The results of Table 7 suggest the following question: Are the turning points in investment that are predicted by the value of the firm synchronized as between corporations? Or, in other words, does the value of the firm predict particularly peaks and troughs that occur in all or most corporations at the same time?

To answer this question, we have constructed Table 9, which shows for each year the number of successes in predicting peaks and troughs observed for the value of the firm at the end of the previous year and for

---

tors of Cyclical Revivals and Recessions ("National Bureau of Economic Research, Occasional Paper," No. 31 [1950]). Moore finds that, of the 11 reference peaks and 11 reference troughs identified in the period 1879–1938, the industrial common-stock price index, Dow-Jones, led in 8 peaks and in 8 troughs. The index lagged in 2 peaks, coincided with 1 reference trough, and lagged behind another. The average lead of the stock-price index for peaks was 6 months, and the average lead for troughs was 7.2 months (*ibid.*, p. 64).

[16] It will be noted that our definition of success in prediction is somewhat one-sided. When the value of the firm shows a decrease but investment in the succeeding year does not decrease, we do not record a failure, and, similarly, we do not record this kind of "failure" for troughs. The question that we have in mind is whether the movements in a certain variable *can* explain or predict turning points in investment. Since we are going to introduce another variable besides the value of the firm as an explanatory variable of investment expenditures, it is reasonable that investment might, for example, not decline even if the value of the firm has declined as long as this other variable exerts a positive effect on investment. But, if investment declines and we do not observe a decline *in any one* of the independent variables, then we have clearly missed in identifying the mechanism that induced the decline in investment.

current profits;[17] in addition, we have recorded the peaks and troughs of aggregate investment of the eight corporations and indicated in each case whether the turning point was predicted successfully by the aggregate value of the eight firms or whether it failed to be predicted by it. Let us concentrate our attention on those years in which four or more corporations experienced a peak in investment expenditures with no corporation experiencing a trough and on those years in which four or more corporations experienced troughs in investment expenditures with no corpora-

[17] It is somewhat of a misnomer to call the co-movement of investment and current profits one year after the occurrence of a turning point a "successful prediction," but it is useful to obtain some uniformity in constructing the table.

TABLE 9

SUCCESS AND FAILURE OF PREDICTING TURNING POINTS IN INVESTMENT
WITH VALUE OF THE FIRM AND CURRENT PROFITS, BY YEARS

YEAR	V_{-1}				P				AGGREGATE $(I$ AND $V_{-1})$
	Pe*		Tr†		Pe		Tr		
	S‡ (1)	F§ (2)	S (3)	F (4)	S (5)	F (6)	S (7)	F (8)	
1935........	0	2	1	0	0	2	1	0	
1936........	0	0	2	1	0	0	2	1	
1937........	8	0	0	0	8	0	0	0	PS
1938........	0	0	4	0	0	0	4	0	TS
1939........	1	1	1	3	1	1	3	1	
1940........	0	0	0	2	0	0	1	1	
1941........	6	0	0	0	6	0	0	0	PS
1942........	0	1	2	1	1	0	2	1	
1943........	0	1	1	0	0	1	0	1	
1944........	0	2	2	1	2	0	2	1	
1945........	0	2	2	1	1	1	2	1	TS
1946........	4	0	0	0	1	3	0	0	PS
1947........	0	0	1	2	0	0	3	0	TF
1948........	1	2	1	0	2	1	1	0	PF
1949........	1	1	1	1	2	0	2	0	TS
1950........	0	0	5	0	0	0	3	2	
1951........	0	0	0	0	0	0	0	0	
1952........	0	1	0	0	0	1	0	0	
1953........	3	1	0	0	3	1	0	0	PS
Total.....	24	14	23	12	27	11	26	9	

* Peak in investment.
† Trough in investment.
‡ Success in prediction.
§ Failure in prediction.

NOTATION

V_{-1} = Real value of firm at end of previous year.
P = Real profits at current year.

tion experiencing a peak. The "synchronized peaks" as defined above occurred in the years 1937, 1941, 1946, and 1953. It will be noted that these 22 peaks were essentially perfectly predicted by the value of the firm. Only 1 peak of the 4 that occurred in 1953 was not predicted. Even more striking is the fact that, of the total 24 successes in predicting peaks by the value of the firm, 21 were predictions of "synchronized peaks." In all these four years there occurred peaks in aggregate investment of the eight corporations, and these 4 aggregate peaks were also successfully predicted by the aggregate value of the firm.

"Synchronized troughs" as defined above occurred in 1938 and 1950. During these two years there occurred only 9 troughs in all the corporations considered. All those synchronized troughs were successfully predicted by the value of the firm. Of these two years, 1938 shows a trough in aggregate investment that is successfully predicted, but 1950 does not show any turning point in the aggregate investment of the eight corporations. In addition, we note that the nine synchronized turning points successfully predicted by the value of the firm are only a small fraction of the total number of 23 troughs successfully predicted by the value of the firm. There were two years, 1936 and 1947, in which no peaks occurred in any one of the corporations, but three corporations experienced troughs in investment expenditures. (These two years were excluded from our preceding discussion because we defined synchronized troughs as being 4 troughs or more.) Of these 6 troughs, only 3 were successfully predicted by the value of the firm.

We have already noted in Section I that peaks in investment seem to be more synchronized than troughs. The preceding discussion reveals that just for this reason "the market value of the firm" is remarkably well suited to explain the occurrence of peaks and troughs in investment. For the peaks in investment behavior which seem to occur in many corporations simultaneously, the value of the firm offers a "synchronized" explanation. In fact the variable seems to summarize only the synchronized forces that cause peaks to occur in investment behavior. However, in the cases of troughs in investment behavior, which seem to be more "private" and unsynchronized, the value of the firm seems to summarize forces that are more unique to the particular corporations.

Current profits show similar characteristics to those found for the value of the firm in that they show a co-movement with investment one year after synchronized peaks. Of the 22 synchronized peaks observed, we find that there were co-movements between investment and profits one year after the peak in 21 cases. Note that rather than to interpret this phenomenon as evidence that profits explain the peaks in investment we could say that the decline in the value of the firm which precedes a peak in investment also predicts a decline in profits in the following year. For the 9 synchronized troughs observed, current profits show a co-movement with investment one year after their occurrence in seven cases. The proportion of co-movements of current profits one year after the occurrence of a synchronized trough to the total number of synchronized troughs (7/9) is nearly identical to the proportion of the number of co-movements one year after non-synchronized troughs to the total number of non-synchronized troughs (19/26).

THE RESULTS OF THE REGRESSION EQUATIONS

In the preceding section we found that the value of the firm shows quite a strong co-movement with investment expenditures. This finding makes the value of the firm a good candidate as a variable to explain investment behavior in a parametric relationship. In principle, we expect the value of the firm to play that role which was attributed in Section II to realized profits, namely, to summarize the relevant information about expected profits. Furthermore, the value of the firm also reflects the rate of interest facing the firm.

To obtain the equation to be estimated, we proceed in the same way as in Section II by stating that the desired stock of capital equipment at time t is a monotonic increasing function of the market value of the firm in time t. Hence as a linear approximation we obtain

$$M^t = a + bV_t,$$

where M^t = desired stock of plant and equipment at the end of period t, and V_t = value of the firm at the end of period t.

If M_t is the existing stock of plant and equipment at the end of period t, then the desired net investment in period $t + 1$ will be

$$M^t - M_t = a + bV_t - M_t.$$

If in period $t + 1$ only a fraction k of the desired investment is carried out, it follows that net investment in period $t + 1$ will be

$$k(M^t - M_t) = ka + kbV_t - kM_t.$$

We further assume that replacement investment plus maintenance and repairs in period $t + 1$ is equal to a fraction g of the existing stock of capital (M_t) and obtain for gross investment plus maintenance and repairs in period $t + 1$:

$$I_{t+1} = k(M^t - M_t) + gM_t = ka + kbV_t + (g - k)M_t.$$

Thus gross investment plus maintenance and repairs is a function of the value of the firm at the end of the preceding year and of the stock of plant and equipment at the end of the preceding year.

Table 10 summarizes the relevant results of such regressions. Row (1) shows the partial coefficients of determination of investment with the value of the firm when the stock of plant and equipment is held constant. Row (2) shows the partial coefficient of determination of investment with the stock of plant and equipment when the value of the firm is held constant. Row (3) shows the multiple coefficients of determination for each regression. One glance at Table 10 reveals that the value of the firm

TABLE 10

PARTIAL COEFFICIENTS OF DETERMINATION OF INVESTMENT, STOCK OF PLANT AND EQUIPMENT, AND VALUE OF THE FIRM

	CORPORATION								AGGRE-GATE OF EIGHT CORPORA-TIONS
	G.M. (1)	G.E. (2)	U.S.S. (3)	A.R. (4)	U.O. (5)	D.M. (6)	G.T.R. (7)	A.S.F. (8)	(9)
(1) $r^2_{IV_{-1} \cdot M_{-1}}$	.532	.145	.246	.322	.096	.000	.225	.128	.535
(2) $r^2_{IM_{-1} \cdot V_{-1}}$	.851	.671	.306	.000	.756	.640	.337	.067	.882
(3) $R^2_{I \cdot M_{-1} V_{-1}}$	.919	.705	.471	.680	.764	.643	.666	.142	.926

NOTATION

I = Real gross investment plus maintenance and repairs.
M_{-1} = Stock of plant and equipment at end of previous year.
V_{-1} = Value of firm at end of previous year.

performs quite well. It certainly explains a larger proportion of investment behavior than either lagged or current profits. No single coefficient of correlation has a negative sign, and all coefficients of determination except two are higher than .1, indicating that they explain for each corporation more than 10 per cent of the variation in investment that is "left over" after the introduction of the stock of plant and equipment.[18]

The value of the firm used in computing all except one of the regression equations in Table 10 is measured at December 31 of each year preceding the investment outlay. The exception is United States Steel, for which we added the average value of equity, over December 31 of the preceding year and January 31 of the same year, to the debt at December 31 of the

[18] If we compute the rank correlation coefficient as among corporations between $r^2_{IV_{-1} \cdot M_{-1}}$ and the size of the corporations we obtain a coefficient of .81. This fact strongly suggests that the value of the firm performs better for larger corporations than for smaller ones. Note also that $r^2_{IV_{-1} \cdot M_{-1}}$ is larger in the regression on the aggregate of all eight corporations than for any single corporation.

preceding year. If we use for United States Steel the value of the firm
at the end of December 31 of the preceding year, the partial coefficient
of determination of investment on the value of the firm, holding the stock
of capital equipment constant, is .090, as compared to .306, obtained
when we use the value of the firm averaged over December and January.
It thus seems likely that the performance of the value of the firm is quite
sensitive to the averaging procedure. We used the averaging procedure
in the scatter-diagram analysis of some other corporations, and they also
showed some improvement in the performance of the value of the firm,
though not so substantial an improvement as in the case of United States
Steel.

The second row of Table 10 reveals that the partial coefficient of determination of investment on the stock of plant and equipment, holding
the value of the firm constant, is larger than .1 for all except two of the
corporations. The partial correlation coefficient is positive for all firms
and for the aggregate of all eight firms. It will be remembered that from
the model that we have developed for investment decisions it is impossible
to deduce on a priori grounds whether the partial correlation coefficient
of investment on the stock of plant and equipment, holding the value of
the firm constant, will be positive or negative. The replacement investment and maintenance and repairs included in the dependent variable
tend to make it positive, and the lagged response of net investment to a
change in expectations tends to make it negative. Our results indicate
that for all the eight corporations considered the "replacement and
maintenance effect" outweighs the "lagged response" effect.[19]

Until now we have considered the performance of the value of the firm
as an explanatory variable of investment by examining its partial correlation coefficient with investment, holding the stock of plant and equipment constant. In the previous section we have examined profits, both
lagged one year and current, in a similar fashion. Comparing the two
variables by looking at their respective partial correlation coefficients in
the *two sets* of regressions, we concluded that the value of the firm offers a
better explanation of investment behavior than profits either in its
lagged form or in its current form. To obtain a more conclusive comparison between the two variables, the value of the firm and profits, we have
introduced them together as two different independent variables beside
the stock of plant and equipment in a regression with investment as the
dependent variable. The main results of these regressions are summarized
in Table 11.

---

[19] For a more thorough examination of this point see Section IV.

Before examining the results of the multiple regression equations, it is interesting to ask how closely the value of the firm is related to profits. Rows (5) and (6) of Table 11 show, respectively, the simple coefficients of determination between profits and the value of the firm at the end of the year (r^2_{PV}) and the simple coefficient of determination between profits and the value of the firm at the end of the previous year $(r^2_{PV_{-1}})$. It will be noted that the size of the correlation between profits and the value of the firm varies from corporation to corporation and on the whole is not very pronounced. In both cases the coefficient of de-

TABLE 11

PARTIAL COEFFICIENTS OF DETERMINATION OF INVESTMENT, VALUE OF THE FIRM, AND PROFITS

	G.M. (1)	G.E. (2)	U.S.S. (3)	A.R. (4)	U.O. (5)	D.M. (6)	G.T.R. (7)	A.S.F. (8)	Aggregate (9)
(1) $r^2_{IP_{-1} \cdot M_{-1}V_{-1}}$	(−).262	.025	.155	(−).088	*	*	.102	.017	(−).008
(2) $r^2_{IV_{-1} \cdot M_{-1}P_{-1}}$	.637	.161	.250	.246	*	*	.247	.115	.548
(3) $r^2_{IP \cdot M_{-1}V_{-1}}$	(−).273	(−).040	.219	.096	.006	(−).049	.097	.142	(−).050
(4) $r^2_{IV_{-1} \cdot M_{-1}P}$	.575	.180	.103	.252	.050	.008	.195	.109	.554
(5) r^2_{PV}	.123	.038	.073	.620	*	*	.339	.000	.056
(6) $r^2_{PV_{-1}}$	.050	.062	.209	.652	.186	.013	.257	.000	.099
(7) $R^2_{I \cdot V_{-1}M_{-1}P_{-1}}$	.941	.714	.555	.680	*	*	.698	.156	.926
(8) $R^2_{I \cdot V_{-1}M_{-1}P}$	.941	.717	.587	.711	.765	.661	.698	.263	.930

* Regression not computed.

NOTATION

I = Real investment plus maintenance and repairs.
V_{-1} = Value of firm at end of previous year.
M_{-1} = Stock of plant and equipment at end of previous year.
P = Current profits.
P_{-1} = Profits lagged one year.

termination is smaller than .1 for the aggregate of the eight corporations. Half of the six coefficients of determination r^2_{PV} for the single corporations which were computed were smaller than .1, and half of the eight coefficients of determination $r^2_{PV_{-1}}$ were smaller than .1. It is therefore quite evident that profits either in lagged or current form does not measure generally the same forces that are measured by the value of the firm.[20]

For lagged profits we again obtain the result that they do not offer a satisfactory explanation of investment outlays (row [1], Table 11). The partial correlation coefficient of lagged profits is negative for the aggregate regression of the eight corporations, and so are the correlation co-

[20] It is interesting to note in this connection that Tinbergen used the "share price index" as a proxy for "profits earned" in those cases in which the profits series were unavailable (see Tinbergen, *op. cit.*, p. 44).

efficients of two of the six corporations for which we have carried out the computations. Of the other four coefficients of determination, two are smaller than .1, and the largest one (for United States Steel) is only .155.[21]

Current profits also do not seem to explain the variance in investment expenditure that is left over after introducing the stock of plant and equipment and the value of the firm (row [4], Table 11). The partial correlation coefficient of current profits in the aggregate regression is negative, and so are three of the eight correlation coefficients of the single corporations. Of the remaining five coefficients of determination, only two exceed .1, and the highest one (again for United States Steel) is .219.

The value of the firm explains a sizable proportion of the variation in investment that is left over after introducing the stock of plant and equipment and profits either in its lagged or in its current form (row [2], Table 11). No one of the partial correlation coefficients is negative, and six of the total of eight coefficients of determination are larger than .1, the largest one being .575. Note also that the partial coefficient of determination of the value of the firm in the aggregate regression is .554.

THE VALUE OF THE FIRM AND THE RATE OF INTEREST

Once the "performance" of the value of the firm as an explanatory variable of investment behavior has been established, we can now go one step further and ask ourselves whether it is possible to obtain some further insight into the relation between these two variables.

Investment may be affected by both changes in expected profits and/or changes in the rate of interest. The value of the firm measures both expected profits and the rate of interest; in fact, as has been noted above, it is equal to the present value of all profits expected in the future, where the "relevant" rate of interest is employed in the computation of the present value. Thus for given expectations about future profits the value of the firm will increase with a decrease of the rate of interest, and for a given rate of interest the value of the firm will increase with an increase in expected profits. Similarly, investment also is positively associated with a shift in expectations and negatively associated with a change in the rate of interest. At this point we have to face a problem that we have previously concealed by using the term the "relevant rate of interest." The rate of interest that is used in finding the present value of the firm's future earnings can be conveniently divided into three parts: (1) the pure rate of interest; (2) the "external" risk premium (or the lender's risk pre-

---

[21] We did not think it worthwhile to invest in the computation of the regressions for the two other corporations because the partial coefficients of determination of lagged profits in the regression excluding the value of the firm were extremely low.

mium); and (3) the internal risk premium (or the borrower's risk premium).[22]

The pure rate of interest is conceptually the rate of interest at which money could be borrowed if the lenders could be *certain* that the full amount of contracted interest and the principle would be paid. The external risk premium is added to the pure rate of interest by lenders to compensate them for the risk that the firm will default on its contracted principle and interest payments. The internal risk premium is added to the pure rate and the external risk premium by the residual income claimants as a payment for the risk involved in the future variations of the income of the firm after principle and interest payments to lenders are made.

The pure rate of interest and the external risk premium are both incorporated in the rate of interest that the firm pays in the bond market which can be measured independently. The internal risk premium presents us with a very difficult problem. Suppose that the bond rate remains constant and that we observe a change in the value of the firm. This increase in the value of the firm may be due to a shift in the mathematical expectation of future earnings or to a decrease in the internal risk premium or both. But a change in the internal risk premium may be regarded as a change in the variance of the probability distribution of expected profits.[23] Thus the "certainty equivalent" of future profits may be affected either by a shift in the mathematical expectation of profits or by a shift in the variance of the probability distribution of profits. Since the only observable magnitude is the "certainty equivalent" of expected profits, the difference between the internal risk premium and a change in expected profits is not operational. We will thus redefine an increase in expected profits as meaning either an increase in the mathematical expectation of future profits or a decrease in internal risk premium or both.

[22] See, e.g., M. Kalecki, "The Principle of Increasing Risk," *Economica*, Vol. IV (new ser., 1937); and S. Wellisz, "Entrepreneur's Risk, Lender's Risk, and Investment," *Review of Economic Studies*, Vol. XI, No. 52 (1952–53).

[23] The probability distribution discussed in the text assigns probabilities to *vectors* of future earnings, where the elements in the vectors are expected earnings for a specific year in the future. The meaning of the expression "an increase in expected profits" presents therefore some very complicated problems that are clearly outside the scope of the present study. For a discussion of some of the terminology used in the text see J. Marschak, "The Role of Liquidity under Complete and Incomplete Information," *American Economic Review, Papers and Proceedings*, Vol. XXXIX, No. 3 (1949); M. Friedman and L. J. Savage, "The Utility Analysis of Choices Involving Risk," *Journal of Political Economy*, Vol. LVI (August, 1948).

Thus the only operational meaning that can be attached to the distinction between the expectation effect as distinguished from the rate of interest effect on investment is to investigate the relation between the performance of the rate of interest in the bond market, as an explanatory variable of investment expenditures, and that of the value of the firm. Ideally, we would like to obtain a time series of bond rates for each corporation over the period studied and substitute this series for the value of the firm in all the regressions computed with this variable. Unfortunately, it was impossible to obtain comparable bond rate series for the single corporations over the period studied.[24] As a way out of this difficulty we noted that most of the corporations included in the sample had had Moody's Aaa bond ratings over most of the period 1935–54. We decided therefore to apply Moody's Aaa bond rate as the relevant bond rate for each one of the corporations and for the aggregate.

Table 12 records the performance of Moody's Aaa bond rate in December of the year preceding the investment outlay, as an explanatory variable of investment. Row (1) shows the simple coefficient of determination of investment and the rate of interest. For all corporations and the aggregate the correlation coefficient is negative, but for most corporations its magnitude is rather small. Row (2) shows the partial coefficients of determination of investment and the Aaa bond rate, holding the stock of plant and equipment constant. These coefficients are all very small (and two of the correlation coefficients have the "wrong sign"), indicating that the simple correlation between investment and the Aaa bond rate for the four corporations in which it has substantial magnitude may be due to a negative correlation between the stock of plant and equipment and the rate of interest during the period studied. One conclusion that can be drawn from this set of results is that, if Moody's Aaa bond rate correctly represents the interest rate at the end of the year preceding the investment outlay, then the performance of the value of the firm as an explanatory variable of investment expenditure cannot be due *only* to the fact that it represents the rate of interest.

The above results do not exclude the possibility that the rate of interest affects investment expenditures. Suppose that the monetary authorities and the suppliers of funds increase the rate of interest in times of boom when expectations about future profits are high and decrease it in times when expectations about future profits are low. Then, even if an

---

[24] To obtain a consistent bond rate over the whole period, it is required that the corporations always have bonds outstanding the yield of which is comparable in terms of the "collateral" and the duration of the loan. No single corporation from those included in the sample had bond issues outstanding during the whole period studied that even remotely fulfilled these "consistency conditions."

increase in the rate of interest will *ceteris paribus* tend to decrease investment expenditures and vice versa, we will not detect this effect with a regression similar to that of Table 12, row (2). The missing variable in this equation which represents the state of expectations will tend to cancel or even reverse the sign of the "true" effect of the rate of interest on investment expenditures. The introduction of the value of the firm as an expectations variable will not settle the issue either, for it incorporates not only expectations factors but also the rate of interest itself.

To see whether the rate of interest does affect investment expenditures, we can try to divide the value of the firm into its "expectation effect" and "rate of interest effect." If expectations about future profits would be in the form of a constant infinite stream, then the value of the firm would be equal to the value of that stream for a certain period divided by the relevant rate of interest. Thus we can approximate a "clean" expectations variable by multiplying the value of the firm by the rate of interest. We can then introduce the rate of interest beside this expectations variable and see what the effect is of the rate of interest on investment, keeping expectations constant. The results of such regressions are shown in row (3) of Table 12. It will be observed that the partial coefficients of determination increase dramatically (as compared to row [2]) and that the partial correlation coefficients have the right sign (negative) except in one case. It is interesting to note that for the three corporations—Diamond Match, Union Oil, and the American Steel Foundries—for which we obtained the poorest results with the value of the firm as an explanatory variable of investment (Table 10, row [1]) we also obtain poor results for the rate of interest. For the rest of the corporations and for the aggregate the effect of the value of the firm on investment seems to be broken down into an expectation effect and a rate of interest effect, both effects showing a substantial influence on investment expenditures. The expectation effect as represented by the partial coefficient of determination of investment and expectations (BV) is presented in row (5) of Table 12. It will be noticed that in all cases in which the value of the firm seemed to explain investment expenditures the expectations variable does so too. Row (4) shows the partial elasticities of investment in respect to the bond rate of interest at the means of the two series. This elasticity seems to vary among corporations, its magnitude varying (for all results significantly different from zero) from $-.74$ to -2.14. These are undoubtedly very substantial elasticities.[25]

[25] The low elasticity in the aggregate regression is a manifestation of Theil's "aggregation error" (see H. Theil, *Linear Aggregation of Economic Relations* [Amsterdam: North-Holland Publishing Co., 1954]).

TABLE 12

PARTIAL COEFFICIENTS OF DETERMINATION, PARTIAL ELASTICITIES, AND MULTIPLE COEFFICIENTS OF DETERMINATION IN REGRESSIONS, INCLUDING RATE OF INTEREST AS AN INDEPENDENT VARIABLE

	G.M.	G.E.	U.S.S.	A.R.	U.O.	D.M.	G.T.R.	A.S.F.	AGGREGATE
(1) $r^2_{iB_{-1}}$	$(-).025$	$(-).179$	$(-).107$	$(-).046$	$(-).113$	$(-).001$	$(-).235$	$(-).058$	$(-).072$
(2) $r^2_{iB_{-1} \cdot M_{-1}}$	$(-).002$	$(-).056$	$(-).056$	.073	.144	$(-).017$	$(-).057$	$(-).043$	.005
(3) $r^2_{iB_{-1} \cdot M_{-1}(BV)_{-1}}$	$(-).182$	$(-).200$	$(-).152$	$(-).085$	.032	$(-).020$	$(-).392$	$(-).037$	$(-).136$
(4) η	$-.743$	-1.290	$-.981$	$-.760$	.549	$-.635$	-2.139	$-.980$	$-.487$
(5) $r^2_{i(BV)_{-1} \cdot B_{-1}M_{-1}}$	.502	.267	.203	.292	.021	.004	.399	.092	.496
(6) $R^2_{i \cdot M_{-1}(BV)_{-1}B_{-1}}$	.914	.761	.472	.691	.781	.650	.756	.145	.920

NOTATION

B_{-1} = Moody's Aaa rate of interest in December of previous year.
M_{-1} = Stock of plant and equipment at end of previous year.
V_{-1} = Value of firm at end of previous year.

$(BV)_{-1}$ = Moody's Aaa rate of interest in December of previous year times value of firm of previous year.
η = Partial elasticity of investment in respect to rate of interest.

Row (6) of Table 12 shows the multiple coefficients of determination in the regressions in which expectations and the rate of interest appear separately. A comparison of these coefficients with the ones obtained when the value of the firm is used as an explantaory variable (Table 10, row [3]) reveals a striking similarity for nearly all firms and also for the aggregate. The over-all power of the value of the firm to explain investment seems to be nearly identical to the combined powers of the expectations variable and the rate of interest.[26]

THE RESIDUALS OF THE REGRESSION EQUATIONS

The co-movement analysis of investment and the value of the firm revealed that the value of the firm seemed to be a promising explanatory variable of investment behavior. The results of the regression equations (and especially the high partial coefficients of determination of investment and the value of the firm) show that we do obtain a "parametric" explanation of investment. The parametric relationship that we have arrived at is a linear regression equation of real investment plus maintenance and repairs on the real stock of plant and equipment and the real value of the firm at the end of the previous year. It is now time to see what kind of explanation the value of the firm really offers.

In our analysis of the residuals we will try mainly to answer the following questions:

1. Do our regression lines explain a larger part of the variations in investment expenditures than the naïve statement, "Investment next year will be equal to investment this year"?

2. How well do the regression lines perform one year after peaks and troughs in investment expenditure, and what is the relation between this performance and our other criteria of a successful "performance" of a variable or a group of variables?

3. Do the eight combined regression lines for all firms yield us more information about aggregate investment than the regression line of aggregate investment on the aggregate variables?

4. Is there evidence that the "disturbances" in our model are serially correlated?

1. *Comparison with the "naïve model."*—If we ask ourselves whether the explanation that our model offers of the variations in investment expenditures is satisfactory, we have to obtain a "standard" by which the

[26] Note that in the second set of regressions mentioned in the text we have one degree of freedom less than in the first set and hence a measure of the coefficient of multiple determination that is corrected for degrees of freedom would show smaller R^2's for the regressions presented in Table 12.

performance of our model can be evaluated. One "standard of comparison" of this kind is the "naïve model." The variation of investment over time shows a pronounced auto-correlation and hence a sizable amount of investment behavior can be "explained" by the naïve statement that investment next year will be the same as investment this year.[27] Does the regression of investment on the stock of plant and equipment and the value of the firm explain the variation in investment expenditures better than this naïve model? To answer this question, let us imagine that two players play the following "game." We take one firm, and each year one player predicts its investment by means of the naïve model and the other player by means of our model. We then compare the two predictions to the actual investment expenditure in the following year, and each player pays to the other the amount of money by which he has missed the actual in-

TABLE 13

COEFFICIENTS OF NET GAIN OF REGRESSION MODEL AGAINST NAÏVE
MODEL—EIGHT CORPORATIONS AND AGGREGATE, 1935–54

	CORPORATION								ALL CORPORA-TIONS	AGGRE-GATE
	G.M.	G.E.	U.S.S.	A.R.	U.O.	D.M.	G.T.R.	A.S.F.		
Coefficient of net gain.....	.33	.18	.17	.77	.38	−.08	.18	.17	.26	.72

vestment expenditure. The predictions are made for the years 1936–54, and the net gain of the player who uses our model, which is defined as positive net gain, is added up over the whole period. To facilitate the comparison of the "net gain" among the corporations, the net gain of each corporation is divided by the sum of the absolute residuals of the regression equation. We will call the ratio obtained for each corporation the "coefficient of net gain." The coefficients of net gain for the eight corporations and for the aggregate are presented in Table 13.

Table 13 reveals that our model offers explanations superior to those of the naïve model in the case of all corporations except one. It is interesting to compare the coefficient of net gain as a criterion for a successful explanation of the variations in investment expenditures to that of the coefficient of multiple determination. If we rank the corporations according to the size of their multiple coefficients of determination and also accord-

[27] See Carl Christ, "A Test of an Econometric Model for the United States, 1921–1947" in *Conference on Business Cycles* (New York: National Bureau of Economic Research, Inc., 1951), pp. 35–105, and comment by Milton Friedman, *ibid.*, pp. 107–14.

ing to the size of their coefficient of net gain, we find that Spearman's rank correlation between the two groupings is .80. The rank correlation is therefore quite substantial, and it seems that the two criteria for judging the success of a regression equation in explaining investment behavior give similar results for our eight corporations.

2. *The "performance" of the regressions at turning points.*—When we carried out the analysis of co-movement between investment, the value of the firm, and the stock of plant and equipment, we asked ourselves whether the independent variables show a downward movement during the year preceding a peak in investment expenditures and an upward movement during the year preceding a trough in investment expenditure. We are now in a position to go one step further and ask ourselves questions about the behavior of the linear combination of the two independent variables as obtained by the criterion of least squares.

TABLE 14

"RIGHT" AND "WRONG" PREDICTIONS OF DIRECTION OF MOVEMENT OF IN-
VESTMENT EXPENDITURES AT TURNING POINTS FOR EIGHT
CORPORATIONS AND FOR THE AGGREGATE

	G.M.	G.E.	U.S.S.	A.R.	U.O.	G.T.R.	D.M.	A.S.F.	Aggregate
Right direction......	5	6	6	12	9	8	9	9	7
Wrong direction......	1	0	1	0	3	3	1	0	1

It may appear as if a good criterion for judging whether the regression lines "predict" the peaks and troughs in investment expenditures would be to see whether they predict the direction of the change in investment at peaks and at troughs. According to this approach, a perfect score would mean that predicted investment at time $t + 1$ is smaller than investment at t for all peaks and that predicted investment at time $t + 1$ is larger than actual investment at t for all troughs. The number of "right" and "wrong" predictions of the direction of change at turning points is presented in Table 14.

Table 14 gives the impression that the performance of the regression lines at turning points is phenomenal. Of a total number of 73 turning points, we obtain 64 predictions of the "right" direction and 9 of the "wrong" direction. But this criterion of measuring the success of a regression in explaining investment is misleading and overstates grossly the real explanatory value of the regression. This fact becomes clear immediately if it is realized that a simple-minded linear trend will, in nearly all cases, have a perfect score in this measure.

There are two ways by which the regression line can fail to predict investment one year after the occurrence of a turning point. The regression may fail to predict any change in direction or may predict a smaller change in direction than really occurred. We will call this first kind of error in prediction "undershooting." The second kind of error in predicting investment will occur when the prediction of investment overstates the fall in investment after a peak or the rise in investment after a trough. This second error in prediction we will call "overshooting." Thus our regression lines will undershoot if we observe that the residuals one year after the occurrence of peaks in investment are positive and if the residuals one year after troughs are negative. Likewise, our regression lines will overshoot if we observe negative residuals one year after the occurrence of a peak and positive residuals one year after the occurrence of a trough. Table 15 shows the number of overshootings of the regression lines one year after a peak or a trough for each corporation and for the aggregate. We find that, of the 38 *peaks* observed, in 13 cases the regression line overshoots and in 25 cases it undershoots.

The proportion of cases in which the regressions predict investment to be too low the year after a peak is noteworthy. We have mentioned earlier that the variable that we expect to predict peaks in investment expenditures is the value of the firm, since the stock of plant and equipment has for nearly all corporations a constantly upward trend. It is therefore interesting to compare the performance of the value of the firm in the co-movement analysis at peaks with the overshooting or undershooting of the regression lines at peaks. To make such a comparison, we rank the eight firms according to the ratio of peaks successfully predicted by the value of the firm (as presented in Table 7), and we also rank the eight firms according to the proportion of peaks for which the regression line overshoots. Spearman's rank correlation between these two rankings turns out to be .68. We conclude that, in corporations for which the value of the firm tends to predict peaks successfully, the regression line tends to overshoot peaks.

Of the 35 *troughs* observed for all eight corporations, the regression line overshoots in 20 cases. The tendency of the regression line to overestimate investment expenditures one year after a trough is clearly due to the pronounced upward trend of the stock of plant and equipment for most corporations. The stock of plant and equipment predicts successfully 26 of the 35 observed troughs, while it predicts only 3 of the 38 peaks observed. If we add the fact that the value of the firm itself predicts successfully 23 of the 35 observed troughs, it becomes quite apparent why the tendency of the regression line to overshoot troughs is so prounounced.

TABLE 15

NUMBER OF UNDERSHOOTINGS AND OVERSHOOTINGS OF REGRESSION LINES ($I = c_0 + c_1 M_{-1} + c_2 V_{-1}$) ONE YEAR AFTER TURNING POINTS IN INVESTMENT

	G.M.		G.E.		U.S.S.		A.R.		U.O.		D.M.		G.T.R.		A.S.F.		AGGREGATE	
	Pe*	Tr†	Pe	Tr	Pe	Tr	Pe	Tr	Pe	Tr	Pe	Tr	Pe	Tr	Pe	Tr	Pe	Tr
O‡ (overshooting)	2	2	2	1	2	1	2	1	0	4	1	4	1	3	2	2	3	3
U§ (undershooting)	1		1	2	2	2	4	5	6	2	4	1	4	1	2	1	3	2

* Peak.   † Trough.   ‡ Overshooting.   § Undershooting.

TABLE 16

COEFFICIENT OF NET GAIN ONE YEAR AFTER TURNING POINTS IN INVESTMENT, FOR EACH CORPORATION, AND FOR THE AGGREGATE OF THE EIGHT CORPORATIONS

G.M.			G.E.			U.S.S.			A.R.			U.O.			D.M.			G.T.R.			A.S.F.			All Corp.			AGGREGATE		
Pe*	Tr†	TP‡	Pe	Tr	TP	Pe	Tr	TP	Pe	Tr	TP	Pe	Tr	TP	Pe	Tr	TP	Pe	Tr	TP	Pe	Tr	TP	Pe	Tr	TP	Pe	Tr	TP
1.06	−.49	.11	−.20	1.36	.26	.47	.86	.63	1.14	1.31	1.23	.21	2.35	.86	.03	.05	.04	−.14	.32	.02	.20	.05	.16	.52	.24	.39	.63	−.41	−.01

* Peak.   † Trough.   ‡ Turning points.

To obtain a measure of the performance of the regression lines at turning points, we can utilize the idea of the coefficient of net gain as defined above. Instead of playing our "game" for all nineteen years, we play it only for the years that succeed turning points in investment expenditures. The coefficient of net gain for turning points obtained for each corporation and for the aggregative regression are shown in Table 16. In addition, we have computed the coefficients of net gain for peaks, troughs, and all turning points that occurred in all corporations during the period of time considered. These coefficients are shown in the next to the last column and will be discussed below.

For each corporation we recorded the coefficient of net gain one year after peaks and one year after troughs separately and the coefficient of net gain for the two types of turning points combined. Let us start our analysis of these results by comparing the coefficients of net gain for all turning points in each corporation to the coefficient of net gain for all years (Table 13). The comparison of the explanatory value of the regression line to that of the naïve model one year after turning points in investment expenditures may seem an "unfair" comparison, since the naïve model will *always* make an error, while the regression line *may* yield a perfect prediction. This disadvantage of the naïve model is not present in the years that do not succeed turning points, since in these years the naïve model *can* yield a perfect prediction. (Put differently, in these years we do not exclude *by definition* the possibility that investment in two adjacent years is equal.) Thus we may expect that the coefficient of net gain will tend to be higher for "turning points" than for "all years." The fact that such a tendency exists but is not a general rule is demonstrated by the result that, of the eight corporations, five have a higher coefficient of net gain for turning points than for all years. But one of the three corporations which shows a higher coefficient of net gain for all years than for turning points is General Motors, a corporation for which the regression line has a better "fit" than for any other corporation and for which the value of the firm yielded perfect "predictions" for all turning points. The small coefficient of net gain for turning points in General Motors is clearly due to the fact that for troughs there is a negative coefficient of net gain. From Table 15, we see that, of the three troughs observed in General Motors, the regression line overshot in two. We are thus led to the conclusion that the negative coefficient of net gain for troughs in General Motors is due to overshooting. This fact is confirmed by the calculation of the coefficient of net gain on which Table 16 is based. Though the naïve model yields superior predictions to the regression line for all three troughs that occurred in General Motors, the main "loss" is due to the two years in which the regression line overshot actual investment expenditures. A similar and even more pronounced result is obtained for the regression line of aggregate investment of the eight corporations. The loss due to overshooting troughs is so large that the coefficient of net gain for all turning points is slightly negative.

The coefficient of net gain one year after turning points is a very different criterion of judging the "fit" of a regression line than the measures usually employed for that purpose. This fact can be demonstrated by comparing the coefficients of multiple determination as among firms to their coefficient of net gain at turning points. If we rank the eight corporations according to these two criteria of success in fitting a regression line, we find that Spearman's coefficient of rank correlation is only .17. The two criteria clearly answer two conceptually different questions. The coefficient of multiple determination treats all deviations without discrimination, since it is based on the variance of all the residuals in relation to the variance of the dependent variable. The coefficient of net gain at turning points discriminates very heavily among the residuals. In fact, it gives zero weight to all the residuals except those that occur one year after turning points. The reason that we are interested in a measure with such a weighting system is that we want to find out whether the claim that our regression lines incorporate expectations is substantiated by our findings. We have claimed previously that the particular points of time at which turning points of investment expenditure occurred are well suited to test our claim that the regression lines do incorporate the relevant expectations factors. But let us recall that in this respect there is an important difference between peaks and troughs. Since most time series were upward sloping over the period under consideration, they naturally "predict" successfully the occurrence of troughs, and hence we cannot regard this success in prediction as evidence that these series incorporate the relevant expectations factors. In the case of peaks the situation is very different. No regression line that merely "catches" the upward trend in investment will predict peaks

We have claimed that the value of the firm incorporates the relevant expectations factors for investment decisions, and we may therefore expect that, the better the "performance" of the value of the firm in the regression equations, the more likely it is that the regression equation will show a higher net gain at peaks. To test this hypothesis, we can rank the eight firms according to the magnitude of the partial coefficient of determination of investment on the value of the firm (Table 10) and also according to the coefficient of net gain at peaks (Table 16). Spearman's coefficient of rank correlation between these two rankings is .57. We have thus confirmed our contention that, in general, the better the "perform-ance" of the value of the firm in the regression equation, the better will be the prediction of peaks in investment expenditures.

Let us now concentrate our attention on troughs of investment ex-penditures. In this case we may ask ourselves two questions:

a) Do the regression lines show a better performance at troughs as compared to the naïve model the higher the partial coefficient of determi-nation of the value of the firm?

b) Do the regression lines show a better performance at troughs as compared to the naïve model the higher the partial coefficient of determi-nation of the stock of plant and equipment?

Our results suggest that both questions should be answered in the negative. The rank correlation between the coefficient of net gain at troughs and the partial coefficient of determination of the value of the firm is −.084. The rank correlation between the coefficient of net gain at troughs and the partial coefficient of determination of the stock of plant and equipment is −.06. It is therefore quite clear that a high partial correlation coefficient for either of the variables does not assure, and, in fact, seems to be detrimental to, the performance of the regression line at troughs relative to the naïve model. We may therefore conclude that neither a large number of successfully predicted troughs in a co-move-ment analysis nor a high partial coefficient of determination for either of the variables is a sufficient indication as to whether a variable or a set of variables will yield a regression that will predict successfully investment expenditures one year after a trough.

The above statement is a demonstration of the fact that our different criteria for a "successful explanation" of investment by means of our variables really stress different aspects of this explanation and may, and, in fact, do, indicate that, while the explanation is satisfactory from one point of view, it is not satisfactory from another point of view. For our purposes, since we are primarily interested in testing the proposition that the value of the firm contains the relevant expectations factors, the fact that the performance of the regression lines is poor at troughs is not of particular relevance. *For that purpose* performance at peaks and perform-ance for all years are the important criteria to be considered.

3. *The aggregate of the regressions and the regression of the aggregate.*—It has already been pointed out previously that the coefficient of multiple determination of the regression of aggregate investment on the aggregate of the stocks of plant and equipment and the aggregate value of the firm is higher than the coefficient of multiple determination obtained for any one of the single corporations. This leads us to ask ourselves whether it is

at all worthwhile to compute regressions for the single corporations if we wish to explain the behavior of aggregate investment.

A method of comparing the performance of the regression equation of the aggregates to the composite performance of the eight regression equations can be derived directly from the residuals of the regression equations.[28]

For the eight corporations considered, the composite coefficient of determination R_2^2 is .906, as compared to a multiple coefficient of determination of the aggregate R_1^2 of .926.

A second way of comparing the explanation for aggregate investment offered by the regression of aggregate investment on the aggregate of the independent variables to that offered by the regression lines for the single corporations can be constructed by utilizing the concept "performance relative to the naïve model."[29] This coefficient can be interpreted in the

---

[28] Add up the residuals for each year over all the eight corporations. Find the variance of these twenty observations and denote it by S_2^2. We now define a composite coefficient of multiple determination in the following way:

$$R_2^2 = 1 - \frac{S_2^2}{S_I^2},$$

where S_I^2 is the variance of aggregate investment.

Since the coefficient of multiple determination for the regression of aggregate investment on the aggregate independent variables is

$$R_1^2 = 1 - \frac{S_0^2}{S_I^2},$$

where S_0^2 is the variance of the residuals of the aggregate regression, we thus obtain

$$R_2^2 = 1 - \frac{S_2^2}{S_0^2}(1 - R_1^2).$$

[29] Denote:

d_{kt} = absolute residual of regression for corporation k in year t (where $k = 1, \ldots, 8$; $t = 1, \ldots, 20$).

S_{kt} = absolute value of first difference of investment for corporation k in year t (where $k = 1, \ldots, 8$; $t = 1, \ldots, 20$).

The coefficient of net gain for any single corporation C_k has been defined as

$$C_k = \frac{\sum_{t=1}^{20} S_{kt} - \sum_{t=1}^{20} d_{kt}}{\sum_{t=1}^{20} d_{kt}}$$

An obvious extension of the concept of the coefficient of net gain is to define a composite following way: the coefficient of net gain for a single corporation (C_k) is equal to the total gain which that player who "plays" the regression equation makes over the twenty years divided by the sum of errors in prediction that he makes over the whole period. In the same way the composite coefficient of net gain (C) is equal to the total gain which that player who "plays" the regression equations makes for all corporations and for all years, divided by the sum of errors in prediction that he makes for all corporations and for all years.

In Table 13 we have shown the composite coefficient of net gain under the heading "All Corporations" and the coefficient of net gain for the aggregate equation under the heading "Aggregate." The composite coefficient of net gain, which is .26, is substantially below the coefficient of net gain for the aggregate regression, which is .72.

It is evident that both criteria for judging the performance of the regression equations in relation to aggregate investment, that of the multiple coefficient of determination and that of the coefficient of net gain, lead to the same conclusion. They both show that the regression of aggregate investment on the aggregate of the stock of plant and equipment and the aggregate of the value of the firm offers a better explanation for aggregate investment than all the eight regression equations on the single corporations combined.

Let us remind ourselves that the above conclusion is based on two criteria that give equal weight to all errors in prediction, and we may ask ourselves whether it will still hold if we concentrate our attention on turning points in investment expenditures. We have seen previously that the coefficient of net gain is well suited to answer this kind of question. Let us therefore define composite coefficients of net gain for peaks and troughs in investment expenditures. These coefficients are similar to the composite coefficient of net gain for all years defined above.[30]

---

coefficient of net gain C for all k corporations over all t years, where

$$C = \frac{\sum\limits_{k=1}^{8} \sum\limits_{t=1}^{20} S_{kt} - \sum\limits_{k=1}^{8} \sum\limits_{t=1}^{20} d_{kt}}{\sum\limits_{k=1}^{8} \sum\limits_{t=1}^{20} d_{kt}}.$$

[30] Denote:

$\hat{d}_{ki}$ = absolute value of residual of regression for corporation k in year i one year after a peak (where $k = 1, \ldots, 8$ and $i = 1, \ldots, P_k$);

$\hat{S}_{ki}$ = absolute value of first difference of investment for corporation k in year i one year after a peak (where $k = 1, \ldots, 8$ and $i = 1, \ldots, P_k$);

In a similar way we can also define a composite coefficient of net gain for all turning points.

In Table 16 we have shown the composite coefficients of net gain for peaks and troughs and for all turning points under the heading "All Corporations." The composite coefficient of net gain is positive for peaks and troughs and for the two types of turning points combined. It is instructive to compare the composite coefficients of net gain at turning points to the coefficient of net gain of the aggregate regression (last column of Table 16). The coefficient of net gain for peaks of the aggregate regression is higher than the composite coefficient of net gain at peaks. But, while the coefficient of net gain for troughs is negative and quite large in absolute value in the aggregate regression, the composite coefficient of net gain at troughs is positive and quite large. It will also be observed that the coefficient of net gain of the aggregate regression for all turning points is slightly negative, indicating that, if one wants to predict

---

P_k = number of peaks of corporation k.

The coefficient of net gain one year after peaks for the corporation has been defined:

$$C_k = \frac{\sum_{i=1}^{P_k} \hat{S}_{ki} - \sum_{i=1}^{P_k} \hat{d}_{ki}}{\sum_{i=1}^{P_k} \hat{d}_{ki}}.$$

The composite coefficient of net gain one year after peaks for all corporations can now be defined:

$$C = \frac{\sum_{k=1}^{8} \sum_{i=1}^{P_k} \hat{S}_{ki} - \sum_{k=1}^{8} \sum_{i=1}^{P_k} \hat{d}_{ki}}{\sum_{k=1}^{8} \sum_{i=1}^{P_k} \hat{d}_{ki}}.$$

By an obvious extension of our notation we define the composite coefficient of net gain one year after troughs:

$$\check{C} = \frac{\sum_{k=1}^{8} \sum_{j=1}^{T_k} \check{S}_{kj} - \sum_{k=1}^{8} \sum_{j=1}^{T_k} \check{d}_{kj}}{\sum_{k=1}^{8} \sum_{j=1}^{T_k} \check{d}_{kj}},$$

where T_k is the number of troughs observed for corporation k.

aggregate investment one year after the occurrence of turning-points, it would be better to employ the "naïve model" than the aggregate regression equation. But, by computing all the regressions for the single corporations and combining the predicted investment expenditures, we obtain a better prediction of investment one year after turning points than by employing the naïve model. This suggests that, if we are interested in predicting aggregate investment one year after turning points, we obtain better results by computing separate regressions for each corporation and then combining the results than by computing a regression for the aggregate variables. If we are interested in predicting investment correctly every year or if we are interested in predicting investment one year after the occurrence of a peak, then we are better off if we compute the aggregate regression rather than aggregate the regressions for the single firms. The paradox that all eight regression lines combined seem to have a lower explanatory power than a single regression on the aggregates can be explained by a reconsideration of the process of formation of expectations that lead to changes in investment. If, in fact, the corporations are directly affected by changes of some large aggregates (e.g., industry or economy variables), and these expectations are not fully reflected in the value of the firm, then, in the process of aggregating the variables over the firms, we actually include this "aggregate effect" into our explanatory model. In this case it is possible that the regression on the aggregative variables includes more relevant information than all the regressions of single firms combined.[31] By introducing the value of all eight firms into the regressions of the single firms, it is possible to obtain an idea of the degree of influence that aggregative or common expectation factors that are not fully included in the private value of the firm have on investment expenditures. In Table 17 we have recorded the relevant results of such regressions.

Row (1) of Table 17 shows the explanatory power of the "private" value of the firm given the "aggregate" value of all eight firms, and row (2) shows the explanatory power of the aggregate value of all eight firms given the private value of the particular firm. It will be seen that the private value of the firm "holds ground" quite well. In six of the eight cases considered the aggregate value of all eight firms does not add any explanation to investment expenditures once the private value of the firm has been taken into account. But for the two oil corporations, Atlantic Refining and Union Oil, the aggregate value of all eight firms seems to

[31] A detailed analysis of such a possibility is presented in Y. Grunfeld and Z. Griliches, "Is Aggregation Necessarily Bad? An Empirical Contribution to the Aggregation Problem," *Review of Economics and Statistics*, XLII, No. 1 (February, 1960), 1–13.

contain more information about the forces that induce investment than is contained in the private value of the firm (in the case of General Electric the two variables seem to contain the same relevant information, and in the case of Diamond Match neither one of them seems to contain any relevant information). Thus we may conclude that, although on the whole the private value of the firm seems to contain the relevant information pertaining to the investment decision that is represented by the aggregate value of the firm and in addition also some forces specific to the corporation, sometimes the "common" forces are not fully measured by it. These cases will improve the explanatory power of the aggregate regression relative to all the regressions of the single corporations combined.

TABLE 17

PARTIAL COEFFICIENTS OF DETERMINATION OF PRIVATE VALUE OF THE
FIRM AND AGGREGATE VALUE OF ALL EIGHT CORPORATIONS

	G.M.	G.E.	U.S.S.	A.R.	U.O.	D.M.	G.T.R.	A.S.F.
(1) $r^2_{Iv_{p-1} \cdot M_{-1}V_{A-1}}$	.300	.001	.159	.079	.000	.017	.184	.119
(2) $r^2_{Iv_{A-1} \cdot M_{-1}V_{p-1}}$	(−).088	.006	(−).006	.130	.116	(−).063	(−).016	(−).014
(3) $r^2_{Iv_{A-1} \cdot M_{-1}} \cdots$	.395	.168	.109	.360	.199	(−).049	.066	.024

NOTATION

I = Real investment plus maintenance and repairs.
M_{-1} = Stock of plant and equipment at end of previous year.
V_{p-1} = Value of firm at end of previous year.
V_{A-1} = Value of all eight firms at end of previous year.

To obtain more direct evidence on whether the influence of the aggregate value of the firms on the investment decisions of the single firms is the reason why we obtained an R^2 of the aggregate that is higher than the composite R^2 for all eight regressions, we can compute a composite R^2 for the regressions of each corporation that contain both the private and the aggregate value of the firms. Such a composite R^2 is equal to .930 as compared to the R^2 of the regression of the aggregates of .926, and to a composite R^2 of .906 when the equations for each corporation do not include the value of all firms. Thus it may be concluded that, if we combine the explanatory power of all the eight regressions containing both the private and the aggregate value of all firms, we obtain a better explanation of aggregate investment than that provided by the regression of the aggregate variables.

Row (3) of Table 17 shows the partial coefficient of determination of investment with the value of all firms, holding the stock of plant and equipment constant. Here the aggregate value of all firms is substituted for the private value of the particular firm as an explanatory variable of investment. It will be noted that this variable does explain quite a sizable proportion of the variation in investment left over after taking account of the variations in the stock of plant and equipment. Aggregate forces are presumably an important element in the formation of expectation of future returns that induce investment.[32]

4. *The serial correlation of the residuals.*—A final step in our analysis of the characteristics of the residuals of the regression equation of investment on the value of the firm and the stock of plant and equipment was to compute the "Durbin-Watson" coefficient of serial correlation.[33] Since there exists a large amount of serial correlation in the dependent variable investment, we may think that it is likely that the "true" disturbances of our model are also serially correlated. This view is incorrect. It will be

TABLE 18

DURBIN-WATSON COEFFICIENT OF SERIAL CORRELATION IN
RESIDUALS OF REGRESSIONS $I = c_0 + c_1 M_{-1} + c_2 V_{-1}$
(For All Corporations and for the Aggregate)

	CORPORATION								AGGRE-GATE
	G.M.	G.E.	U.S.S.	A.R.	U.O.	D.M.	G.T.R.	A.S.F.	
Coefficient of serial correlation........	.88	1.07	1.12	2.37	.76	1.08	1.25	.99	1.26

recalled that in the "model" from which we derived the regression equation we have taken account of the fact that investment in each year is dependent on investment during the previous years. In fact, one of the main roles of the variable "the stock of plant and equipment" was to take explicit account of that dependence. Consequently, we may conclude that, if our model offers a reasonably close approximation to reality, we should not expect that there will exist serial correlation in the disturbances of the equation. But it should also be remembered that we have never claimed that our investment model was a "full model" in the sense that it incorporates *all* the factors that affect investment decisions. If we have "left out" a variable that incorporates such additional factors and if this variable is itself serially correlated, then we may expect serial correlation in the disturbances of our equation.

[32] Note that the performance of the value of all eight firms cannot be just a reflection of the rate-of-interest effect. Recall that the rate of interest performs very poorly when substituted for the value of the firm as an explanatory variable of investment.

[33] J. Durbin and G. S. Watson, "Testing for Serial Correlation in Least Squares Regression," *Biometrica*, XXXVIII (1951), 159–77.

The Durbin-Watson coefficient for the regression for each corporation and the aggregate is shown in Table 18. There is only one corporation for which we can conclude that there exists positive serial correlation in the disturbances at the 5 per cent significance level.[34] This corporation is Union Oil. It will be noted that the regression equation of the aggregate yields a coefficient that lies in the "indeterminate region," as do the coefficients of six of the corporations. Only in the case of Atlantic Refining Corporation can we reject the hypothesis that there exists serial correlation in the disturbances.

IV. FURTHER EXAMINATION AND TESTS OF THE MODEL

THE REGRESSION COEFFICIENTS

In the preceding section we presented all our results in terms of partial coefficients of determination. These coefficients are suitable to measure the explanatory power of the variables. A further insight into the plausibility of our model can be obtained by examining the regression coefficients, which are given in Table 19.

The partial regression coefficient of the stock and plant and equipment reflects both the effect of replacement investment and the dynamic adjustment to previous stimuli. Since the dynamic adjustment to previous changes in expectations is expected to produce a negative coefficient for the stock of plant and equipment, we may conclude that the calculated coefficient c_1 and also the sum of the coefficients c_1 and c_2 are underestimates of the replacement and maintenance and repairs effect.[35]

A glance at the values of c_1 obtained for the different firms reveals that the coefficient is too large for General Motors, United States Steel, and Diamond Match. It seems unreasonable to believe that depreciation and maintenance comprise more than 30 per cent of the existing stock of plant and equipment. Even if we take into consideration that the coefficients

---

[34] For twenty observations and two independent variables the 5 per cent level of significance is bracketed by $d_L = .89$ and $d_U = 1.55$. Denoting the computed coefficient of serial correlation by d, then

> if $\quad d < d_L \rightarrow$ positive serial correlation
> if $4 - d < d_L \rightarrow$ negative serial correlation
> if $\quad d > d_U$ and $4 - d > d_U \rightarrow$ no serial correlation

In all other cases the test is inconclusive.

[35] If g = replacement and maintenance as a ratio of the existing stock of capital,
$\quad k$ = dynamic adjustment coefficient,
$\quad b$ = the ratio of an increase in the desired stock of plant and equipment to an increase in the value of the firm,
then $c_1 = g - k$, $c_2 = kb$, and $c_1 + c_2 = g + (b - 1)k$.
We assume that $k > 0$ and $0 < b < 1$.

are only sample estimates and also that there is some multicollinearity between the two independent variables, we can still conclude that the rate of replacement and maintenance implied by the regression coefficients is too high.[36] In the cases of United States Steel and Diamond

TABLE 19

PARTIAL REGRESSION COEFFICIENTS OF REGRESSION OF INVESTMENT ON STOCK OF PLANT AND EQUIPMENT AND VALUE OF THE FIRM

$$I = a + c_1 M_{-1} + c_2 V_{-1}$$

(Eight Firms, 1935–54)

	CORPORATION								AGGRE-GATE
	G.M.	G.E.	U.S.S.	A.R.	U.O.	G.T.R.	D.M.	A.S.F.	
c_1	.400	.152	.390	.003	.124	.082	.437	.084	.281
	(.041)*	(.026)	(.142)	(.022)	(.017)	(.028)	(.080)	(.083)	(.025)
c_2	.116	.027	.175	.162	.087	.075	.005	.065	.097
	(.026)	(.016)	(.074)	(.057)	(.066)	(.034)	(.027)	(.042)	(.022)
r^2_{VM}	.196	.014	.028	.756	.001	.367	(−).022	(−).089	.140
R^2	.919	.705	.471	.680	.764	.666	.643	.142	.926

* Numbers in parentheses equal standard error.

NOTATION

c_1 = Partial regression coefficient of the stock of plant and equipment.
c_2 = Partial regression coefficient of value of firm.
R^2 = Coefficient of multiple determination.
r^2_{VM} = Coefficient of determination of value of firm on the stcok of plant and equipment.

Match the high regression coefficient for the stock of plant and equipment can be due to the fact that for those corporations the value of the firm seems to include only a minor part of the determinants of investment.[37]

[36] For both General Motors and Diamond Match, c_1 is significantly larger than .3 in a one-tailed test with a 5 per cent significance level. The sum of the coefficients $c_1 + c_2$ is also significantly larger than .3 in the case of General Motors and United States Steel. This test can be constructed as follows: Denote the estimate of the variance of c_1 by $s^2_{c_1}$, the estimate of the variance of c_2 by $s^2_{c_2}$, and the estimate of the covariance between c_1 and c_2 by $S_{c_1 c_2}$. Then

$$s_{c_1 + c_2} = \sqrt{s^2_{c_1} + s^2_{c_2} + 2\, s_{c_1 c_2}}$$

is the standard error of $c_1 + c_2$.

$$\frac{c_1 + c_2 - .3}{\sqrt{s^2_{c_1} + s^2_{c_2} + 2\, s_{c_1 c_2}}}$$

is distributed as "Student's" t.

[37] Recall that for Diamond Match the partial coefficient of determination of the value of the firm is essentially zero and that in the case of United States Steel profits

But in the case of General Motors we could not find any satisfactory explanation for the apparent high rate of maintenance and replacement expenditures. This fact casts some doubt on the adequacy of our model to explain investment expenditures. Some important effect of size on the decision to invest may exist which has not been incorporated formally into the investment model constructed in the previous section [38]

PREDICTION OF INVESTMENT EXPENDITURE IN 1955 AND 1956

The quality of the prediction of investment expenditures obtained for the years 1955 and 1956, which were not included in the original observations for which the regressions were computed, serves as another test of the explanatory value of our investment equations. It should be stressed that the quality of prediction is only one criterion by which the explanatory value of our regressions can be judged; it is not the only or even the most important one. It would be strange to base our criterion of a successful explanation of investment behavior on two particular years. Nevertheless, the quality of prediction is a useful criterion if it is added to the ones that we have discussed in Section IV.

It is quite evident that the linear functions that we have fitted to our data give only a linear approximation in a certain neighborhood to an essentially non-linear relation. It is especially unreasonable to believe that the dynamic adjustment coefficient is really a constant as we have assumed in the construction of the regression equations. One would expect that the adjustment coefficient decreases as a function of the change in expectations, or, in other words, that net investment as a percentage of the difference between the desired stock of plant and equipment and the existing stock of plant and equipment decreases as this difference increases. Furthermore, we would on other grounds expect predictions to be worse, the farther the independent variables deviate in the prediction years from their range during the period of observation.

Actually, in predicting investment expenditures for 1955 and 1956, we found both that the differences between actual and desired stock were very large *and* that the observations on the independent variables were in many cases far from their range of earlier years. The entries in Table 20

---

seem to explain a sizable part of the variations in investment after the effect of the value of the firm has been taken into account. In the case of United States Steel for the regression equation that includes both the value of the firm and lagged profits the regression coefficient of the stock of plant and equipment is .238.

[38] Note also that there seems to be a slight positive association between the size of a corporation and the regression coefficient of the stock of plant and equipment. The coefficient of rank correlation between these two characteristics is .29.

were constructed in the following way: first we took the difference between the magnitude of each one of the independent variables in the two prediction years and the *maximum* magnitude that they attained in the observation period. These differences were then expressed as percentages of the *range* of the independent variables in the observation period.

Table 20 reveals that some of the corporations experienced huge variations in their independent variables during the prediction years that shifted them far away from the range of experience during the observation period. For example, the value of the firm of General Motors was higher in 1954 than the maximum which it attained in the period 1934–53 (in 1952)

TABLE 20

DIFFERENCE BETWEEN INDEPENDENT VARIABLES AT PREDICTION YEARS
AND MAXIMUM VALUE DURING REGRESSION YEARS AS PERCENTAGE
OF RANGE OF INDEPENDENT VARIABLE DURING REGRESSION YEARS

Corporation	V 1954	V 1955	M 1954	M 1955
General Motors............	68	153	29	48
General Electric............	63	*	13	*
United States Steel.........	−27	0	−11	−23
Atlantic Refining...........	− 4	2	7	10
Union Oil..................	98	70	6	13
Goodyear Tire and Rubber...	74	126	11	0
Diamond Match............	−38	175	6	−12
American Steel Foundries....	− 6	0	6	−13

* Not computed.

by more than two-thirds of the over-all range of the value of the firm during the observation period. Furthermore, in 1955 the value of the firm exceeded the "range of experience" by more than one and a half times the "range of experience." Of the eight corporations considered, in five the value of the firm shows deviations from its range of experience in one or both prediction years comparable to that of General Motors.

The stock of plant and equipment is, on the whole, closer during the prediction year to its range of experience during the observation period than the value of the firm. One exception is the stock of plant and equipment of General Motors, which shows in the prediction period substantial deviations from the range of experience during the observation period.

1. *The standard errors of forecast.*—The first question that we will ask about the predicted values of investment expenditures in 1955 and 1956 is whether they are consistent with the regression equations computed for the period of observation. More precisely, we will test the null hypothesis

that the observations in the prediction period were generated by the same linear relations in the populations that had generated the observations for which we have computed the regression equations.[39]

The standard error of forecast was computed for each prediction year and for each corporation. The difference between actual investment and predicted investment was divided by its standard error of forecast for each prediction year. This ratio is distributed as "Student's" t. The test is, strictly speaking, applicable only if we make a forecast for one year. Since we forecast two years for each corporation, we had to take account of the "covariance of forecast" between the years. The appropriate statistic to be tested in this case has Fisher's variance ratio distribution (F).[40]

Table 21 summarizes the prediction tests for all corporations and for the aggregate of all eight corporations. The only corporation for which we reject the hypothesis (at the 5 per cent level of significance) that the observations of the prediction period have been generated by the same linear relationship in the population as the observations in the observation period is General Motors. (At a level of significance of 20 per cent we reject the null hypothesis in the case of two corporations.) For all other corporations we found that the error in forecast is not large enough to justify the conclusion that the regression equations computed for them

---

[39] There are two kinds of alternative hypotheses that we may have in mind: (1) we could "maintain" the assumption of linearity and test the hypothesis that the same set of parameters in the population could have generated the observations in the observation period and in the prediction period, or (2) our alternative hypothesis may combine a change in parameters and a non-linearity statement. Since the assumption of linearity in our case is questionable, it is better to choose for our purpose the second alternative hypothesis. The choice of the alternative hypothesis will matter only in those cases in which we reject the null hypothesis.

[40] If $\sigma^2\Omega$ is the variance-covariance matrix of the errors of forecast in the prediction period, where σ^2 is the population variance of the disturbances, and if U is the column vector of errors of forecast then

$$A = \frac{\hat{U}'\Omega^{-1}\hat{U}}{\sigma^2}$$

will be distributed as $\chi^2(n)$ where n is the number of years in the prediction period. If we denote the unbiased estimate of the variance of residuals of the regression equations by s^2 then $B = Ns^2/\sigma^2$ will also be distributed as $\chi^2(N - K)$, where $N - K$ = number of degrees of freedom in the regression equation. Hence

$$\frac{A}{B} = F(n, N - K).$$

This test was suggested to me by Carl Christ. For the standard error of forecast in the case of one observation see A. M. Mood, *Introduction to the Theory of Statistics* (New York: McGraw-Hill Book Co., 1950), pp. 304–5.

are inconsistent with the investment expenditure observed in the prediction period. Put differently, for these seven (or six, depending on the level of significance one prefers) corporations our success in prediction is not worse than might be expected from our regression equations.[41] It will be noticed that the power of the test of prediction is higher the higher the coefficient of multiple correlation of the regressions. Thus for those corporations for which the regression equations do not show a "good fit," we may not be able to reject the null hypothesis even if the errors in prediction are quite substantial. Some evidence on this point can be obtained by ranking the corporations according to their respective magnitudes of

TABLE 21

t VALUES, F VALUES, AND TWO-TAILED PROBABILITIES FOR TEST OF HYPOTHESIS
THAT INVESTMENT DURING PREDICTION PERIOD WAS GENERATED BY
SAME LINEAR EQUATIONS AS INVESTMENT IN OBSERVATION PERIOD

CORPORATION	1955		1956		COMBINED	
	t	Prob-ability	*t*	Prob-ability	F	Probability
General Motors.......	3.20	.006	3.81	.002	7.73	.001 < P < .01
General Electric......	.88	.380	N.a.*	N.a.	......	....
United States Steel....	.68	.580	.65	.526	.37	P > .20
Atlantic Refining.....	−1.32	.200	1.69	.108	3.02	.10 > P > .05
Union Oil............	.19	.844	.67	.516	.25	P > .20
Goodyear Tire and Rubber............	.04	.999	.23	.824	.04	P > .20
Diamond Match......	.24	.808	.06	.997	.03	P > .20
American Steel Foundries..........	− .22	.332	− .99	.828	.49	P > .20
Aggregate........	2.78	.012	....	....	.....	....

* Not available.

F, as in Table 21 (note that we have computed the *F* ratio only for seven corporations), and according to their coefficient of multiple determination. Spearman's rank coefficient of correlation between these two rankings is .32. It is therefore possible that the fact that we reject the null hypothesis in the case of General Motors is due to the high coefficient of multiple correlation that we have obtained for this corporation. We have argued in the preceding section that it is unreasonable that for General Motors and some other corporations the linear approximation repre-

[41] The importance of General Motors in the sample is again demonstrated by the fact that we reject the null hypothesis in predicting for the year 1955 by the aggregate equation at the 2 per cent level of significance.

sented by the regression equations will hold in face of the huge deviations of the independent variables in the prediction period from their range of experience in the observation period. Our tests seem to confirm this supposition in the case of General Motors but not in the case of the other corporations that have also experienced large variations in their independent variables during the testing period. But at this point it is important to insert a note of caution. The accounts of General Motors underwent a very fundamental revision in the year 1954. In that year General Motors' subsidiaries in England and Germany were included for the first time into the consolidated accounts. More important, a radical revision was made in the calculation of depreciation.[42]

2. *Comparison with the naïve model.*—We can obtain a further insight into the errors in prediction by looking at actual and predicted investment in 1955 and 1956 and by employing again the idea of the naïve model and the coefficient of net gain. Table 22 shows actual investment in the years 1954, 1955, and 1956 and predicted investment for the years 1955 and 1956. In addition, we have computed the coefficient of net gain for the two years for each corporation (for General Electric investment expenditures in 1956 were not available to us, and we computed the coefficient of net gain only for 1955). The picture revealed by Table 22 is certainly not very encouraging. Of the eight corporations examined, four have negative coefficients of net gain. The regression equations of those corporations which yield good predictions for 1955 seem also to perform well in 1956. The striking fact about the predictions for the different corporations is that those corporations for which we obtained the best fit in the regression yield the worst predictions. If we rank the eight corporations according to their coefficients of multiple determination and according to the coefficients of net gain for the years 1955 and 1956, we obtain a Spearman's coefficient of rank correlation between the two rankings of $-.55$. Here we have demonstrated again a theme that runs through our whole study. The "goodness" of an explanation of investment behavior should be judged only in the light of the question that it is supposed to answer. Nearly any criterion that we have used for judging the quality of the investment equations has yielded a different answer.

The coefficients of net gain for the prediction period represent a much more severe test of the quality of prediction than the standard errors of forecast, but the two criteria rank the corporations according to the success in prediction in a similar way. If we rank the corporations according to their respective magnitudes of the coefficient of net gain during the prediction period (Table 22) and according to the magnitude of the vari-

[42] See *General Motors Annual Report, 1954*, pp. 47–48.

ance ratio *F* in Table 21, then Spearman's rank correlation coefficient between the two rankings is −.71 (here again we excluded General Electric from the comparison). There is, therefore, a substantial degree of agreement between the two measures of goodness of prediction.

Our tests of the predictive quality of our regression equations can be summed up as follows: The errors of prediction obtained in the two years tested were not in excess of what might have been expected from the

TABLE 22

ACTUAL AND PREDICTED REAL INVESTMENT PLUS MAINTENANCE AND
REPAIRS (IN 10^6) AND COEFFICIENT OF NET GAIN

CORPORATION	ACTUAL INVESTMENT			PREDICTED INVESTMENT		COEFFICIENT OF NET GAIN
	1954	1955	1956	1955	1956	
General Motors.....	$1,486.7	$1,470.1	$1,673.6	$1,961.2	$2,516.4	−.84
General Electric....	189.6	195.8	N.a.*	238.6	....	−.86
United States Steel.	459.3	496.1	549.0	577.2	679.5	−.58
Atlantic Refining...	81.4	73.9	114.4	88.5	110.7	1.62
Union Oil.........	89.5	86.7	91.2	89.7	81.2	−.44
Goodyear Tire and Rubber..........	49.3	82.6	89.8	82.9	93.8	8.42
Diamond Match....	5.1	6.7	6.3	6.8	6.3	19.00
American Steel Foundries........	6.3	11.1	8.0	10.0	9.8	1.72

* Not available.

quality of the regression equations themselves (except for the case of General Motors). But the errors in prediction are quite substantial in absolute magnitude for a majority of the corporations tested.

APPLICATION OF THE MODEL TO THREE ADDITIONAL CORPORATIONS

The reader will undoubtedly feel by this time that our analysis of the eight corporations has passed by far the point of "diminishing returns." It seems, therefore, desirable to continue our investigation by introducing some additional corporations into the picture. The corporations on which we have experimented and from the behavior of which we have derived the hypotheses were mainly very large corporations. It is therefore reasonable to choose some additional large corporations and see whether their behavior conforms to our previous findings. The only other requirement that these new corporations have to fulfil is that their accounts should be conistent over the period. We chose the following three corporations: International Business Machines (I.B.M.), Chrysler, and Westinghouse. Our hypothesis is that the variations in the value of the firm together with the variation in the stock of plant and equipment explain a sizable part of the variation in investment expenditures over time. We also claim that the value of the firm is a superior explanatory variable of investment behavior to profits in either its lagged or its current form. At this stage of our study we did not feel that it was worthwhile to examine the three corporations by means of a co-movement analysis, and we proceeded directly to compute the regression equations that are required in order to test our hypothesis.

TABLE 23

PARTIAL COEFFICIENT OF DETERMINATION OF REGRESSIONS OF INVESTMENT ON THE STOCK OF PLANT AND EQUIPMENT, THE VALUE OF THE FIRM, AND PROFITS, INTERNATIONAL BUSINESS MACHINES, CHRYSLER, AND WESTINGHOUSE, 1935–54

Corporation	Regression	M_{t-1}	P_{t-1}	P	V_{t-1}	R^2
International Business Machines...........	1	.68	.06			.908
	2	.04			.51	.952
	3	.04		.00	.45	.952
Chrysler..............	1	.83	.16			861
	2	.87			.47	.913
	3	.88		.03	.44	.916
Westinghouse.........	1	.33	.00			.575
	2	.14			.39	.744
	3	.12		$(-).02$	.40	.748

NOTATION

M_{t-1} = Stock of plant and equipment at end of previous year.
P_{t-1} = Profits lagged one year.
P = Profits current.
V_{t-1} = Value of firm lagged one year.

The general hypothesis can be tested by computing the following three regression equations for each corporation: (1) investment on lagged stock of plant and equipment and lagged profits; (2) investment on lagged stock of plant and equipment and the lagged value of the firm; and (3) investment on the lagged stock of plant and equipment, the lagged value of the firm, and current profits. The partial coefficients of determination of each of the variables in the various regression equations are shown in Table 23.

The results presented in Table 23 confirm very strikingly our main hypothesis that the value of the firm serves as a superior explanatory variable of investment to profits in either form. In fact, the results obtained for the performance of the value of the firm in the three corporations are better than those obtained for the eight corporations from which we derived the hypotheses. The partial coefficients of determination of the value of the firm range from around .4 to around .5 in all cases. This shows that the value of the firm explains a large proportion of the variance "left over" by the stock of plant and equipment. In the present context we can also say that all the partial regression coefficients of the value of the firm are different from zero at a very high level of significance (.001). In contrast, consider first the partial coefficients of determination of lagged profits (regression 1). In two cases it is practically zero,

TABLE 24

PARTIAL REGRESSION COEFFICIENTS AND THEIR STANDARD ERRORS OF REGRESSION OF INVESTMENT ON LAGGED STOCK OF PLANT AND EQUIPMENT AND VALUE OF THE FIRM, INTERNATIONAL BUSINESS MACHINES, CHRYSLER, AND WESTINGHOUSE, 1935–54

Corporation	M_{t-1}	V_{t-1}
International Business Machines..........	.085 (1.00)*	.131 (.031)
Chrysler.............................	.316 (.029)	.078 (.020)
Westinghouse........................	.093 (.056)	.053 (.016)

* Standard error.

NOTATION

M_{t-1} = Stock of plant and equipment at end of previous year.
V_{t-1} = Value of firm at end of previous year.

and in the third case it is .16. All three regression coefficients of lagged profits are not significantly different from zero at the .05 level of significance. Finally, the really striking finding in the regression analysis is the poor performance of current profits as measured by its partial coefficient of determination when it is introduced in a regression equation with the stock of plant and equipment and the value of the firm. All partial coefficients of determination of current profits are practically zero.

One important reason why the three corporations show such a good performance for the variable "the value of the firm" as compared to its performance for the eight corporations analyzed previously lies in the fact that, in measuring the stock of plant and equipment and the value of the firm for three additional corporations, we have used the "best" methods at our disposal. In measuring the stock of plant and equipment, we have used all the different corrections discussed in Section III, and in measuring the value of the firm we used average stock quotations of

December 31 and January 31 instead of the single quotations of December 31 used for seven of the eight corporations analyzed previously.

The partial regression coefficients obtained for the regression of investment on the stock of plant and equipment and the value of the firm for the three corporations are presented in Table 24. The regressions for International Business Machines and Westinghouse have reasonable coefficients for the stock of plant and equipment. The sum of the two regression coefficients of Chrysler exceeds .3.[43]

V. Conclusion

Did we find a satisfactory explanation for investment expenditures?

It seems that at least one conclusion that we can draw from our study is that it is impossible to give a unique answer to this question. It all depends on what we mean by "satisfactory."

We have seen that our explanatory variables, the market value of the firm and stock of plant and equipment, show strong co-movements with investment expenditure over time. In particular, we observe that the value of the firm tends to rise in years preceding troughs in investment and to fall in years preceding peaks, thus, in a sense, predicting peaks and troughs. This last finding confirmed our belief that the value of the firm incorporates expectation factors that are relevant for investment behavior. In the regression equations we saw that our model performs quite well in terms of the magnitudes of the partial coefficients of determination of the independent variables. By breaking up the value of the firm into two components, one registering expectations about future earnings and the other the rate of interest, we were able to identify the effect on investment expenditures of each one of these two factors. The examination of the residuals of the regression equations showed that we have explained a sizable part of the variation of investment expenditures for most firms and that our explanation holds quite well for turning points in investment expenditures. We saw also that, if we predict the investment expenditure of each corporation for two additional years, then, on the whole, our predictions are not worse than might be expected from the original regression equations. Finally, we convinced ourselves that our explanation applies to three corporations that were not included in our original sample.

---

[43] It is interesting to observe, though it may be a mere coincidence, that the two corporations which fail to meet our requirement that the sum of the coefficients should be less than .3, General Motors and Chrysler, are of the same industry. In the case of Chrysler, too, the sum of the coefficients is significantly larger than .3. The statistic t is equal to 3.19.

We have also encountered some evidence that sheds some doubt on the adequacy of our model to explain investment expenditures. In the first place, we saw that our predictions were not good enough to be employed in any practical situation, since in many cases they were worse than those obtained by the "naïve model," and this in spite of the fact that the observed investment expenditures were within the "prediction intervals." In the second place, some of the regression coefficients that we have obtained did not seem reasonable on a priori grounds.

The results of our study suggest and leave unanswered two major problems that seem to be a fruitful avenue of further research. There are some indications that the performance of our model improves when it is applied to larger aggregates. It is clearly very interesting to ask how it will perform for the United States economy as a whole. Such a test of our model, though liable to yield high returns, will also involve large costs, since it will not be easy to obtain the relevant data in a consistent form for the economy as a whole. A second problem and perhaps the most important one is inherent in the key explanatory variable that we have used: the value of the firm. The explanation of the variation in investment expenditures by the variations in the value of the firm leaves us with the important problem of determining the causes of the variations in the value of the firm. In particular, we were apparently able to identify and record the expectations about future conditions that are relevant to the investment decision of the firm, but we have not dealt with the problem of determining the way in which these expectations are formed.

Index

Index

PRINTED IN U.S.A.